utopian television

Utopian Television

ROSSELLINI, WATKINS, AND GODARD BEYOND CINEMA

Michael Cramer

UNIVERSITY OF MINNESOTA PRESS
Minneapolis • London

Portions of chapter 2 appeared in "Roberto Rossellini's History Lessons," *New Left Review* 78 (November/December 2012): 115–34.

Published by the University of Minnesota Press
111 Third Avenue South, Suite 290
Minneapolis, MN 55401-2520
http://www.upress.umn.edu

Printed in the United States of America on acid-free paper

The University of Minnesota is an equal-opportunity educator and employer.

23 22 21 20 19 18 17   10 9 8 7 6 5 4 3 2 1

Library of Congress Cataloging-in-Publication Data
Cramer, Michael, author.
Utopian television : Rossellini, Watkins, and Godard beyond cinema / Michael Cramer.
Minneapolis : University of Minnesota Press, [2017] | Includes bibliographical references and index.
Identifiers: LCCN 2016022213 | ISBN 978-1-5179-0038-0 (hc) | ISBN 978-1-5179-0039-7 (pb)
Subjects: LCSH: Television—Production and direction—Europe. | Television—Philosophy. | Rossellini, Roberto, 1906–1977—Criticism and interpretation. | Watkins, Peter, 1935– —Criticism and interpretation. | Godard, Jean-Luc, 1930– —Criticism and interpretation.
Classification: LCC PN1992.3.E78 C73 2017 | DDC 791.45/094—dc23
LC record available at https://lccn.loc.gov/2016022213

Contents

INTRODUCTION

The Land beyond Cinema

TELEVISION AND UTOPIAN METHOD

In 1959, Roberto Rossellini produced his first television show, *L'India vista da Rossellini,* which provided an account of his recent travels in India. By 1964, the director had made television his permanent home, abandoning cinema almost completely. Jean-Luc Godard, too, would leave the cinema behind later in the decade, first producing largely unbroadcast films for television with the Dziga Vertov Group and then carrying out two large-scale TV series with Anne-Marie Miéville during the 1970s. In 1965, meanwhile, a young British director named Peter Watkins was catapulted to fame by his controversial (and also unbroadcast) BBC film *The War Game,* making him one of the first filmmakers to gain widespread recognition on the basis of works made for television. TV, it seemed, was becoming an increasingly attractive medium for some of the most talented Western European filmmakers of the day, both young and old. All three directors, however, created television programs that bore little resemblance to those that surrounded them: as suggested by the fact that some never hit the airwaves at all, these works challenged preconceptions about what television could be and often directly attacked its existing manifestations. Television, if it was to be the privileged audiovisual medium of the future, would need to be transformed into something considerably different than what it had become in its formative years.

For Rossellini, Godard, and Watkins, television represented a space of disillusionment but also one of hope. All three attached utopian aspirations to the medium, although it was Rossellini who was the most insistent in his use of the word *utopia.* For him, television was potentially utopian insofar as it offered a technological means through which knowledge—primarily knowledge about history and philosophy—could be disseminated to millions, creating a new, enlightened society. To fulfill this task, however, television would also need to reconceptualize audiovisual language itself, breaking with cinema and starting over again. Rossellini's television utopia was thus at once technological, formal–linguistic, and cultural, bringing together a new device, a new language, and a new cultural site and function for the moving image. His coupling of the terms *utopia* and *television,* despite his project's failure to bring about the mass enlightenment he hoped for, continues to intrigue, figuring in the title of a number of projects relating to his works: among these are Adriano Aprà's collection of Rossellini's texts on television, *La Télévision comme utopie* (Television as utopia), published in 2001 in conjunction with a retrospective and colloquium held at the Louvre, and Jean-Louis Comolli's 2006 television documentary *La Dernière utopie: la télévision selon Rossellini* (The last utopia: Television according to Rossellini).[1] One wonders if the current fascination with Rossellini's conjunction of these terms might have something to do with the very strangeness and improbability that it holds for our twenty-first-century ears, as though it had gained in appeal precisely because it suggests something so radically different from our present conception of television. Put otherwise, the project's truly utopian character has emerged more fully in its failure—a notion I will return to later.

In what senses can (or could) television be considered utopian? This question, of course, cannot be answered in any simple or direct way, because the term *utopian* is itself so fluid and polyvalent. One might call television utopian due to its promise of total visibility, a world present to itself, or due to its temporal powers, its ability to instantaneously transmit an event to millions viewing simultaneously. It could equally be seen as utopian, as it was for Rossellini, as a result of its educational or formative potential, as a device that relocates the functions of church, school, and state institutions into the home. In each of these cases, though, one can just as easily detect a negative valence: the notion of total visibility inevitably evokes the threat of a wholly "spectacularized" society, one in which the image becomes the site of the world's complete submission to ideology, while the possibility of addressing millions at the same time and "forming" them through television points toward an Adornian nightmare of mass psychological control. Even in these very broad examples, the powers of television appear to be highly ambivalent, and more often than not (at least in leftist intellectual traditions), they have been viewed as negative. To make television utopian, though, as I will argue that Rossellini, Watkins, and Godard sought to do, was not to reject what it was but rather to find within both its actually existing manifestations and the broader cultural conditions it had created the raw materials for imagining what it could be.

Although I will not adhere exclusively to a single definition of *utopia* or *utopianism* here—primarily because the word means different things depending on who is using it—my usage of the term is most highly informed by the works of Ernst Bloch and Fredric Jameson. Ruth Levitas has argued that one can characterize any given definition of *utopia* by determining to what extent it refers to a particular content, form, or function.[2] It is the third that will be of the greatest concern to me here, insofar as I use the term to designate a certain type of thought and practice rather than a literal depiction of some ideal world; this practice, however, can of course not exist without drawing on and articulating itself through specific forms. What I call "utopian television" is not characterized as such due to its representation of an imaginary future or any sort of ideal community or social structure but rather because of its application of "utopia as method" to the raw materials provided by television as it existed. The phrase "utopia as method," however, has also been used in several different ways: the "method" that will guide my thinking (and that guided the directors treated here, I will argue) is not that of Levitas, which always involves the "Imaginary Reconstitution of Society," but that of Jameson.[3] For Jameson, "utopia as method" is a mode of thinking through which "what is currently negative can also be imagined as positive in that immense changing of the valences that is the utopian future."[4] He defines it as "neither a hermeneutic nor political program, but rather something like the structural inversion of what Foucault, following Nietzsche, called the genealogy."[5] It entails a "revalencing" of a phenomenon regarded as negative by locating within it a positive moment or attribute that could, through a temporal projection forward, be seen as the initial condition or raw material of a more positive future state. Utopia as method seeks "to declare positive things which are clearly negative in our own world, to affirm that dystopia is in reality Utopia if examined more closely, to isolate specific features in our empirical present so as to read them as components of a different system."[6] This is, then, a use of the term in which *utopia* always refers to temporality and futurity rather than to a separate space. Although I would note here that one need not see the "target" of the utopian method as necessarily or wholly negative (because the identification of negative or positive elements within it is an act that presupposes the coexistence and unity of the two as well as the possibility of a negative element being converted into a positive one given its character as process rather than as fixed quality), this is indeed the attitude with which television was approached by Rossellini, Watkins, and Godard.

Of course, Rossellini, Watkins, and Godard were not aware of Jameson's method (or that of Ernst Bloch, to which I will return shortly). My claim that they practiced it is thus in itself an interpretative act: despite the wide differences between the three directors, I believe that we can find a common set of strategies shared between them and that these strategies can best be understood as an application of utopian method. Although the chapters that follow will examine this method in its specific instances, I will here offer a broad sketch of how it functions, a distillation or schema that will serve as a map to navigate the pages ahead. In the works of all three directors, a critique of television is often joined by a "revalencing" of the very elements criticized; what is condemned as negative is not simply opposed or negated but rather dialectically transformed into something else. The end product of the utopian method when applied to television is the imagining of what television could be, not merely posited in theory but created as an audiovisual text (although the word *television* itself, of course, can hardly be delimited to signify only a collection of audiovisual texts, as I will return to in chapter 1). The application of the method thus entails two steps: first, the identification of elements of television that make certain "promises" (much like Ernst Bloch's identifications of such elements in a wide variety of phenomena in his *Principle of Hope*) and that can be imagined as taking on a new meaning when read as "components of different system," and second, the creation of television programs that fully draw out or realize these elements.[7] A moment of recognition (of what could be, of the seeds that are immanent in what is) is thus followed by a moment of correction or substitution. The first moment, which we might call the "Blochian" component of this process, assumes that whatever exists is not fixed eternally, but rather part of an overall process of becoming, and thus contains within it the seeds of what it could become; a subject identifies and, we might say, fertilizes these seeds, but they nonetheless must be objectively present for there to be sufficient grounds for what Bloch calls *docta spes,* or "educated hope."[8] The utopian imagination, Bloch writes, "does not play around and get lost in an Empty-Possible, but psychologically anticipates a Real-Possible," and its ideas "extend, in an anticipating way, existing material into the future possibilities of being different and better."[9] The television works of Rossellini, Watkins, and Godard, however, are not simply psychological anticipations. Though they are the result of the kind of anticipatory extension Bloch describes, they are also concrete and perceivable (and here "utopia as method" begins to give way to something more akin to a represented utopia, albeit weakly) fragments of a hypothetical future state that suggests a broader utopian totality of which they could be a part. We might say, in other words, that they show us a future. This future is, of course, not one whose advent we are intended to expect; it remains hypothetical and provisional (although quite proximate for Rossellini), an imagining of what future media could be if they were not blocked by present constraints.

None of this, however, explains what the utopian elements of television were, or why Rossellini, Watkins, and Godard should be the privileged authors in a study of utopian television. The answer to this first question is of course a historically specific one; television is no longer, I will argue here, a privileged site or raw material for the exercise of the utopian imagination, but for a particular period of time, it certainly was. This book will deal with the promise and potential that were located in television in post–World War II Western Europe (and in the United Kingdom, France, and Italy, in particular, given the national origin of the directors under consideration), where it was often treated as a powerful means of reconstruction and modernization. The first, and perhaps most important, element that made television so well suited to utopian thinking can be found in one of the guiding institutional principles of broadcasting in Western Europe, namely, the model of public service (and corresponding state monopoly) that was dominant from the postwar period until the 1980s. I am not by any means suggesting that the public service model was, in practice, a predominantly positive endeavor but rather that it contained certain elements that could be seen as anticipations or "promises" of something that it was unable to achieve. What "public service" itself meant was often extremely ill defined, which in turn rendered it highly elastic and politically manipulable. While the forms it took on in different nations varied and practice often fell short of stated goals, even scholars who demonstrate a great skepticism about the coherence of the idea itself acknowledge that public service broadcasters in Europe consistently embraced education and culture as their guiding principles from its beginnings until the 1990s.[10] Among European broadcasting institutions, the BBC made the greatest efforts to define the term; as formulated by John Reith, the highly influential director-general of the BBC (albeit prior to the first BBC television broadcasts), public service positioned itself, Jérôme Bourdon argues, as "the direct heir of a humanist dream of mass education, born of the nineteenth century."[11] It sought to implement, in a manner that certainly suggests a strong connection to utopian programs, a carefully controlled effort to shape the social subject, albeit one strongly marked—both for those who would seek to undermine it from the right as elitist or pedantic and those on the left who found it insufferably classist and universalizing—by its national and class character. This by no means, however, rules out the possibility that some future (or imagined) variation of it might be able to keep the promises that it made, locating within them what Bloch calls a "cultural surplus," that unrealized idea present in excess of any ideological function.[12] As a notion that had already deeply defined what television was or could be by the early 1960s, public service broadcasting provided many of the raw materials that allowed the utopian imagination to seize upon television as a fertile site for its exercise as well as an economic and institutional framework within which visions of another television, if only occasionally, could be executed and broadcast to a large public.

It was not only the often ill-defined and abstract concept of public service that made television a fertile site for the exercise of utopian imagination; it also enacted a dramatic shift in the ways in which images and audiovisual communication (previously dominated by the cinema) could be conceptualized, and it reconfigured the relationship between different categories of practice and experience. Of central concern to me here will be the way that television allowed for a rethinking of the relationship between image and knowledge, between aesthetics and information, and how it suggested the possibility of new ways of knowing through its frequent alignment (in its own practices and institutional self-characterization) with the category of "information" or the "informational." One of the most significant aspects of its utopian character was the way in which it remapped the boundaries between seeing and knowing, between practices considered to be instrumental or informative and those believed instead simply to entertain or facilitate aesthetic experience.

Although I will return in far more detail to the tendency of television (at once as technology, as institution, and as a set of texts) to narrow or eliminate the gaps between different categories of practice and apprehension, I briefly mention it here to introduce one of the other main theoretical reference points that will appear frequently in what follows. This tendency allows television both to suggest and to enact changes in what Jacques Rancière calls the *partage du sensible,* or "distribution of the sensible," defined as "a delimitation of spaces and times, of the visible and the invisible, of speech and noise."[13] Rancière's term is a complex and multivalent one, which can be inflected differently depending on the conceptual work it is called on to accomplish. Two different senses are suggested by the verb *partager* alone, which denotes both the separations or divisions within the sensible and their status as shared; the term refers, Rancière explains, to "the system of self-evident facts of sense perception that simultaneously discloses the existence of something in common and the delimitations that define the respective parts and positions within it."[14] He first uses the term to describe the "aesthetics of politics," or how the political "revolves around what is seen and what can be said about it, around who has the ability to see and the talent to speak, around the properties of spaces and the possibilities of time."[15] This same conception of aesthetics can then be used to analyze artworks, insofar as artworks "intervene in the general distribution of ways of doing and making as well as in the relationships they maintain to modes of being and forms of visibility."[16] The *partage du sensible* provides a way to rethink how precisely we might speak of an artwork as being political, not on the basis of its content but rather in terms of how it challenges existing distributions of the sensible and proposes another, creating what Rancière calls "dissensus" (a term equally applicable to political forms of contestation). My usage of the concept here will focus particularly on how it links different forms of making, seeing, and experiencing to different forms of knowing. In political terms, we could read these different "ways of knowing" as informed by class, education, and so forth: some forms of expression and experience "count" as knowledge in any given *partage du sensible,* whereas others do not. This given order, however, can be challenged: the positing of a dissensus within the *partage du sensible,* as Davide Panagia puts it, serves as an "interruption of the ways in which we establish the criteria of knowledge."[17] Applied to the audiovisual, we can use the idea of a *partage du sensible*—taking it to refer to the lines drawn between different forms of seeing, hearing, doing, and experiencing, as well as the discourses that encourage a particular interpretation or evaluation of these elements of the sensible—to consider how different forms of audiovisual text are categorized and understood to be ontologically and functionally different from one another, but also how images and sounds themselves are placed within a wider "sensible" context. Television, I will contend in what follows, disrupts the existing distribution of the sensible in its contestation and transformation of the boundaries between different practices (e.g., sports, dramatic performance, news), the forms of visibility and audibility they take on, and the ways they are experienced.

Rancière's ideas about how the *partage du sensible* lays down certain rules for making, experiencing, and understanding art in particular will also prove useful here. He has attempted to demonstrate how the *partage du sensible* determines how the category of "art" is identified and what it is believed to do, identifying three dominant "regimes" that circumscribe the ways in which art can be thought, a regime being defined as "a specific type of connection between ways of producing works of art or developing practices, forms of visibility that disclose them, and ways of conceptualizing the former and the latter."[18] I will draw on the concept of the regime here both to describe dominant ways of thinking about what art did or was thought to do, as Rancière does, and to show how television challenged any "regimentation" or fixed distribution, how it undermined certain laws about what images could or should do, and how art and the aesthetic could be related to other types of discourse, ways of making, experiencing, and knowing. Whereas art, then, occupies a position of privilege for Rancière, illuminating and transforming the *partage du sensible* because it "intervene[s] in the general distribution of ways of doing and making," I will be equally concerned with what is defined as non-art and the moments at which such definitions seem to bend or break under pressure.[19]

The question arises, then, of how the concepts of the *partage du sensible* and the regime might relate to the concept of utopia as employed by thinkers like Jameson and Bloch. First, the connection arises in the way in which different *partages* allow for different types of practice and thinking: some uses of the moving image, at given historical moments, might seem completely devoid of utopian potential, whereas a subsequent *repartage* (i.e., the undoing or reconfiguration of the *partage du sensible*) or dissensus, whether realized or simply imagined or anticipated, may change this situation completely. More subtly, different ways of imagining the divisions between various forms of making, experiencing, and knowing might lead to different types of utopian imagining, insofar as these never emerge, in Jameson's schema, ex nihilo, but rather from a reconfiguration or bricolage of existing raw materials; the *partage du sensible* will thus inform and delimit what sort of future may be anticipated.[20] Second, one can join the concepts of utopia and the *partage du sensible* by attending to the way in which the utopian method, at least when applied to television, imagines a different *partage du sensible* on the basis of television's raw materials. For example, in many cases, the utopian transformations of television examined here are characterized by a desire to break down the barriers between existing practices, erasing the lines between different types of text (the fiction film, the newscast, the pedagogical lesson), experience (aesthetic or nonaesthetic, quotidian or exceptional), and apprehension (whether one "knows" through rational faculties, through the senses or emotions, or through a process that can be identified with supposedly aesthetic faculties). The utopian work they do is thus particularly closely related to the idea of a redistribution of the sensible, albeit one that remains anticipatory rather than actual; it depends, however, on a redistribution (sometimes more tentative or contained than others, as we will see) that television itself has already begun to carry out. Rancière's concept of the regime, meanwhile, will be useful here insofar as it provides a set of models whose disruption or dissolution will be suggested or carried out through the works of utopian television. To more succinctly join the concept of the *partage du sensible* with the utopian method of these works as described earlier, we could rearticulate the two steps of this method as follows: the first entails identifying raw materials and a particular challenge to the existing *partage du sensible* that make television an appealing site for the exercise of utopian thought, while the second entails a projecting forward of these raw materials to imagine a *partage du sensible* that has yet to come.

While I hope the chapters that follow will provide ample justification for my decision to focus on Rossellini, Watkins, and Godard, let me give a very brief sketch of how the work of these directors enacts the method I have outlined. All three seize upon characteristics of television and the discourse around it. They then either attempt to draw out latent characteristics perceived as positive, realizing their promise, as it were (e.g., in Rossellini's insistence upon the "pure" informational character of his programs), or to "reverse" characteristics perceived as negative through their dialectical transformation into positives (television's confusion of informational and noninformational discourse for Watkins or its placement in the home for both Watkins and Godard). This also frequently involves a practice of blurring the difference between or deliberately heightening the contradictions between two terms, whether they be types of audiovisual text (documentary vs. fiction), cultural functions (information vs. entertainment), or modes of experience (rational apprehension vs. aesthetic experience). In short, existing modes of "commonsense" thinking are challenged through dialectical thought. Although the results of this process vary greatly between our three directors, it thus tends to illustrate the historical contingency (and ultimate untenability) of existing categories of thought, perception, and practice in a way that points to a neutralized opposition, or even an anticipated Hegelian *Aufhebung* or sublation, of existing elements, insofar as it involves an imagining of a future state that contains the present within it (as Hegel puts it, "to sublate" on "one hand . . . means to preserve, to maintain, and equally it also means to cause to cease, to put an end to").[21] The utopian television of Rossellini, Watkins, and Godard does not simply imagine the future; it imagines a future in which television itself would no longer be identifiable as such, even if its attributes (as well as those of cinema) could still be located in some subsequent form of audiovisual practice.

Other identifiably utopian elements animate the works of Rossellini, Watkins, and Godard in a way that has less to do with utopia as method and that brings them into closer relation with utopian programs. The utopian program, in Jameson's schema, can be opposed to utopia as method or the Blochian utopian impulse in that it seeks a concrete transformation of reality that is in some sense achieved through its own practice: "it can range from a whole social revolution, on a national or even world scale, all the way down to the design of the uniquely Utopian space of a building or a garden."[22] The presence of a program is evident in Rossellini, who is explicit about his desire to replace existing television with his own renovation of it, and about his vision of the enlightened future that will result from this process. Watkins's later works *(The Journey, La Commune)* draw even closer to concrete utopian programs in their efforts to establish new communities in the very process of their realization. Godard, meanwhile, also aspires (most clearly in *Six fois deux,* directed with Anne-Marie Miéville) to create a kind of "replacement" television but remains quite conscious of its provisional status; here we see where the lines between a project and an imagining begin to blur, particularly if we take the intention behind any particular utopian endeavor into account.

The gap between utopian programs, on one hand, and utopia as method and a kind of anticipatory imagining, on the other, however blurry it might become, thus demarcates a major fault line between the works covered in this book. Yet even works that seem to belong in the first category may be approached from a different perspective to reveal something through their own limitations. We might read Rossellini's television project, for example, as animated by a more obscure utopian impulse than the one clearly visible on the surface, one that, despite its clear participation in various forms of ideological mystification, necessitates a hermeneutic operation that searches for its deeper meaning elsewhere than in the program it declares. While not all failures are the same, one can perhaps also unite works that actually practice a utopian program and those that merely anticipate or imagine a future state through their shared failures. Both a failed utopian program and an imagining or anticipatory use of utopia as method (always a failure insofar as it anticipates rather than realizes) can carry out a more diagnostic function, allowing us to see the limitations of imagination at any given time (itself, as Jameson would argue, a hermeneutic function) and what possible "salvageable" material exists in the present.[23] This diagnostic and critical function depends on the work's failure qua utopian plan to prove its utopian character. This failure also conjures up the totality in which the attempted plan or the hypothesized anticipatory extension might succeed, one that would have to be realized not through the means of that failed plan or imagining itself but through a more holistic political transformation. Whether it is aware of it (Godard) or not (Rossellini) (Watkins, as we will see, moves between the two poles), utopian television is not so much an attempt to transform television, let alone the world, as it is a use of television as raw material to think about the forms that this transformation might take—and to spur our desire for it.

Despite the importance of television as a technology and institution in eliciting and shaping utopian thought, then, this book is not really an account of either of these as something that could actually achieve or enable a new social or political structure. Nonetheless, what might ultimately be achieved in the future and what has been or can be imagined are closely linked, particularly if one believes in the possibility of a Blochian "educated hope"; even if, as Jameson puts it, "the positing of alternate futures is not itself a political program nor even a political practice . . . it is hard to see how any durable or effective political action could come into being without it."[24] Utopian television tells us what could be posited, and it is this positing and its historicity, the way in which what can be thought is always what can be thought in a certain place and time, that will concern me here. Any historical moment, to again follow Jameson, has its specific system, one that "opens a set of creative possibilities . . . as well as tracing ultimate limits of praxis that are also the limits of thought and imaginative projection."[25] Here, however, I do not simply attempt to sketch a synchronic cross-section; rather, I assume that the changes undergone by television and what it allowed to be thought can be most productively read as part of a series of transformations and developments. I thus also attend both to the early or pretelevision era (the 1920s and 1930s) and the era in which television took on, at least in Europe, a dramatically different form (the 1980s). As I have already suggested, if television was indeed a "utopian machine," it may also at a certain point have ceased to be one, most likely in the 1980s, after the opening of the airwaves to private capital and the marginalization of public service radically altered the limits of practice and thought.

On the other hand, we might say that it was precisely at this moment that public service, and even television as a more abstract notion, now historically delimitable due to its disappearance, fully revealed their utopian character. Bourdon notes that public service now seems "more a utopia than an ambition that would be at least partially realizable."[26] His use of the term "utopia" here is more or less synonymous with "impossibility," but this unrealizability, this severing of the idea from any real form of practice, may itself allow us to better grasp the utopian thinking enabled by television. As it emerges as utopian to our retrospective view, it breaks free of the actuality that might have seemed at the time to compromise or "contaminate" it, making its utopian potential clearer. The same applies to the works of utopian television that sought to draw out this utopian potential but still, at least in some cases, remained steeped in an ideology that threatened to obscure their value. This book is not simply descriptive but critical, and it assumes that the projects it seeks to analyze are hardly self-evident. They require interpretation and critique, but in a way that brings their own potential as utopian raw material to light and invites us to find their analogues in a present that perhaps remains more obscure.

I follow Bloch in assuming that the utopian value a work presents to us now may not have been visible at the time it appeared: the cultural material of the past, he argues, may "provide a philosophy which has surmounted the bourgeois barrier of knowledge with possibly progressive inherited material, even though, as is obvious, this material particularly requires elucidation, critical acquisition, functional change."[27] It is to the past, then, that we must look if we wish to see the future: "unbecome future becomes visible in the past, avenged and inherited, mediated and fulfilled past in the future."[28]

The current value of any "unbecome future" in past television or its anticipatory doubles, not to mention how (or where) one seeks to apply their lessons, may depend on what one makes of the current state of television. If the signifier was always a rather fluid one, it has become positively protean in the past fifteen years or so. Television is now often invoked either as a model for today's "new media" or as a privileged site for the study of the mutations and changing cultural functions of audiovisual practice (toward interactivity, choice, new forms of media delivery and viewing experience, etc.).[29] Against this characterization of television as a still-developing and increasingly important medium, I will here consider it—primarily, but not exclusively, in its public service form—to be one whose time has largely passed or that can at least be considered to have vanished in one distinct historical form. In the title of his film on Rossellini, Comolli describes television as the *last* utopia. One hopes that this is incorrect, but we might build off of this title to ask what media or practices might serve the same functions that television did from roughly the mid-1950s to the early 1980s. As I will discuss at greater length in chapter 5, I do not believe that one can simply transfer the same utopian qualities that were found in television onto another medium. This is not because "new media" do not or cannot possess utopian potential but rather because our historical situation, and the role of media within it, has changed so dramatically. The life-span of public service television, if we date its rise to the postwar and its decline to the mid- to late 1980s, corresponds closely to a specific historical trajectory: that of the Western European welfare state and its dismantling, along with the changes in modes of production and forms of labor that accompanied its rise and fall.[30] The demise of public service television, furthermore, was certainly not unrelated to the corresponding demise of the forms of European Socialism and Communism that were such powerful forces in the postwar period—in the cases of France and Italy, it was largely the Socialist parties that buried public service, even if its grave was being dug for many years before—and the dual collapse of the two held deep implications for the forms that the utopian impulse could take.[31] If, as Comolli suggests, television can indeed be called the last utopia, perhaps it was more precisely the last utopia of a specific geographical and political formation and a particular historical era, one that could be traced as far back as the French Revolution or the Enlightenment. Any "unbecome future" in utopian television cannot therefore be mobilized by a mere reanimation or reapplication but will instead require a kind of translation into the idiom of the present, allowing us to recognize the potential in phenomena whose utopian character may be obscured today by giving us a greater appreciation of the utopian thinking of the past. Though this translation to the present is not the main concern of this book, I will offer some additional thoughts on it in chapter 5.

While such questions—and, indeed, the theoretical premises I have laid out in this introduction more broadly—remain quite abstract, most of this book, in contrast, will take a far more specific approach, attending to the cases of individual audiovisual practitioners ("filmmakers" feels like a far too conventional and un-utopian term here, so I will generally opt for the still-problematic "directors") and examining their ideas, their works, and their manner of grappling with the questions they found before them at precise points in space and time. My focus on the specific cases of Rossellini, Watkins, and Godard should not be taken to imply any exclusivity; there are almost certainly other chapters that could have been added to this book, most obviously one on Alexander Kluge, whom I will briefly consider in chapter 5. The centrality of the author that this approach implies, however, also raises the question of whether this is in fact an "auteurist" study. While it is indeed largely organized around the works and ideas of individual authors, the ultimate aim guiding my inquiry into each filmmaker is to find out how their answers to the questions raised by television and their ways of thinking with or through it might contribute to our understanding both of their period's cultural logic and that of our own, rather than looking directly *to* them for solutions or answers about what television was or could be. Nor is my choice to focus on individual filmmakers meant to suggest that we need to understand their work through a face-value acceptance of the author's intentions, as I have suggested in respect to Rossellini. Rather, my preoccupation with the words and ideas of the filmmakers themselves, with what they believed they were doing and how they were able to conceptualize their interventions, is meant to provide a sense of how the problems they dealt with could be configured at a specific historical moment, what assumptions underlie their thoughts and works, and how processes that seek to alter cultural practice occur in historical and subjective contexts. Although I do wish to use my observations about these three directors to build up to the broader perspective and argument I have outlined here, the individual case studies take precedence. They are not so much "proof" of a particular dynamic or development (although taken together, I believe they allow us to observe one) as they are examples of cultural practice as response to some desire or need, as the answer to questions that were not limited to these individuals.

The middle three chapters of this book focus on individual authors (Rossellini, Watkins, and Godard), while the two that bookend them take a broader perspective. Chapter 1 considers how television allowed for new ways of conceiving of the relationship between aesthetic and informational practices, explores how these related to models of art's "usefulness," and examines the tensions and oppositions that characterized discourse surrounding it. Chapter 2 focuses on the "historical encyclopedia" of Roberto Rossellini, comprising more than forty hours of programming created for television between 1962 and the director's death in 1977. Here I attempt to treat these works as an ensemble, discussing the rationale behind Rossellini's rejection of cinema in favor of television, the project's conception and formal construction, and, most importantly, how it grappled with the legacy of avant-garde and modernist conceptions of art and their relationship with utopian thought and desire. Chapter 3 focuses on the two films made by Peter Watkins for BBC television, *Culloden* and *The War Game*, and, to a lesser extent, on his 1971 film *Punishment Park*.

It argues that Watkins's practices, which draw heavily on television forms, both critique and repurpose those forms, and inquires as to how they might be positioned in relation to the 1930s work of John Grierson and the British Documentary Film Movement, an earlier attempt to create a "useful" civic art that was in many ways similar to public service television. Chapter 4 engages with numerous works created by Jean-Luc Godard and his collaborators (Jean-Henri Roger, Jean-Pierre Gorin, and Anne-Marie Miéville) from 1969 to 1977, after his rejection of commercial art cinema in the post-1968 period. Looking at Godard's output over an extended period of time, I trace the development of a recurring set of questions or problems (aesthetic, semiotic, political) that emerge first in his works with the Dziga Vertov Group and are then radically reframed in his subsequent collaborations with Miéville. Both sets of works engage with television, in the first case as both a source of funding and an object of critique (both directly and obliquely), in the second as a set of forms and practices to be drawn on and repurposed in the imagining of television's utopian double. Chapter 5, finally, deals with later works by Watkins and Godard as well as the television productions of Alexander Kluge. More broadly, it seeks to discern the relationship between cinema, television, and utopian thinking after the opening of the European airwaves to private interests and the declining power and influence of public service broadcasting in the 1980s. Cinema and new media emerge as central concerns in this chapter as well: what does it mean to speak about the death of cinema or television, about old and new media, and what might the ways that we construe their relationships say about our historical placement and the ways we are able to conceptualize the past and the future? By attending to the media of today through the lens of the "lost" utopias of cinema and television, I hope to develop a set of tools through which we can better grasp our present, looking toward the future by returning to the past.

1

The Promise of Television

MAKING UTOPIA POSSIBLE

The associations between television and utopia are hardly limited to the kinds of transformations of the medium carried out by directors like Rossellini, Watkins, and Godard. Indeed, as Jonathan Bignell and Andreas Fickers note in their introduction to the first scholarly study of television from a pan-European perspective, one of the central attributes of the medium was its intimate connection with hopes for the future: it played a key role in broader processes of modernization and functioned in Europe "as a totem or currency representing greater transformations."[1] Early narrative accounts of television's invention tend to focus on the technological marvel of the device, casting it as emblematic of a better future, while many of those who laid the foundations of the major European state television networks, as I will return to shortly, saw it as a powerful tool for holistic social transformation.[2] Such hopes, however, were almost always accompanied by a fear of the new medium, with even those who sought to make use of it viewing it as a kind of monster to be tamed.[3] Even in its early years, and particularly from a left-wing perspective, television was often cast not as a symbol of a better future but as the emblematic device of an age in which both art and communications had lost their revolutionary or utopian potential. As Siegfried Zielinski puts it, "after World War II, the televisual living room medium of familial privateness became established rapidly as the (mass) communicative vanishing point of a considerably disillusioned modern age."[4] Television here is characterized as both the instrument of an individualist consumerism that held out the promise of happiness in spectacle and commodity and a facilitator of increasing isolation, "a concomitant and result of people's retreat into the

1

intimacy of their own four walls."[5] This image recalls Gunther Anders's characterization of television as giving rise to the "mass-produced hermit," an atomized viewer identical to every other.[6] Whether from a hopeful or pessimistic standpoint, television was invested with a symbolic significance that inextricably linked it not only with the future but also with the kind of individuals that might dwell there, as though, for better or for worse, it would be television that would change the world. Utopian and dystopian attitudes toward television can thus be read not as highly polarized opposing positions but as different placements within a common discursive field that projected anxieties or hopes onto the medium due to its association with the future. Characterizations like the one described by Zielinski thus hardly negate or contradict the fact that television represented for many, whether taken at face value or as a set of possibilities to be developed, a valuable tool and a potential site for the renewal of those very hopes whose defeat it was so often called on to signify.

A hope that television might lead not to an atomized or commodified society but rather to a more coherent and enlightened one was more palpable in Europe than in the United States, owing both to television's more purely commercial character in the latter and to its status as state monopoly and its persistent association with public service in the former. One finds numerous examples of extremely bold claims about television's social and political potential made in postwar Europe, particularly in Italy, where television was seized on by Catholic politicians and intellectuals, such as Radiotelevisione Italiana (RAI; originally Radio Audizioni Italiane) director Filiberto Guala, as a means to rebuild national culture after the war and as an ideal tool for the linguistic unification of the nation.[7] Pope Pius XII himself addressed French and American viewers in 1949 to hail the "marvel" of the new medium and its power to allow us to witness events at the moment they occur.[8] Jean d'Arcy, director of programming at France's Radiodiffusion-Télévision Française (RTF), appealed to television as a key tool for ensuring the fulfillment of human rights and needs established in the United Nations's 1948 Universal Declaration of Human Rights.[9] While a full unpacking of this claim will have to wait until the conclusion of this chapter and an analysis of Rossellini's television project in the next, one might say that the large-scale utopian projects of the interwar period, often associated with the historical avant-garde, were absorbed by or mutated into the state-sponsored mass communications projects of the postwar, albeit with the left often dismissing such projects as a blunt instrument of the same forces that the earlier avant-gardes had aimed to overthrow.

When viewed from the present, the bold claims made for the power of television in the 1940s and 1950s seem to ascribe an improbable amount of agency and responsibility to the mass media. They indicate the seriousness and ambition with which the project of European television was developed and provide a good sense of why it might have seemed to be a useful tool for strengthening social cohesion and building a new society after the war. Regardless of one's attitude toward such ideas, then, it is thus not difficult to imagine their appeal to individuals working in audiovisual media, who could invoke them as a way to ascribe a greater importance or a new social function or placement to their own work. The sort of promise one found in television depended, of course, on the perspective from which one was looking, so we might begin by considering why television might have appealed to directors associated primarily with the cinema, such as Rossellini and Godard.[10]

In what way might television have facilitated the development of a form of moving image practice qualitatively different from that of cinema, and what precisely would have to be transformed to leave the cinema behind? Any notion of a succession or historical unfolding of media risks being tautological, yet such notions are undoubtedly instrumental in informing both media practice (how, the practitioner asks, can I go *beyond*?) and any attempts to retrospectively understand past shifts between media ecologies. They suggest a process in which mediums or *dispositifs* rise and fall over time, each one somehow corresponding to the epoch that it dominates. In this sense, many would accept the idea that television succeeds cinema, replacing it as the primary form of mass entertainment. But thinking about television as coming after cinema also suggests a potential development, an overcoming and absorption of what came before. It is this latter sense that I will privilege here, treating television as the site of the imagining—if not the actual enactment or realization—of the art that would come after cinema. A contrast between what was achievable or thinkable through cinema, on one hand, and through television, on the other, allows us to see how television had opened up new possibilities for audiovisual practice that were inaccessible to cinema and perhaps only latent in or implied by existing television practices.

In what follows, I will consider not only how the conditions and raw materials created by television (as technology, as institution, as a set of textual practices) made the projection of its utopian double possible but also how they allowed for the reframing of a number of long-standing questions related to art and to cinema specifically (the "uses" of art, its relationship to information and other pedagogical practices, the conceptualization and cultural placement of the moving image). In other words, just as important as the new variables introduced by television were the needs and desires that they addressed. If television was to be seen as providing the starting point for a new, utopian form of audiovisual media, it was not simply because it provided solutions to long-standing problems but also because it allowed those problems themselves to be conceptualized in new terms.

To arrive at a narrative in which television fulfills or improves on cinema, we will need to begin by considering how the transition between the two media might fit into the negative or dystopian one invoked by Zielinski. The negative narrative might argue that even if television had at some point harbored utopian promise, this had been destroyed by the 1960s; the associations between television and isolation, depoliticization, and consumerism expressed in Zielinski's formulation provide a good sense of how television was viewed by a considerable number of intellectuals (left, liberal, and right), even in its early years. If anything, television seemed to have perfected and rendered even more culturally ubiquitous the functions of escapism and ideological maintenance often attributed to cinema. From this perspective, it seemed not to have come to challenge cinema but rather to better fulfill its aims. T. W. Adorno, perhaps television's fiercest critic on the left, had concluded by 1953 that, thanks to its growing ubiquity, "the gap between private existence and the culture industry, which had remained as long as the latter did not omnipresently dominate all dimensions of the visible, is now being plugged."[11] What cinema had started, television finished. Television, for Adorno, was the apotheosis of a culture industry that had successfully placed all aspects of daily life under its sway, the greatest form of totalitarian manipulation ever realized, transforming "modern mass culture into a medium of undreamed of psychological control."[12]

Although a narrative that sees television as something like the realization of cinema's commercial, escapist, and ideological functions is undoubtedly correct in some senses (particularly when applied to the United States), one can nonetheless dialectically complement it with another, in which the very same processes identified as negative in the first account become at least potentially positive in the second. We might thus complement the preceding narrative with one in which television comes to fulfill the utopian promises of cinema rather than simply further developing its ideological functions. Cinema, of course, *had* been utopian, and perhaps in some sense still is, as Christopher Pavsek has recently argued. Cinema, Pavsek writes, has long been associated with "an idea of utopia in which the hope for and aspiration toward the establishment of a social utopia is deeply bound up with the commitment to unfolding the promises contained in the history of film."[13] These promises, however—those found in Eisenstein's *Battleship Potemkin* in its twin commitment to the achievement of a new society and a new, total work of art—were certainly less present in the late 1950s and early 1960s than they had been in the 1920s, as was the political context of revolutionary fervor that facilitated them.[14] The way in which the pioneers of public service television seem to have latched on to promises of social usefulness that were at one time associated with cinema (one thinks here not only of Vertov but also of John Grierson), however, suggests the displacement of hope from one medium to another—although one could also construct this narrative as one in which cinema itself is a sort of mistake or commercial aberration that diverges from the longer trajectory of radio and television as useful media. But if cinema was no longer the site—or at least not the most fertile site—for the imagining of the future, what would allow television to serve this function?

In the simplest terms, television could be seen as offering not so much new aesthetic or even technological specificities as a second chance to fulfill the social function that had been abdicated by the cinema. Zielinski cites a commentator writing in a 1929 issue of the journal of the Volksverband für Filmkunst (Popular Film Society), who, after attending Dénes von Mihály's demonstration of television technology in Berlin, asked,

> Will *Fernkino* [tele-cinema] simply serve to present us with the desolate state of film art all over again, shall we, as state-sanctioned home-cinemagoers, be spoon-fed harmless picture-book films like good children, uplifting us to become docile and devout subjects of the state, or will television also open up intellectual spheres to our gaze that have so far been denied to us by cinema?[15]

The commentator recognizes the all-too-familiar pattern in which novelty only means more of the same, the old oppression dressed in new technological clothes. Such a recognition suggests that any form of cultural practice coming after cinema could only seriously contest it by questioning the cultural role it had come to play, by replacing an anodyne medium of escapism and pleasure with one that opened up new "intellectual spheres." In this case, the new medium would have represented hope not so much because it offered any particular capacities lacking in the old ones but rather because it constituted an area of openness and opportunity not entirely solidified and dominated by capital, another chance to intervene on the cultural front.

The broad set of ideals and practices gathered under the umbrella of public service broadcasting provided a response to some, but hardly all, of the hopes articulated by Zielinski's commentator: public service broadcasting was even more "state sanctioned" than the cinema, given that it granted a monopoly on broadcasting to the state and was managed (indirectly or directly, depending on the case) by the state. It did offer, however, a space for imagining what a postcinematic moving image practice might look like, most importantly in terms of how its function might be conceived. While the ideals and practices of public service broadcasting are rather difficult to pin down (given the distance between principle and practice, local variations, and major changes over time), they provided the principal framework for thinking about what television was and what it could do in postwar Europe. In short, if there were any cardinal points from which to chart the path to utopian television, public service broadcasting was certainly one of them. By sketching the contours of the main ideas and practices associated with public service and tracing their migration from their initial point of conception, the United Kingdom, to France and Italy (these being the three countries that will be our primary focus in what follows), we can begin to see how they provided raw materials for the imagining of a utopian television, not only in making a number of promises about what television could and should do but also by radically destabilizing the very terms and practices that television invoked to constitute its identity as a medium.

PUBLIC SERVICE AND MONOPOLY

Some of the earliest formulations of the principles of public service broadcasting, written even before the advent of television itself, position broadcasting as radically different in function from cinema, yet still in some sense the inheritor of hopes that the older medium had failed to deliver on. John Reith, first director-general of the BBC, imagined broadcasting as a force that would act as a cultural bulwark against cinema and other forms of popular culture that had abandoned the task of enlightenment. As he writes in his 1924 book *Broadcast over Britain*, "the possibilities of the 'pictures' were enormous, and at the outset it was firmly believed that here was to be found the means of educating the masses. The ethical and educational value of the cinematograph was allowed to be superseded by sensationalism."[16] Reith's belief that broadcasting should be different from cinema—and that this difference would be located in function rather than in technological capacity or any other form of medium specificity—illustrates the extent to which a narrative of succession (and improvement), conceived of in terms of sociopolitical use-value, informed early broadcasting's self-characterization and contributed to its association with usefulness and information.

Any definitive definition of public service, even from an empirical perspective, is rendered difficult by the fact, as Richard Collins notes, that its mission has often been more informed by tradition than by legal documents.[17] Indeed, while Reith's writings provide a canonical account of public service, one can discern relatively little about the BBC's mission or its institutional character by reading its first Royal Charter of 1927, which only alludes in passing to broadcasting as a "means of education and entertainment ... in the national interest."[18] Nonetheless, some broad generalizations are possible: in one of the most frequently cited attempts to define public service broadcasting, Jay G. Blumler identifies six characteristic features. First, public service is "comprehensive," and thus committed to broadcasting a wide range of programming for a wide range of purposes, serving "such multiple goals as education, information and entertainment; range, quality and popularity."[19] Second, public service broadcasters act according to "generalized mandates": because their founding legal documents are almost always rather vague, they enjoy considerable power and flexibility in carrying out their mission. Third, and closely related to the first point, public service strives to serve a diverse audience, catering not only to majority taste but to the tastes of minorities as well, as opposed to a commercial system in which programming is designed to attract the largest possible number of viewers. Fourth, public service television serves a "cultural vocation," often conceived of as "a responsibility for sustaining and renewing the society's characteristic cultural capital and cement." Fifth, it plays a major role in national political life, granting ample time to political debate and news coverage. Sixth, and finally, it is noncommercial, generally funded by license fees paid by viewers and listeners, and attempts to "keep market forces at bay and to ensure that they [do] not unduly dominate or distort program making."[20]

Though these defining characteristics give a good sense of the general parameters of public service broadcasting, it will be useful to supplement them with more specific attention to the ways in which the principles underlying public service, first formulated by Reith, informed ideals and practices in Italy and France. While Reith's ideas were first developed in relation to radio, they provided the BBC with a mission that would continue to be upheld and invoked when it moved into television broadcasting, and it is in respect to television that I will examine the spread of his ideas. The core of Reith's characterization of public broadcasting, as suggested by his quote about cinema above, lies in a conception of enlightenment that sees television's function as primarily educational and its public as something like a group of students; this function could only be carried out free from the pressures of a commercial system. To use broadcasting merely for entertainment, he believed, would be a terrible waste, a "prostitution of its powers and an insult to the character and intelligence of the people";[21] instead, its vocation was to "carry into the greatest possible number of homes everything that is best in every department of human knowledge, endeavor, or achievement."[22] Reith's attitude toward the public set the tone that the BBC, as its detractors so often noted, would maintain in the following decades: public service was not to be a matter of giving the public what they wanted but rather what they needed. As Reith put it, "few know what they want and very few what they need. . . . In any case it is better to overestimate the mentality of the public than to underestimate it."[23] As Asa Briggs notes, one can easily observe a continuity between the ideas of Matthew Arnold and those of Reith; both strongly believed in the notion of an elect who shouldered a "burden" to enlighten the masses.[24]

Reith's conception of broadcasting as a noncommercial instrument of public enlightenment, albeit with different inflections and particularities, was shared by the pioneers of Italian and French public service broadcasting, particularly in their postwar construction of national television services. The highly influential Filiberto Guala, mentioned previously, treated it as powerful means to modernize Italian society. Guala's vision of television, as Franco Monteleone notes, established the pedagogical foundation that would serve as the basis for Italian broadcasting, casting it as "a collective educator . . . deeply rooted in the moderate, Catholic, sentimental identity of the majority of Italians."[25] In line with the ideology of Italy's Christian Democrats, television aimed to smooth over the gaps between modern society and Italian cultural and religious traditions, "integrating" the working class and leading it away from Communism.[26] Guala was followed by a figure who dominated Italian broadcasting throughout the 1960s, the slightly more moderate Ettore Bernabei. Bernabei too saw television primarily as a means of education and declared, "The spectators are 20 million fools, and our job is to educate them."[27] Like Reith, Bernabei believed that the custodians of television should be a cultural elite, using mass communications to shape society according to their vision.

Guala and Bernabei found their French equivalents in Wladimir Porché, director-general of RTF from 1949 to 1957, and Jean d'Arcy, his programming director from 1952 to 1959. Porché and d'Arcy struck a more egalitarian tone than Guala and Bernabei, with the former casting television as means for the "abolition of intellectual castes"[28] and the latter, closely linked to the popular education organization Peuple et Culture, treating it as a means to achieve more equal access to knowledge and to "awaken the men of this country to the destiny that lies before them."[29] D'Arcy's programming followed the public service practice of seeking to at once "inform, educate, and entertain" (a slogan frequently used by the BBC), although the RTF's mission was not formalized in any legal documents until its reorganization as the Office de Radiodiffusion Télévision Française (ORTF) in 1964, at which point the BBC was used as an explicit model.[30] Privileged genres in early French television included those of "cultural popularization," historical drama, and adaptations of French literary classics.[31] Despite d'Arcy and Porché's aspirations toward a cultural leveling, then, French public service was, like the British and Italian variations, "highly prescriptive" and "based on the assumption that radio and television should promote a certain idea of culture and not necessarily try to cater to the immediate tastes of the majority."[32] In all three cases, we find a blending of a large-scale project of cultural uplift and integration with a very traditional and class-specific definition of culture.

All three countries, at least at the outset of their television services, were alike in that the state held a monopoly on broadcasting. By the late 1940s, a fairly standard model had emerged, in which

> broadcasting was centralized in a public institution with a monopoly over television and radio. This organization provided two or three channels of television for the entire country. . . . It was (and still is) usually not run under direct government control, but through a semi-independent board appointed directly or indirectly by the government or, more frequently, by the national legislature. . . . Financing derives from a periodic license fee on television and radio sets, supplemented by advertising revenues.[33]

A monopoly, of course, rendered television an essentially noncommercial operation (although advertising would be introduced in some instances;

I will return briefly to the Italian case). Unlike film producers, then, state television monopolies had no obligation to sell anything; they were almost entirely insulated from any competition, with the exception of the United Kingdom, which operated under a public–private duopoly system, itself still a very limited form of competition, as of 1956.[34] The monopoly likewise allowed the spectator to be conceived of in a very different way than in the cinema, more as "a public or set of publics to be served than as a market to be exploited, less as a mass being pulled toward a predominant focal point of gravity and more as a set of overlapping tastes and interests," as Blumler puts it.[35] As we will see in chapter 5, it was the challenge to state monopolies on broadcasting that largely changed the face of public service broadcasting, forcing it both to redefine its relationship to commercialism and to reconceptualize its spectators.

I will not attempt here to pass judgment on every element of public service broadcasting or to consider the gap between its ambitions and its achievements. Even so, one can hardly fail to note the extent to which the entire project was bound up with a classist ideology of "integration" and national authority, dressed up in the sacred vestments of culture. While one could easily see public service as "a relocation of a nineteenth-century humanistic dream," this dream itself was driven by a fear of the masses, one that we could easily link to a "cultivating" function motivated by a perceived need for their control and pacification.[36] This ambition further suggests a desire to universalize the bourgeois subject in a condescending manner not unknown, as we have seen, among major figures in public service broadcasting. Reith himself described his project as the effort of a "practical idealist who builds up his Utopia on the foundations, and with materials, already to hand."[37] Yet can one really call "utopian" a project so steeped in an authoritarian, classist, and statist agenda? If we are speaking of utopia as method, there is no reason why not; as Bloch and others have demonstrated, the "utopian impulse" by no means limits itself to manifestations that appear progressive or emancipatory, nor is the utopian value of any given phenomenon negated by its ideological functions. To return to a notion I alluded to in the introduction, we might draw on Bloch's concept of the "cultural surplus" to see the ideology of public service as serving but not delimited by its own ideological function. Bloch argues that even ideologies that initially served to create false consciousness can contain utopian elements that articulate valid hopes yet to be fulfilled.[38] We can thus find within the ideology and practices of public service both material practices that can be easily revalenced to draw out their utopian character (as the three directors treated here do) and promises that it suggested but never realized (of a harmonious collective, a "people that sees itself," a kind of audiovisual media that would remain accountable to the public good). From a utopian perspective, what counts—not only for those who imagined its superior double in the past but also for our present and our future—is not how public service and the discourse around it functioned ideologically but rather what that ideology allowed to be thought or projected beyond what actually existed. In short, even if one believes that the directors of the BBC, RAI, and ORTF had no interest or ability whatsoever (whether for ideological or political reasons) in advancing an emancipatory project through their monopoly and its accompanying cultural and educational imperatives, this does not mean that the notion of public service broadcasting or television more broadly does not make legitimate promises that we can call on the future to fulfill.

The characteristics of television as defined by public broadcasting institutions and their discourses provide a good starting point for understanding how and why one might place television after cinema in a succession of media forms—and why it might have appealed to practitioners of utopian thought and method. Taking its proclamations at face value, however, whether one believes they were fulfilled or not, only begins to scratch the surface of the enormous cultural changes that television had set in motion; though public service made grandiose promises that sparked the utopian imagination, many of the processes that it set into motion were carried out far less overtly. They did not take the shape of explicit utopian promises but rather produced new conflicts and contradictions that created the conditions for new ways of thinking about the image, its relationship to other forms of information, and its possible uses.

The discourses and practices of public service broadcasting, even as they tried to construct a stable identity and function for television, often threatened to disrupt and destabilize some of the central terms they used to do so. This destabilization was the result of two primary (and closely related) phenomena: the first was television's supposed affinity for and association with information. In making information a central part of its identity, television raised the question of what distinguished an "informational" use of the audiovisual from any other one: does an informational image look different from an entertaining one or one meant to provide an aesthetic experience? Is it possible to predetermine the mode of reading that will be applied to an "informational" image to make sure it is understood as intended? My point here is not so much that viewers can decode television messages in multiple ways, as argued by Stuart Hall, as it is that "information" itself is suddenly revealed, when used as a criterion of distinction, to be a highly relative category (whether applied to a particular text, a particular medium, or a particular way of decoding), difficult to definitively separate from its others.[39] To be clear, my use of the word *informational* throughout this book is not meant to suggest any essential or empirical referent; rather, I assume it to be a fluid and historically variable category, whose identifiability depends on its supposed difference from some equally fluid other category. Part of what television makes visible, as I will return to later, is precisely how much such categories depend on a historically specific *partage du sensible* whose lines of demarcation are subject to change.

The second major destabilizing element was located in the "comprehensive" quality of public service, particularly in the way it insisted that an informational function be complemented by others (entertainment, cultural dissemination). At stake here was not only the difficulty of discerning the informational from its others but also the broader question of the effects and implications of television's absorption of so many different functions, forms of text, and forms of spectatorial engagement. As Raymond Williams notes, "the cinema had remained at an earlier level of social definition; it was and remains a special kind of theatre, offering specific and discrete works of one general kind. Broadcasting, by contrast, offered a whole social intake: music, news, entertainment, sport."[40] The consolidation of one institution depended on the radical disruption of almost all others but also called into question whether these separate fields and functions would (or could) retain their distinction when quite literally located (from the viewer's perspective) in the same place.

The very ideas that public service broadcasting invokes to define and justify itself are thus extremely fragile and potentially disruptive; attempting to achieve them risks revealing the fact that they are based on abstractions and categorizations that the medium itself threatens to do away with. The same fragility or indeterminacy can likewise be located in television as technology. Television was, William Urrichio notes,

> a medium, even before its institutional consolidation around 1950, that was related to telephone, radio, and film technologies; that drew upon journalistic, theatrical, and (documentary) filmmaking practices; that was variously understood as domestic like radio, public like film, or person-to-person like the telephone; that was live and recorded, high definition and low, large screen and small.[41]

As their proximity in Urrichio's description suggests, the collapsing or merging of functions or forms of practice (journalism, theater, filmmaking) and the hybrid character (film, telephone, radio) of television's technological functions were intimately connected; both disrupted the existing divisions between ways of making and doing, seeing and experiencing, and challenged the categories through which these were identified and kept separate.

Far beyond simply offering a new venue in which informational media could develop itself, television thus carried out a kind of cultural remapping, in which different forms of discourse, different modes of reception, and different cultural levels could be brought together. In this sense, it offered a way to shift the lines of demarcation that accomplish Rancière's *partage du sensible,* altering not only what could be seen and by whom but also how different types of practice and experience (watching the news, watching a televised play, watching a sports match) were placed in relation to one another, particularly in terms of their supposed function or value. This remapping deeply informed the shape of the utopian projects that television could inspire. It was not only cinema, in other words, that television held out the promise (or threat) of absorbing into itself: through its commitment to comprehensiveness and its centralizing of formerly separate functions and activities within the same institution (and for the viewer, within a single device), it evoked the possibility of a future state in which the boundaries between them might be dissolved.

Why, precisely, television's cultural remapping might have been seen as holding utopian promise, however, only becomes fully clear in light of the cultural needs that it might have served and the broader problems to which it might have responded. I will provide a far more detailed account of how television destabilized and reconfigured the *partage du sensible* in this chapter's final section. Before doing so, however, I would like to take a slight detour and sketch the basic contours of some of the major postwar debates about art and information and the deadlocks or problems that they generated. By examining how filmmakers attempted to respond to these problems both before and after the consolidation of television, we will be able to see more precisely how the redistribution of the sensible that it carried out provided the raw materials for new, utopian solutions to be posited.

ART, INFORMATION, AND "USEFULNESS"

Television's unique attributes not only facilitated the remapping of cultural categories and displaced existing lines of demarcation between practices, institutions, and experiences but, in doing so, offered a new way to frame—and hence respond to—long-standing questions concerning art's "usefulness" and where it "belonged." While the idea that art should have a clear social purpose had been at the heart of many of the key developments of interwar art (the "historical avant-garde" as defined by Peter Bürger, Brechtian theater, the British Documentary Film Movement), it had fallen into a more dubious position in the postwar period.[42] Certainly conceptions of art that assigned it a social or political imperative—Socialist Realism, Sartrean *engagement*—continued to exist, but they were largely outflanked by the anti-instrumental position espoused by Adorno and by a modernism that derived its power from its externality to any specific ends and its distance from any easily identifiable or reducible meaning. Much debate revolved around the question of whether art's social or political function lay in an instrumental usage of its ability to accurately represent and inform (Sartre) or in its nonsubordination to meaning and purpose (Adorno). "Eulogists of 'relevance,'" Adorno writes, "are more likely to find Sartre's *Huis clos* profound, than to listen patiently to a text whose language challenges signification and by its very distance from meaning revolts in advance against positivist subordination to meaning."[43] For Adorno, art's importance lies not in its meaning or its positing of political solutions but in its resistance to them: "It is not the office of art to spotlight alternatives, but to resist by its form alone the course of the world, which permanently puts a pistol to men's heads."[44] One wonders, however, if Adorno's position may not be undergirded by the same logic that responds to disillusionment by retreating within four walls, into the warm glow of the television; the pistol-to-the-head of modern life is not characterized as something that one might in any way alter or that might set the stage for some future development but rather is something that should be resisted "by form alone."

Sartre's alternative, meanwhile, does little to solve the problem. The engaged artist—for Sartre, above all a writer, thanks to literature's supposed capacity for communication, a capacity that is certainly more often emphasized by television than by cinema—can reveal to the reader both the world and himself. Richard Wright, for example, in addressing African American readers, "mediates, names, and shows them the life they lead from day to day in its immediacy" by raising himself "from the immediate to the reflective recapturing of his condition."[45] Ideally, the readers of the engaged work are, in reading it, "able to get their bearings, to see themselves and see their situation . . . the work of art, taken in the totality of its exigencies is not a simple description of the present but a judgment of this present in the name of a future."[46] The possibility of this future, in turn, reveals to the reader his freedom to build it: "we must reveal to the reader his power, in each concrete case, of doing and undoing, in short of acting."[47] Sartre's program, then, is one in which a writer constructs a representation that serves as a "reflective recapturing" for the reader, which in turn leads to a particular behavior ("acting"). There is little importance attributed to aesthetic specificity here or to that form that for Adorno constitutes art's defining attribute. Instead, the artist's medium is treated as transparent and communicative and capable of achieving a predictable result. This model essentially follows the logic of what Rancière has termed the "representational regime," still espoused by much self-avowedly "political" art, in which

> what the viewer sees—on a stage no less than in a photographic exhibition or an installation—is a set of signs formed according to an artist's intention. By recognizing these signs the spectator is supposedly induced into a specific reading of the world around us, leading, in turn, to the feeling of a certain proximity or distance, and ultimately to the spectator's intervening into the situation staged by the author.[48]

Of course, in Sartre's case, we are dealing primarily with words rather than with visual representations, but the logic is the same: the artwork's usefulness lies in its supposed capacity to create a representation that conveys particular ideas or "a specific reading of the world." These ideas, in turn, elicit a certain action on the part of the spectator or reader.

As Rancière notes, this schema was called into question as long ago as the eighteenth century by Jean-Jacques Rousseau, who "argues against the presumption of a direct relation running from the performance of bodies on stage to its effects on the minds of spectators and its consequences for their behavior outside the theatre."[49] Adorno shares Rousseau's skepticism: it is not only that such a system does not work that poses a problem but also the fact that any effort to instantiate it detracts from art's legitimate function. For him, the logic of art and the logic of information or didacticism are simply incommensurable, and both suffer in any attempt to join the two. Adorno illustrates this argument through an analysis of the works of Brecht, in which "the process of aesthetic reduction [of individuated characters into 'the agents of social processes and functions'] that he pursues for the sake of political truth, in fact gets in its way. For this truth involves innumerable mediations, which Brecht disdains."[50] Similarly, in *Mother Courage*, "the picture-book technique which Brecht needs to spell out his thesis prevents him from proving it."[51] The "political truth" and conceptual theses Brecht wishes to convey are for Adorno incommensurable with aesthetic form. Similarly, a concern with information disrupts the work's formal power for expressing more abstract "essences": "the more preoccupied Brecht becomes with information, the more he misses the essence of capitalism which the parable [of *Saint Joan*] is supposed to present."[52] Form, finally, reasserts itself after all, as "the primacy of lesson over pure form, which Brecht intended to achieve, became a formal device itself.... The correction of form by external conditions, with the elimination of ornament in the service of function, only increases its autonomy."[53] Adorno seems to have all of the bases covered: information and "political truth" are inevitably simplified or falsified when subjected to an aesthetic form, art-as-form is weakened by any attempt to convey information, and attempts to foreground "lesson" only turn it into another element of form rather than a means of conveying information.

For Adorno, then, any coexistence of informational and aesthetic imperatives is impossible. In attempting to bring the two closer together and to eradicate their specificity, an artist like Brecht fails on all counts. Even if Brecht's concern with form exceeds that of Sartre, he is no more capable of solving the problem. For Adorno, art's capacity for social meaning and "resistance" is instead to be found in one of the characteristics that Rancière identifies with the "aesthetic regime," a mode of thinking about art that finds its roots in the eighteenth century, particularly in the German context (Kant, Schiller), and persists today, namely, its appeal to a discrete sensorium, "a specific form of sensory apprehension."[54] Rancière argues that any notion that this separate form of sensory apprehension could be completely autonomous and apolitical, however, is contradicted by another tendency, in which the work of art suggests "the autonomy of a life in which art has no separate existence—in which its productions are in fact self-expressions of life."[55] One of the dialectics characteristic of the aesthetic regime, then, is that between an art whose separateness marks its "resistance" to all else that exists and an art that elicits a transformation of the world into one in which the "other life" suggested by it would become a reality. Adorno's position in relation to these two poles is a complex one—he does indeed believe that art cannot simply represent total otherness, pure resistance, lest it tumble from "a determinate negation of meaning" into "a bad positivism of meaninglessness"[56]— but it does clearly require that art maintain its distinctiveness to avoid subordination to meaning, its complete co-option by the state or the culture industry, or the total destruction of any separate sensorium: art must be saved from "its transformation into a metapolitical act and from its assimilation into the forms of aestheticized life. It is this demand that is encapsulated in Adorno's aesthetics."[57] The idea of an "other life" remains, but on the condition that this otherness accept no demands from that which does exist. As Rancière writes, "in this logic, the promise of emancipation is retained, but the cost of doing so entails refusing every form of reconciliation, or maintaining the gap between the dissensual form of the work and the forms of ordinary experience."[58]

For Rancière, the very logic of the aesthetic regime necessitates that for something to be identifiable as art, it must be discernibly "separate" from that which surrounds it, yet this very separateness elicits a desire to change the world to more fully approximate the condition of the work of art. Any instrumental or informational use of art, then, risks turning art into its opposite (i.e., part of the dominant sensorium, whether that of an aestheticized politics, the culture industry, or the instrumentalist register of the "informational"), draining it of any specificity as form of practice or experience (as in the case of Sartre) or severely compromising both aesthetic and informational functions (as in the case of Brecht). Adorno's position, coupled with Rancière's analysis of the foundations that subtend it, clearly articulates the deadlock that art and artists found themselves in regarding their potential "usefulness" during the postwar period, one that derived both from the ways of thinking about art firmly entrenched by the aesthetic regime over the past two centuries and, more proximately, from the supposed failure of the historical avant-gardes and efforts to reconstitute life as art that had taken place in the 1920s and 1930s, in both Fascist and Communist regimes.

This deadlock, however, is not necessarily an insurmountable one; it depends, at least in part, on the acceptance of a certain *partage du sensible* that may in fact be alterable, nor is it an eternal, ahistorical one (any more than the Sartre–Adorno polemic represents a clash between conflicting eternal truths). After all, as Jameson reminds us, "the taboo on the didactic in art (which we moderns, we 'Western' moderns, take for granted) is in fact itself a feature of our own modernity."[59] The aesthetic regime, meanwhile, can be interpreted in a way that admits its own sort of usefulness, whether in the form of Adorno's "resistance" or of Schiller's "aesthetic education." While it is the representational regime that Ran-cière associates with a "pedagogical model," the aesthetic regime clearly has its didacticism and pedagogies as well, whether they deal with an experience of radical freedom that invites its own realization beyond the sphere of art or posit the aesthetic as offering a specific kind of knowledge. There are, finally, works that reject the pedagogical models of both the representational *and* the aesthetic regimes, while still maintaining some conception of usefulness.

ART AND INFORMATION IN VERTOV AND GRIERSON

In many senses, the works of Rossellini, Watkins, and Godard fit this definition, even if they are able to imagine their exit from these paradigms more than they are able to achieve it. They were hardly the first, however, to attempt to conceptualize the moving image's usefulness in respect to its aesthetic and informational properties. I will contend here that it was the cultural operations carried out by television that provided the context and the concepts through which they did so, but other attempts both predate television's large-scale instantiation and gesture toward the same end. The two efforts I have in mind are the work during the 1920s and 1930s of Dziga Vertov, in the Soviet Union, and of John Grierson, in the United Kingdom. I pause to consider them here for several reasons: first, they provide key reference points, and even "models," for the televi-sion works that followed (Vertov for Godard; Grierson, more tacitly, for Watkins; and both, I would argue, for Rossellini). Second, they serve as useful points of historical comparison: what was thinkable in the 1920s and 1930s that was not in the 1950s and 1960s, or vice versa, and what might television have to do with it? Third, they demonstrate that the kind of overcoming of separate forms of practice and apprehension that characterizes the utopian television of the 1960s and 1970s is not specifi-cally dependent on television as technology but rather *makes use* of it, just as Vertov and Grierson made use of the cinema; it is a cultural operation rather than a technological one, or one that depends on anything like medium specificity, even if different mediums suggest different ways of solving the problem. By examining the way that Vertov and Grierson approach the art–information relationship prior to the consolidation of television, and then considering the same problems they confronted within the later context of the changes television had brought about, we can begin to see how the *partage du sensible* had been reconfigured and what sort of promise this reconfiguration held.

Both Vertov and Grierson used the cinema to attempt to renegotiate the relationship between aesthetics and information. At the same time, they defined their practice in opposition to both, refusing to identify with practices clearly associated with either the informational or the aesthetic. Grierson contrasts the documentary—a form which for him is more one to be realized than it is something that actually exists—with the newsreel, which displays "a purely journalistic skill," and "lecture films," which "describe, and even expose, but in any aesthetic sense, only rarely reveal."[60] The documentary, unlike the newsreel or lecture film, he argues, is an artistic product, "a new and vital art form," yet confronts problems to which art is supposedly unaccustomed.[61] As he puts it in a statement that makes one suspect he had not read too many British novels, he writes, "Realist documentary, with its streets and cities and slums and markets and exchanges and factories, has given itself the job of making poetry where no poet has gone before it, and where no ends, sufficient for the purposes of art, are easily observed."[62] Despite this, Grierson is unwilling to consider his project an aesthetic one: "In our world," he writes, "it is specially necessary to guard against the aesthetic argument. . . . Documentary was from the beginning—when we first separated our public purpose theories from those of Flaherty—an 'anti-aesthetic' movement. . . . What confuses the history is that we had always the good sense to use the aesthetes."[63] Even if one finds Grierson's vacillation concerning the aesthetic status of the documentary to be the result of political exigencies or theoretical inconsistency, it is clear that his project brought the aesthetic and the anti-aesthetic, art and information, into a proximity that threw their relationship into question. I would, on this matter, strongly disagree with the critiques against Grierson leveled by Brian Winston, who dismisses his efforts to couple art and actuality as "an obvious contradiction"[64] and argues that "Grierson's social responsibility rhetoric was largely negated by the artistic privileges implicitly and explicitly claimed by this 'creative' person."[65] While Grierson's project was of course subject to compromise, and can be legitimately attacked (as it is by Winston) on political grounds, this does not diminish the significance of his efforts to discern how one might relate (and possibly synthesize) art and information; what matters here is less whether the problem Grierson posed was solved and more the fact that he felt the need to pose it in the first place, and the sorts of solutions he and his colleagues were able to imagine. Indeed, his inconsistency itself suggests that the form of practice that he sought to develop would necessitate a synthesis and overcoming, the accession to a position in which different imperatives and different practices were no longer regarded as separate and in tension with one another. At times, Grierson seems to resolve the problem by reverting to a hierarchical schema in which information simply "uses" the aesthetes, but this solution leaves plenty of questions unanswered: if one needs to "use" the aesthetes, is it merely to make the information go down easier; or, as Ian Aitken has argued, does Grierson's ideal have a far more sophisticated philosophical foundation, drawing upon the British philosopher F. H. Bradley as well as Kant and Hegel?[66] And might not the idea of "using the aesthetes" in itself potentially pose a challenge to major assumptions of both the representational regime (insofar as knowledge is no longer conceived of as transparently transmissible through some neutral form of representation) and the aesthetic regime (insofar as giving meaning to the aesthetic requires attaching it to a process of communication and the targeted transmission of a message)?

Vertov was less prone to such solutions and fully aware of the status of his work as challenging existing boundaries between practices and modes of apprehension. On one hand, he clearly rejects "art" as it currently exists: "Yes, comrades, as many of you know, we relegate 'art' to the periphery of our consciousness. . . . Instead of surrogates for life (theatrical performances, film-drama), we bring to the workers' consciousness facts (large and small), carefully selected, recorded, and organized."[67] The task of his "kino-eye" is not an "artistic" one, he argues, but rather an informational one: the "influencing" of workers "is done through facts, not through acting, dances, or verse, it means we devote very little attention to so-called art."[68] At the same time, Vertov refuses, like Grierson, to identify his practice with established "informing" ones: although he refers to his *Kino-pravda* films as newsreels, he notes their difference from other newsreels of the time—"the newsreels from Pathé and Gaumont (newspaper chronicles)"[69]—and calls, anticipating Grierson, for a newsreel that would "triumph as well in art."[70] Despite the fact that Vertov generally situated his own practice as informing and useful, then, its conception of utility had little to do with existing notions about the transparency of information. Indeed, for him the existing models needed to be replaced by new forms of seeing and new ways of producing and arranging images, formal innovations that appealed to the creation of a specific sensorium and necessitated something like an art. This new practice depended on the fusion of man and technology—the "concerted action of the liberated and perfected camera and the strategic brain of man directing"[71]—but was just as importantly an attempt to blur the lines between aesthetic and informational practice, with an emphasis on giving a clear use-value to the former, as evidenced by Vertov's claim that he created something more like shoes than an "artistic film." His films, he argues, are "perhaps clumsy, awkward, lacking shine, perhaps somewhat flawed, but still necessary objects, vital objects, aimed at life and needed in life."[72] Even if Vertov tends, like Grierson, to give the "informational" the upper hand, there is a clear reaching toward a synthesis of information and aesthetics, which attests both to the possibility and desirability of an overcoming and the difficulty of achieving one, as though the concepts, words, and practices for doing so were still unreachable, located at some inaccessible point in the future. The ultimate goal entails something like a redistribution of the sensible, a reconfiguration of ways of making, doing, seeing, and knowing, that would suit the new socialist society of the USSR.

What if the tool that could accomplish this goal were television, or at least its ideal utopian version? As has often been noted, many of Vertov's concerns—the idea of an all-seeing "kino-eye," continuously recording and minimizing the temporal gap between filming and viewing—gesture toward television, a medium whose possible uses he anticipated.[73] As Zielinksi notes, "although technically it only existed in rudimentary form and aesthetically only as a utopia, what he described, what he practiced from the principle of production and with regard to an audience's perception, was essentially *tele-vision*."[74] Less than the idea that Vertov anticipated or imagined uses for technology that was yet to come, though, what interests me here is that the idea of a transcendence—of leaving the *dispositif* of cinema behind—suggests the need, for Vertov, for new words, new cultural materials to work with, and what we might call a new site or even a utopian enclave. In other words, while it is certainly significant that Vertov's imagination attached itself to new, utopian forms of technology, and particularly those that would allow for the proto-televisual linkage of workers around the world, it is perhaps even more significant that these technologies (whether televisual or otherwise) were at least in part appealing because they offered a solution to what was essentially a cultural rather than technical problem: to go beyond the current separation of art and other forms of production and reception, beyond an impoverished art and an ineffective informational practice, one needs to imagine a site at which this separation could be overcome. As it emerged in the postwar period, television offered such a site—and a new set of materials for solving the problems that Vertov and Grierson had posed in respect to cinema.

THE DISRUPTIVE FORCE OF TELEVISION

The experiments of Grierson and Vertov, of course, could not simply be repeated in the television age. On one hand, the technological possibilities available to those working with moving images had changed dramatically; on the other, the lines separating art from non-art, and a conception of art as formally "resistant" rather than instrumental (as in the representational regime) or world transforming (as in the transformational moment of the aesthetic regime), were more firmly entrenched. Nor were these two factors separate: from an Adornian point of view, it was television that had finally succeeded in transforming the world into "appearance," into a self-evident phenomenon easily graspable from one's own living room. For Adorno, television marks the technological realization of a completely visible world, whose ideology hinges on this very visibility: "the more completely the world becomes appearance, the more imperviously the appearance becomes ideology."[75] What would later be called the "ideology of the visible," in which visibility is falsely equated with access, understanding, and self-evidence, becomes ubiquitous thanks to the broadcasting capacities of television and its new centrality within the home.[76] One can thus argue that any form of visibility that manifests itself within this context will almost invariably fall sway to its rules and logic, so any effort to "use" it can only fall deeper into ideology.

Furthermore, this visible world, as Gunther Anders argues, is nothing more than a commodity, one that viewers consume from a position of passive detachment.[77] Vertov's dream of a world visible to itself is thus recast as the apotheosis of ideology and the complete penetration of the world by the logic of the commodity, whereas any effort to bring art closer to other cultural practices becomes, as Peter Bürger puts it, a "false sublation," in which art does indeed become "useful" but serves the purposes of consumer capitalism.[78] Furthermore, Adorno identifies television as an illustration of how utopian hopes always fail: in a 1964 conversation with Bloch, he notes that it represents one of the "numerous so-called utopian dreams" to have been fulfilled, whose fulfillment itself has made it take on "a peculiar character of sobriety, of the spirit of positivism, of boredom."[79] TV claims to fulfill our wishes, but "instead of the wish-image providing access to the erotic utopia, one sees in the best of circumstances some kind of more or less pretty pop singer, who continues to deceive the spectator in regard to her prettiness insofar as she sings some kind of nonsense instead of showing it."[80] Television, in short, is a tease, as are any utopian promises it might make.

We might, then, be tempted to dismiss the 1960s as far less hospitable to any new form of art than the decades that preceded it. What efforts at synthesis like those of Grierson and Vertov gestured toward seemed to have become not more proximate thanks to the development of new technology but rather betrayed or revealed as negative due to cultural transformations in which television had played an instrumental role. The "television age," as noted at the outset of this chapter, would thus be cast as the end of a particular narrative, as a state of paralysis and depoliticization that forbid efforts at cultural renovation that had previously seemed possible. But if we superimpose a utopian narrative upon this one, we can begin to look at television as something that had at this moment not yet happened; we can project it forward, turning it into a true *tele-vision* or *Fernsehen*, in which what it discloses to us in its actuality is something yet to come, a far-off place that can nonetheless be glimpsed *through* the actual rather than being obscured by it. This far-off place is the utopia toward which utopian television turns its gaze; it is not so much, as discussed in the introduction, an imagined future that it glimpses but rather the anticipatory projection of elements of the present.

What emerged from the first decades of television's history that could then be used to challenge the ways in which information, art, and their relationship to each other, or the social role of the moving image more broadly, could be thought? As noted earlier, I believe that the two factors that contributed the most to new ways of conceptualizing such questions were, first, television's status as a kind of cultural "catch-all," in which previously separate cultural functions, types of discourse, and forms of experience or apprehension converged, and, second, its powerful association with information and communications. Both in its early stages of development and in the fixed *dispositif* that it established after World War II, television—as a technology, a set of institutions, and a set of textual practices—consistently ran up against problems concerning the relationship of the terms *art* and *information* (or others that could be closely associated with them), so much so that these problems themselves became central to its self-definition as medium. Following this tripartite definition of television as a technology, set of institutions, and set of textual practices, I want to now examine how conceptions of what television was and what it could do were generated in each of these three areas. It was these conceptions that provided the starting point for a utopian television, one that aimed beyond cinema and beyond television as it existed but, unlike the earlier projects of Grierson and Vertov, exploited the new cultural topography of the television age, taking the very processes that television had carried out, even the most seemingly devastating ones, as the raw materials for utopian thinking.

As a technology, and in the very components that define its materiality as a device, television invited associations with information to a greater extent than cinema. This affinity is evident in television's technological genealogy, as a technology that developed alongside cinema but with very different goals. While this genealogy itself by no means dictated the cultural forms television ultimately took, it had a decisive impact upon how it was subsequently thought, where it was placed culturally, and what other practices it was associated with. The primary distinction between a "cinematic" genealogy and a "televisual" one, Zielinski argues, is one between technologies of preservation and presentation, on one hand, and technologies of instantaneous communication, on the other, with television falling into the latter category, along with telegraphy and

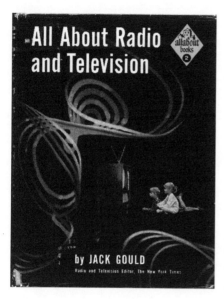

FIGURE I. Television depicted as a visible screen and invisible waves on the cover of Jack Gould's *All about Radio and Television* (1959).

telephony.[81] As it developed, television was thus located, practically and conceptually, alongside technologies of communication, far from early cinema's placement alongside either scientific analysis (the closer examination of physiological functions, as in Muybridge and Marey) or public entertainment. Rather than a visible object or the generator of visible objects, of "preserved images," television was first and foremost a *process*.

Even on a conceptual level, however, television-as-technology was not merely represented as a kind of empty process of communication, in need of some other substance to transmit. Rather, the television set's status as a kind of synecdochal representation of a larger communications system suggested an inherent duality, one that offered a new way to imagine and give figuration to the relationship between the aesthetic and the informational, among other binaries. This duality is clearly perceivable in an image used by David Joselit to demonstrate television's status as both network and commodity, the cover of Jack Gould's 1959 *All about Radio and Television* (Figure 1). For Joselit, the cover of Gould's book—an image of a television set surrounded by giant colored waves—depicts "the gap between the television commodity, represented photographically, and the network, represented in abstract wave patterns."[82] This duality, Joselit argues, suggests the possibilities of resisting or displacing the commodity form and turning it back into process, reasserting "the trajective principle by dissolving things into networks."[83] This is certainly one way of locating utopian potential in aspects of the technology that have been suppressed (or are being occulted) by its current usages, but we could also add another layer to Joselit's reading that would connect it more explicitly to the concept of information: the waves here suggest both the process of broadcasting and the idea of a kind of pure informationality, a nonphysical, nonvisible substance that exists alongside or behind the visible screen of the television-as-object (and presumably the speakers of the radio, not shown here). The signifier "television" itself thus encompasses two very different levels of substance: the nonmaterial "wave" and the material, visible "box" or "screen"—and the latter necessarily implies or calls to mind the former.

This basic configuration lends itself to a number of projections, a series of oppositions that could be mapped onto its components and subsequently inform the way that television and its functions might be thought. The perceivable surface of the screen, not dissimilar from the movie screen or the flat surface of a painted canvas or wall, invites associations with art and the aesthetic. The invisible wave, meanwhile, stands as a kind of pure knowledge, perhaps even as a challenge or rebuke to the all-too-accessible truth of the visible. One can easily see how such a configuration recapitulates and strongly underscores the idea that there is indeed some tension between the realm of information and the realm of the visible, also the realm in which the (visual) art object manifests itself. This tension or contradiction can be inflected in a number of different ways: one might, for example, take the associations I have suggested here to indicate that the visible world of television is nothing more than a degraded form of truth or real information, and even that art more broadly is essentially nontruth. Such a position, itself subject to a range of inflections (iconoclasm, Debordian critique of spectacle), would broadly position television as a sort of betrayal of truth and a negation of information (of course, one could just as easily adhere to this position while dispensing with the idea that "information" and "truth" are in any way the same thing). Yet one could take the opposite route as well, seeing this duality as a sign not of contradiction or opposition but of an effective communications process; in this case, television would *gain* informational or truth value due to its status as "translator" or "concretizer" of nonvisible data into perceptible images. Television, from this point of view, becomes a good icon, one whose visibility does not betray truth but incarnates it. Of course, one need not be so abstract: perhaps the most common association that grows out of this particular opposition is one that casts television as a practical device that carries information to and fro, as opposed to the cinema and other "static" technologies. I do not intend, of course, to suggest that any of these qualities are actually "in" television, nor that the oppositions I have sketched out have any kind of empirical existence. They do, however, deeply inform how television can be thought, particularly in terms of its capacity to unify or contain oppositions or contradictions, especially those between information and its others. We find the mobilization of these oppositions, to name just a few examples for the moment, in Rossellini's appeal to television as a machine capable of transmitting pure (i.e., disinterested, nonideological) information through its translation into and sensory manifestation as sound and image, in Watkins's exploration of the ways in which knowledge could be made visible through a critique of visibility itself, and in Godard's search for knowledge not in but between or through visible images. Television, more than cinema, then, lends itself to a conception of the moving image as in some way incarnating or translating the nonvisible, often identified with knowledge or information. We might say it *mediates* in a different way than film or, more specifically, that it tends to be thought of as a process that involves a change of substance, a transcoding rather than an analogical recording or storage, to recall Zielinski's opposition between transmission (television) and preservation (cinema).

The associations and oppositions I have outlined thus far, of course, are subject to a wide range of forms of encouragement or discouragement; how they are inflected depends not only on the philosophical and cultural frameworks that one projects upon them but also upon institutional claims and practices concerning television. Here the distinction between American and European broadcasting institutions also takes on a high degree of importance. In Europe, broadcasting (first of radio signals, then of television signals) was first associated on an institutional level with practical communications rather than art or entertainment, to such an extent that when, in the United Kingdom, "the Marconi company began broadcasting in 1920, there were complaints that this use for entertainment of what was primarily a commercial and transport-control medium was frivolous and dangerous, and there was even a temporary ban."[84] Critics of early broadcasts in the United Kingdom argued that "wireless, which was ideally equipped to be the 'servant of mankind,' was being treated as a 'toy to amuse children.'"[85] Here we begin to see how the question of what sorts of functions were permitted to broadcasting, and what other sorts of institutions it should be associated with, were highly contested ones. This contestation shows the extent to which radio, and then television, as sites of cultural negotiation provided an opportunity for the remapping of cultural functions. Would broadcasting be a tool of "service" or a means of entertainment? Even if one could clearly define either of these terms, both suggested further difficulties: would broadcasting take over the functions of the press or, for that matter, those of the music industry or the theater? What could be seen or heard, where, and by whom? A dramatic redistribution of the sensible was at stake. The extent to which this was considered a major problem, even on a purely economic level, is clear in Reith's chapter-long efforts in *Broadcast over Britain* to assure individuals working in the press, music, and theater that these fields would not be destroyed by broadcasting.[86] This was hardly, however, a solely economic problem, and the anxiety produced by broadcasting's seemingly infinite capacities to displace and materially reconfigure (or perhaps even dematerialize) existing institutions and their functions is symptomatic of the enormous yet largely unacknowledged cultural disruption that it was carrying out.

Reith's assurances notwithstanding, European broadcasting, in its adherence to a public service mission, most often assigned itself the tasks of communication, education, and socialization, later situating television as the heir, as Williams notes, not only to the newspaper but also to institutions such as church and school.[87] Much of the institutional discourse surrounding television in its early years, however, far from simply promoting this merging of functions and cultural fields within a single institution and device, aimed to contain it or render it less disruptive. The various functions television could serve were literally "channeled" and hierarchized, as though to insist on the separateness of types of texts, types of reception, and various cultural tasks; bulwarks were thrown up to restore order in the face of an overly radical redistribution of the sensible. The tension between a preservation of order and difference, on one hand, and a chaotic merging of categories, on the other, is immediately apparent in one of public service's most famous slogans. In the well-known British formulation, television was to "inform, educate, and entertain." Here, Bourdon argues, "the order plays a central role: entertainment was secondary with respect to the other two missions."[88] In France, meanwhile, the formulation was similar, but slightly modified, with "education" and "entertainment" coming after "satisfying needs of information and culture."[89] The precise orderings and variations here are less important than the fact that the need for some sort of hierarchization was felt, as though a wide range of texts and functions could not possibly be permitted to become equal or reducible to each other. This anxiety was so powerful that BBC director-general William Haley (Reith's successor) firmly opposed BBC Television head Maurice Gorham's request to begin television news service after the end of World War II, arguing that television's "entertainment" value threatened to overwhelm its informative capacity:

> I doubt whether the implications of a completely visual news bulletin and a newsreel have been fully comprehended. [Radio] is a vital public service charged with responsibilities of all kinds. [Television], in essence, is entertainment.... The necessity would arise to subordinate the primary functions of the news to the needs of visual presentation.[90]

When television news did begin to appear in the United Kingdom, it tended to alternate between two formats: an image filling the entire screen, occasionally accompanied by voice-over, or an image of news presenters simply reading the news bulletin; the latter practice was likewise the norm on German television. These tendencies to divide word and image, as though information could not be permitted to be visual, demonstrate what Bourdon calls "a repulsion for the moving image, judged to be incompatible with 'serious' information."[91] Here, then, functional hierarchy and the first point raised earlier—the duality of visible and invisible, here verbal/aural information and visual entertainment—converge. The attempt at separation between the two both signals the deep impact that their mixing had, as a cultural force disrupting long-standing distinctions, and points toward an ultimate state of radical nonseparation. This much-feared disruption creates an opening in which new utopian configurations—especially ones involving a synthesis or sublation—can be imagined, even as it threatens a kind of totalitarian homogenization, a prospect I will return to later.

The question of separation and hierarchization took on particular urgency in the early 1960s, for several reasons. First of all, the question of a balanced program, and the ways in which different types of television programs could be associated with different types of cultural tasks, was foregrounded by the creation of additional television channels (new public channels were launched in West Germany and Italy in 1961 and in France and the United Kingdom in 1964). In the case of the United Kingdom, a battle was waged regarding whether the new channel would be a public or private one, with the former eventually winning the day. The presence of multiple channels, however, presented new problems: should channels make programming choices separately or, as began to be standard practice with Italy's RAI networks in the 1960s, program in tandem to place a "weak" program against a "strong" one, thereby preserving a commitment to cultural programming while providing a "popular" alternative?[92] Would the two channels take on different "profiles" or both show a mix of entertainment and cultural/educational programming? The tension between convergence and separation, containment and total promiscuity, reemerged once again as a fundamental question, as a new form of separation or "channeling" became a possibility.

Throwing an additional layer of complexity into the problem of separation was the issue of advertising: with the exception of those shown on the United Kingdom's ITV (Europe's only private television channel in the 1950s), ads had to be clearly separated from programs, and could not interrupt them (a screen marking the beginning and end of advertisements is still common practice on European television).[93] As with the more general efforts at ordering and hierarchization discussed previously, here we once again see an effort to prevent a full collapse of functions: commercial imperatives would not be allowed to mix too freely with educational or cultural ones, and this separation seems to be predicated on the idea that the spectator's modes of reading the two might somehow converge. The case of advertisements, however, demonstrates the untenable character of any such efforts at separation: Italy's RAI instituted an all-advertisement program, *Carosello*, in 1957. The idea that a special time slot would be provided for ads suggests a careful effort to avoid contamination—an effort that is, of course, necessary only because a somehow-unacceptable convergence has already occurred. Despite the separation, however, advertisements themselves were turned into texts that resembled other types of programs; they were marked off through their self-containment and designated time slot but at the same time drew on "all sorts of televisual resources, the cartoon, a short theatrical scene, variety . . ."[94] While on the surface level, this might seem like a sort of pretext—a kind of sweetener to make advertising less objectionable, as Walter Veltroni puts it when he argues that, in contrast to America, "in Italy advertising had to find mediating aesthetic models, it had to be hidden, justified"[95]—it more tellingly demonstrates the convergence of all forms of texts and modes of apprehension on television; one is addressed by, understands, and is moved by an ad in the same way one would understand and be moved by a cartoon or a theatrical scene, to the point that any distinction between them becomes negligible. *Carosello* furthermore functioned as a kind of microcosm for the cultural agglomeration—the gathering of everything in a single place—carried out by television more broadly: the program enacted a kind of promiscuous montage or collage, Aldo Grasso explains, gathering together pieces of existing theatrical, cinematic, or televisual texts in a sort of travesty of the "constructive techniques of the avant-garde."[96] This phenomenon is a sign of the fact that efforts at separation and noncontamination were largely ineffective but likewise suggests that such convergence was part of the deeper underlying logic of television, that the blurring of boundaries and movement toward complete indistinguishability of modes of address, textual forms, and modes of reading and interpretation were perhaps its most important characteristics.

That such mixing could, however, have a utopian character is hinted at by the presence of what were previously avant-garde techniques, providing a connection to the art of the 1920s that we will also find in Rossellini's works. What is odd here, however, is that the very institution that proclaims the importance of and enforces separation depends on its failure. I will return to the implications of this contradiction between the overt behavior of the institution, its proclaimed logic, and its actual functioning shortly, but suffice it to say for the moment that this oscillation between convergence and separation marked another one of the main ways that television invited a rethinking of how different types of cultural function could be integrated and how the social function served and experiences engendered by the moving image could be conceived.

Beyond its technological basis and its institutional framework, television's capacity to transform the ways in which the relationship between information and its others could be conceived of was affected by the use of textual forms that insisted on its uniquely informational function and demarcated it from cinema. As Mary Ann Doane has observed, "television does not so much represent as it informs. Theories of representation painstakingly elaborated in relation to film are clearly inadequate."[97] Television, in other words, has both a different function and a different set of forms that ostensibly correspond to that function. This was, of course, already a defining characteristic of television on the technological and institutional level, but one that had to be promoted and solidified through specific textual practices. A notion of the informational permeates the forms of televisual discourse and is not isolated to overtly informational programs: as Doane notes,

> Information would specify the steady stream of daily "newsworthy" events characterized by their regularity if not predictability. Although news programs would constitute its most common source, it is also dispersed among a number of other types of programs.... The content of information is ever-changing, but information, as genre, is always *there*.[98]

In other words, what one might expect to be one specific mode or category (and, indeed, one whose integrity and reliability depend on its separation from other modes or categories) in fact bleeds over into others, thus gesturing toward the impossibility of maintaining separation but also the potential merging of all modes into a single one. Doane goes on to note that this informationality seems to resist identification with any particular form: "information, unlike narrative, is not chained to a particular organization of the signifier or a specific style of address."[99] While this was certainly less true of European television in the 1950s and 1960s than it was of the 1980s American television that Doane focuses on, her observation suggests that television ultimately makes "information" itself harder to identify as a discrete category precisely due to its supposed ubiquity.

Even within the framework of programs that clearly marked themselves as "informational," one finds an anxiety about the instability of this category and efforts to prevent it from being destabilized. For example, the information–visibility opposition—which for William Haley prevented television from being as viable a news source as radio had been—might be mapped onto that of voice–body, with the visible body of the television speaker threatening to disrupt or contaminate the informational character of the voice. The bodies belonging to the television speaker had to be carefully selected, as though to contain them: as André Bazin notes, the television presenter or "speakerine" "must be pretty and gracious, but in no way lead the tele-spectator to imaginary adultery."[100] The idea that the visual image and appeal of a presenter—whether male or female—might present some threat to the informational integrity of television was likewise reflected in European television's early news broadcasts, which refused a "star-system" and, in some cases, deliberately neglected to name the presenters.[101] These efforts suggest not only an awareness of the precariousness of the informational—as genre, as guarantee, as prescribing a single mode of viewing—but perhaps even a fear that television was constitutionally incapable of delivering what was perhaps the most important element of its own self-definition.

On a similar note, Raymond Williams notes the frequent concern, raised in relation to "drama-documentary" programs, that viewers would somehow confuse the informational elements with noninformational ones. On the surface, this seems like another effort at containment, on the level of the individual program rather than of the schedule, an effort to make sure that separate textual forms, their associated functions, and the modes of apprehension they encourage do not collapse into one another.

Yet Williams argues that, much like those failures at containment that a program like *Carosello* depended on, this fear represents an ideological effort to preserve the illusion of separation: "some of the complaint about 'confusion between reality and fiction' is naïve or disingenuous. This attempt to hold a hard line between absolutely separated categories seems to depend on a fiction about reality itself. It depends also on the convention that 'factual' television simply shows, neutrally, what is happening."[102] Both of these issues—the separation between informational and noninformational text, and the relationship between reality and fiction—will, as we will see, play a central role in the television works of Peter Watkins, which question the boundaries between these categories while still adhering to an informational imperative.

Such efforts to separate or "channel" different types of content and modes of reading demonstrate the fragility of the assumptions about inherent differences between different forms of text or audiovisual data that television at once affirmed and contradicted. Television would seem to be a duplicitous medium, one that acts one way on the surface while relying on a contrary logic on a deeper level, calling for separation while benefiting from its impossibility. This contradiction stems in part, as Williams suggests, from an ideological need to preserve the illusion of television's "neutrality," its association with pure information. The truth hidden by the efforts of containment, then, would be that television is never neutral, never informational, but always self-consciously exploiting its ability to mix types of text, functions, and modes of viewing. The truth of television would be something like Williams's concept of "flow," the idea that texts are not in fact separate but part of an integrated program whose overall logic shapes their individual form. Instead of a system in which "each unit could be thought of discretely, and the work of programming was a serial assembly of these units," television becomes one "in which the true series is not the published sequence of programme items but this sequence transformed by the inclusion of another kind of sequence, so that these sequences together compose the real flow, the real 'broadcasting.'"[103] I would inflect Williams's much-discussed term somewhat differently than he does, though, to emphasize not that flow is a kind of organizational principle and viewing experience specific to television but rather that it can itself serve as a metonym for the way that television productively refuses separation while formally adhering to or even performing it. The collapse that underlies television's efforts at separation is not some subversive force, some disruption that destabilizes a surface stability, but rather its organizing principle.

The collapse between institutions, forms of discourse, types of audiovisual texts, and modes of reading that television brings about—a process that I would argue can be productively understood, following Rancière, as a redistribution of the sensible—is hardly one that has gone unnoticed, yet my intention here has been to present a rather different account of it. Here, again, it might be useful to think in terms of competing or dialectically complementary narratives: while one can read this process as one that moves toward a violent eradication of all difference, one might also see it as leading to a different end or providing the raw materials for imagining one. The more familiar negative narrative is visible in a thinker like Jean Baudrillard, who argues that television and the other instruments of mass media subject all events to the same form; what would have formerly been separate types of texts and functions are reduced to a single, hegemonic logic. As Baudrillard puts it, the mass media is "not an ensemble of techniques for the diffusion of messages, but the imposition of models."[104] If news, entertainment, and ads all look the same, such a conclusion suggests, it is because television represents their political subjection to the force of ruling-class ideology, a subjection that produces homogeneity in cultural products, just as in human beings.

This account, however, would once again position television at the end of a narrative; it settles on a negative reading in which the cultural operations of convergence I have been describing, in their ultimate realization, have an essentially negative valence. The possibility of a remapping of cultural functions that they offer is foreclosed, because this is presumed to have led to nothing other than total homogeneity. There are several lines of thought with which we could challenge this narrative. We might find within the homogenization Baudrillard speaks of a suggestion of its utopian double: a process conceived of not as a top-down imposition of form and function but rather as a synthesis of previously separate forms and functions, into which the preexisting elements have been sublated.

This reading would suggest the possibility of a different television, but one that draws on the same constitutive processes and takes the conceptual and ideological bases of actually existing television quite seriously. We might also envision a television in which the untenability of the concepts through which the medium defines itself and the futility of its efforts to draw boundaries between different forms of text and different modes of spectatorship would be revealed, but not with the end goal of simply showing the duplicitous character of television. Rather, this critique would be accompanied by an effort to rethink how the disruptive power of television and the redistribution of the sensible that it enacts could be drawn out and exploited for different ends.

These lines of thought were followed by Rossellini, Watkins, and Godard. Rossellini took the first approach, not directly attacking the conceptual and ideological bases of television but rather treating them as promises that existing television had failed to fulfill. He attempted to save television by placing faith in its promise of a world in which appearance and truth, image and information, would all be one. In this case, television becomes its own kind of abandoned ideal, another new medium that has failed to deliver on what it claimed to offer, but whose offer itself deserves another attempt at fulfillment. Watkins (in his 1960s and 1970s work) and Godard, meanwhile, took the second route and attempted to mobilize the contradictions that emerged from the cultural convergence enacted by television, simultaneously revealing and exploiting the medium's underlying logic and its capacity to generate new ways of knowing, identifiable with neither the representational nor the aesthetic regime.

Whether one strives for a true synthesis (Rossellini), a "good" one to oppose the "false sublation" of the culture industry, or uses the inherent ambiguities and contradictions generated by television's dialectic of separation–convergence and its supposed informationality as the raw material for both a critique of television as it exists and the utopian imagining of its other (Watkins, Godard), television thus provides a new set of conditions for rethinking the question of the character and limits of art, its relationship to information, and its ultimate social utility. The conceptual field opened up by television was, at least for a time, quite undecided and fluid: while the terms called into play by or projected onto this field could ultimately position or define themselves, as I have suggested, in a wide range of opposing and even contradictory ways, key here is that the terms themselves are *mobilized,* quite literally, and their habitual positions disturbed or rendered less clearly identifiable. It is, meanwhile, the most apparently negative or threatening operation that takes place in this process of mobilization—the potential homogenization of previously separate cultural tasks into a single form, collected in a single venue—that offers the greatest opportunity, through a dialectical move that would transform the collapsing and homogenizing effects of television and the cultural logic it enacts into the signs or even embryonic forms of a utopian future state in which the collapse of art and information, aesthetic and pedagogical practice, would be used as a means of genuine public service.

The promise of television, of course, was not only a conceptual one. For the filmmaker, it also offered a site of production free of many of the constraints of working in the commercial cinema: no tickets needed to be sold, one had a more or less guaranteed audience, and funding was often provided by the state. It reached millions of viewers at once, guaranteeing an audience larger than many films would find in their entire commercial run during the course of a single evening. If an engaged, informational, and mass art was still possible—the kind of art that Grierson and Vertov had dreamed of—it would be on television rather than in the cinema. Here the moving image practitioner could take on a new identity, rejecting that of the art film auteur in favor of something far more protean and experimental. It was from this space, an actually existing, institutionally situated one, that another utopian space—that of an art after cinema, after television as it was, and perhaps after the falling away of any distinction that would even allow art to remain identifiable as a discrete category of cultural practice—could be glimpsed.

2

Television as Enlightenment
ROBERTO ROSSELLINI'S HISTORY LESSONS

Prior to his turn toward television in the early 1960s, Roberto Rossellini had been a central figure in the Italian neorealist movement and then director of a string of idiosyncratic works *(Stromboli, Europa '51, Voyage to Italy)* that would prove a major influence on the European art cinema of the coming years. He began to speak frequently of television as an alternative to cinema in the late 1950s, telling interlocutors André Bazin and Jean Renoir in a 1958 interview on the subject, "Modern society and modern art have been destructive of man; but television is an aid to his rediscovery. Television, an art without traditions, dares to go out and look for man."[1] For Rossellini, television's usefulness thus appeared first and foremost in its status as an open space or enclave, an "art without traditions," and hence a site upon which the foundations of a new art and society might be laid. Conversely, Rossellini's statement to Bazin and Renoir suggests a move backward: the new technology of television could be used not only to forge the future but to do so by recovering the lost hopes of the past, *re*-discovering the now-degraded figure of "man." Rossellini's utopianism thus entailed not simply looking forward or projecting from the present but also imagining connections between past and future, allowing the now-eclipsed possibilities of history to manifest themselves once again. Looking toward a future utopia required, in Blochian fashion, a return to the unfulfilled promises of the past. For Rossellini, man could be recovered or "rediscovered" through television, but only if one could find a way to save television itself, to keep it from wandering down the garden path of cinema, a medium that he associated with commercial escapism and a hermetic modernist art.

Rossellini committed himself to this task during the last fourteen years of his career, from 1962 to 1976, making exclusively what he considered to be "pedagogical" films, in all but two cases for television. According to their director, these films constituted a major break with the existing cinema: they were neither art nor entertainment, and he himself wished to be considered "not an artist but a pedagogue," expressing a desire to leave behind both cinema and the role of the *auteur*.[2] The television films tackle historical subjects that go far beyond the scope of the usual costume drama: notable titles include *The Taking of Power by Louis XIV, Acts of the Apostles, Socrates, Cartesius,* and the twelve-hour, history-spanning *Man's Struggle for Survival* (conceived by Rossellini but directed by his son Renzo). They were broadcast on European television, most often on Italy's RAI, reaching in some instances as many as 16 million viewers.[3] They resemble in their form neither the historical epic nor the "illustrated lecture" of didactic television; rather, they create a language all their own, as though cinema's cultural function could not be left behind without forging a new audiovisual language. Shot very quickly, the films rely on extremely long single takes, full of sinuous camera movements coupled with Rossellini's self-invented remote-control zoom. Narrative is only occasionally and weakly present, lengthy sequences of expository dialogue abound, and the acting shows little regard for naturalistic conventions.[4] Totaling more than forty hours, the television films constitute about half of Rossellini's entire output, a rather surprising figure given that he is remembered almost exclusively, even within scholarly circles, for his seminal neorealist films like *Open City* and *Paisà*. Until a recent resurgence of interest at the beginning of this century, even the French cinephile circles in which Rossellini has long been a canonical figure generally neglected these late films in favor of the maestro's works of the early 1950s. In part, the lack of attention given to them may result from their long unavailability, but even upon their initial broadcast, former Rossellini supporters like François Truffaut dismissed them entirely.[5] The relative lack of attention given to these films, and the discomfort or qualification that often accompanies their discussion, suggests not so much a case of neglect based on inaccessibility as a distaste and even rejection of Rossellini's claims to be moving beyond art, beyond cinema, and beyond his own *auteur* status. These claims were an outright provocation to both film directors and cinephiles, suggesting as they did the cultural and political bankruptcy of the kinds of moving image production in which they had invested themselves. They constituted an unequivocal rejection of cinema—as both an audiovisual language and a cultural and commercial institution—and an insistence that it be superseded and replaced by television. We might even conceive of this replacement as an overcoming or sublation; as Raymond Bellour notes, Rossellini's career path seems to suggest such a process, moving as it did "from the invention of modern cinema to its programmed disappearance in television."[6] One must, then, take seriously Rossellini's attempt to move beyond cinema; if audiovisual practice was to have any utopian potential, it was not, for him, to be found in the realm of cinema—an art that he had increasingly come to associate with the absence of communication—but in television, a medium whose communicative potential had not yet been fully exploited.

The puzzlement with which many of Rossellini's contemporaries responded to his pedagogical project has largely been mirrored by academic studies of his work, a situation that seems to me to suggest their exceptionality and their resistance to conventional forms of evaluation; academic discourse, we might say, has largely kept Rossellini on precisely the same ground from which he sought to depart. First, and understandably, the television project has been treated almost exclusively within the context of auteurist studies of Rossellini. Emphasis has therefore been placed on close readings of individual films and their "artistic" aspects, with less attention devoted to the project's theoretical positioning and its broader cultural and historical contexts.[7] Even studies that do address the theoretical framework (for example, many of the essays in the 2012 volume *Roberto Rossellini: de la fiction à l'histoire*) too often merely summarize Rossellini's thoughts or seek to judge their validity rather than attempting a deeper interpretation or historical positioning of them.[8] Second, the television films have been characterized by Rossellini's English-language biographer Tag Gallagher, who acts as a kind of official interpreter through his liner notes and "video essays" on the American DVD releases of the films, as little more than a modernist art cinema in disguise. Gallagher's line is typical of the resistance that

Rossellini's pedagogical project has so frequently encountered: despite his appreciation for the films, he downplays their difference from the rest of the director's works, dismissing the ambitious conceptual framework with which they were surrounded as a mere cover for business as usual. For Gallagher, Rossellini's claims of moving beyond art cinema are "patent hypocrisy":[9] "He wanted to do non-art but only succeeded at art."[10] I will attempt to counteract these tendencies here, both by placing Rossellini's project in a broader historical framework and by insisting on the importance of its theoretical underpinnings and its difference from art cinema. The project's greatest significance lies, I believe, in its status as an epochal effort to rejoin art and pedagogy, to meld together aesthetic (although Rossellini himself rejected the word) and informational practices, whose cross-contamination had been so vehemently rejected by Adorno in his critiques of Sartre and Brecht. In its attempts to do so, Rossellini's project represents a deeply revealing symptom of a historical moment at which the creation of a useful mass art with sociopolitical agency seemed unlikely yet still possible; as such, it can be seen as a late effort to salvage both twentieth-century modernity and Enlightenment ideals, much like public service television itself. The tools that Rossellini used, however, were those of his moment: he depended on the cultural operations of convergence or collapsing that television had carried out and on a conceptualization of television deeply inflected by the associations that had grown up around the medium since its inception. In other words, his efforts to create a utopian television would not have been possible in the absence of many of the same attributes of modernity that he decried.

For Rossellini himself, the television project's difference from what preceded it, and from all other audiovisual texts that surrounded it, was hardly in question. Indeed, it is the director's insistence that his television films constituted a major break with existing modes and institutions of cultural production that suggests the need to treat them not as a series of individual texts but as a concerted effort to redefine the form, function, and placement of audiovisual media, not to mention the status of the artist. Rossellini's stated desire to be "not an artist but a pedagogue" signals both the decisiveness of the transition and the presumed nonidentity of these two roles.[11] Accompanying this shift in identity or role was a renunciation of and separation from the cinema as an industry and institution, signaled by the declaration, "I wish to withdraw from the profession."[12] Accompanying this withdrawal, Rossellini believed, would be a tabula rasa on which to rebuild from scratch a new kind of art (or perhaps something challenging any possible definition of art): "I believe that what is necessary today is to prepare, in full liberty, to reexamine everything from the beginning, in order to be able to embark on a path with completely different foundations."[13] This path, Rossellini hoped, would lead to what he frequently referred to as a "utopia," as in the title of his 1974 book *Utopia autopsia 10^{10}* (with 10^{10} referring to the supposed number of neurons in the human brain; I will return to the implications of *autopsia* later).[14] As the title suggests, the utopia Rossellini had in mind would be one based on knowledge acquired through vision but can most concisely be characterized as a society in possession of a total knowledge of history, philosophy, and science, which he believed could be disseminated via television. The path to the future, then, could only proceed through a "reexamination" of the past, as though television itself had come to redeem a failed modernity and reinvest it with the utopian glow it once possessed.

AGAINST THE CULTURE INDUSTRY

While Rossellini's public declarations forcefully declared his intentions and symbolically enacted his rupture with the domain of cinema and art, they were preceded by theoretical reflections that more clearly reveal the motivations behind his television project and its historical stakes. These reflections are rooted in the opposition between high and low culture, between modernism and kitsch, that so strongly structured discourse around cultural production in the 1950s and 1960s. Rossellini's project begins as a proposed antidote to one of the terms of this opposition, namely, the products of the culture industry. His position on mass culture essentially echoes the Frankfurt School critique voiced so strongly by Adorno and Horkheimer, although the conclusions to which it leads him are uniquely his own, drawing out the emancipatory potential of forces that were, for his German forerunners, wholly oppressive.[15] While there is no evidence to suggest that Rossellini ever read Adorno and Horkheimer directly, he repeatedly cites the American cultural critic Dwight MacDonald's "A Theory of Mass Culture," which adopts Clement Greenberg's distinction between high art and kitsch and the Frankfurt School critics' viewpoint that mass culture is used by the ruling classes to "exploit the cultural needs of the masses in order to make a profit and/or to maintain their class rule," and both of these concepts are central to his thinking.[16]

Initially, Rossellini took a position typical of postwar modernists, affirming the artist's self-expression and individuality as a form of opposition to industrialized mass culture. Film, he argues in a late 1950s interview, must resist being co-opted by mass culture, which creates products "whose distinctive character is that of an article destined for mass consumption, like chewing gum, and which exploits, rather than satisfies, the cultural needs of the masses."[17] Furthermore, Rossellini contends, the products of mass culture serve as propaganda for "imposing the ideal of the American way of life onto the world" and encourage ignorance.[18] Cinema could resist these tendencies, he believed, by serving as a means of authentic and disinterested self-expression. It should do so, the filmmaker proposed, by occupying the familiar cultural position of high art, explaining in October 1958 that he was in favor of an authorially produced and artisanal art cinema: "I absolutely do not believe in working in a team, and I absolutely do not believe in the work of 'specialists' of art. To make chewing gum, to make shoes, yes, but not in art."[19] The dominance of an impersonal, mass-produced cinema that exploits rather than satisfies cultural needs, Rossellini argued, necessitated a firm response from filmmakers that could be implemented on a wide enough scale to represent a real challenge, and he led the charge by declaring, "My great project is to fight seriously and systematically against the 'official' cinema."[20] From its beginnings, then, Rossellini's project was systematic. It was not conceived of as an act of personal resistance to the hegemony of the "official cinema" but rather as an entirely new paradigm that had to be instantiated collectively.[21] As a systematic endeavor, it not only affirmed its kinship with utopian projects but also recalled Grierson's attempt to develop a noncommercial educational cinema, an attempt Rossellini references in noting that "Grierson had the genius to identify what the needs were, and then to organize a system in which to develop the thought, to satisfy those needs."[22] What

Rossellini had in mind, much like Grierson, was a large-scale project that would radically differ from cinema in terms of its form, function, and modes of production and distribution.

Rossellini at first believed that the French New Wave could become such a project and took a relatively hands-off but nonetheless engaged approach in guiding it.[23] He was disappointed with the results, but this disappointment indicated to him a need for something other than modernism or high culture. While the New Wave provided an alternative to a more industrial commercial cinema, it simply put personal neuroses and fetishes on display and had little social use: "What good is it to liberate cinema from the forces of money," Rossellini asks, "if it is only to open it to those of individual fantasy?"[24] The existing "art cinema," such as that of the New Wave or Fellini or Antonioni, may not have been culture industry propaganda, but it demonstrated a crippling degree of introversion and pessimism: "Today, art is either moaning and groaning or cruelty," he declares in 1963.[25] "The highest moral stance contemporary artists have taken has been to speak of incommunicability and alienation, that is to say, of two phenomena that are absolutely negative."[26] Such dissatisfaction with the individual self-expression characteristic of the European modernist cinema signaled Rossellini's first step away from a Greenbergian dualism and motivated a fierce and repeated denunciation of modernist art that condemned its inability to communicate and the alienation of the artist from his society: "I can understand an abstract painter, but I cannot understand how abstract art could become the official art form since it is the least intelligible."[27] Rossellini's rejection of modernism, disrupting the dualism that previously informed both his own thinking and that of so many other cultural critics of the period, in turn necessitated the formulation of a new set of oppositions that would structure his television project, as he took both high art and mass culture as negative objects against which he defined his own work. This new oppositional structure could have conceivably led Rossellini to take one of several familiar positions: one could easily see it falling into alignment with a Lukácsian rejection of modernism, a Sartrean insistence on communication and *engagement*, a Zhdanovite insistence on transparently didactic and idealizing art (i.e., Socialist Realism), or a position in which art ensures a kind of uncritical humanism compatible with what Marcuse calls "affirmative culture."[28] Rossellini's theoretical solution to the opposition and the works that it generated, however, escaped all of these positions, marking his exit from familiar ways of conceptualizing cultural production. It is in this exit, and in the attempts to break free of any existing paradigms, that we find the novelty and the importance of his project and its reasons for employing television.

Rossellini's rejection of both mass culture and modernism was born of a sense of their underlying kinship: both were symptomatic of the same processes of reification, of atomization, and of individualism.[29] Art cinema and modernism were seen as sterile oppositions to mass culture precisely because they reflected its constitutive social conditions and could only be read as symptoms of alienation: "Art has basically always had the aim of understanding as well as expressing certain things," Rossellini laments in 1965. "But what does the art of today learn or teach? It is the expression of a certain malaise, of a state of unhappiness and incomprehension but no more."[30] Neither alternative offers a vision of artistic production as potentially emancipatory or utopian, precisely because they both reflect the same worldview, that of an ahistorical timelessness that no longer sees itself as part of a historical narrative that reaches into the future:

> We have arrived at the point at which everyone, even the ruling classes, has lost the optimism that animated humanity at the moment at which it was convinced that the wave of industrialization, science, technology and intrinsic rationality of production, joined with the effects of knowledge and the expansion of capitalism to a global level, would guarantee uninterrupted social progress.[31]

Here is where the imagining of the future enabled by utopian thinking becomes central to Rossellini's task: the antidote to mass culture and modernism would be a form of cultural production that affirmed a historical narrative taking the form of "uninterrupted social progress" and embraced advances in technology and science but that extended beyond the stasis of the present moment, characterized by a lack of any belief in a better future. The problems that it would need to consider would not be self-expression or aesthetic experimentation but rather "how to disseminate the knowledge of things and ideas, how to arouse people's curiosity about what they don't know."[32]

The central aim motivating the choice of subject matter in Rossellini's pedagogical films is thus to reestablish a historical narrative that continues through the present and into the future, stretching from Pascal's calculator to the IBM computer and beyond. As he explained during a colloquium at Rome's Centro Sperimentale di Cinematografia in December 1963, the content his films depict attempts to produce an understanding of the modern world by returning to its origins, moving toward the future via the past: "Cinema, I believe, and all art in general, all modern intellectual activity, insists on observing immediate phenomena; I on the other hand seek to go back to the components of these phenomena."[33] The historical events and personages that Rossellini depicts were chosen "not because they had attracted or excited [him] in a particular way, but only because they represent the articulation and the unfolding of fundamental ways of thinking."[34] *Acts of the Apostles*, for instance, examines the origins of a Pauline Christian worldview, *The Age of the Medici* the flowering of Renaissance humanism and modern capitalism, and *Cartesius* the foundations of a philosophical paradigm that would endure for centuries. In other cases, Rossellini chose his subjects in light of their particular relevance to his own era: *Augustine of Hippo*, for example, depicts the last days of the Roman Empire, a period that mirrors Rossellini's view of the decadent present: "we too are reaching the end of a civilization, and it seems to me that it could be very useful for the men of today to reflect upon a historical moment in which, like today, a new age was about to begin."[35] Statements like this also reflect Rossellini's ability to find hope in a seemingly desolate present: if modernity had taken the wrong path and led to "the end of a civilization," this in turn would open the way toward its enlightened reconstruction, which would only become possible through a reconsideration of the past.

Rossellini strove to create audiovisual texts whose character as cultural productions mirrored their content: a historical narrative emphasizing rationality and progress was to be conveyed by a type of text that merged formerly integrated practices (art, pedagogy, science, history) he believed to have been separated by modernity's destructive irrationality, which had also led to the advent of what he called, echoing Max Weber, "specialized man."[36] Rossellini's new audiovisual practice, rather than art or pedagogy, could perhaps be called "enlightenment," as his films overwhelmingly focus on that historical moment and its legacy, insisting on the importance of the insights of Descartes, Pascal, and their Renaissance humanist predecessors like Leon Battista Alberti. *This* Enlightenment, however, both as a historical period and a narrative that stretches into the present, would be clearly opposed to modernity as we know it, represented for Rossellini by bureaucratic specialization, the culture industry, and a sterile modernism. In Blochian terms, we might say that Rossellini seeks to draw out the surplus utopian content that lies at origins of phenomena that can only be seen in the present as negative. The project thus illuminates the very narrative at whose end it places itself, bringing to light the signposts toward the future that have been obscured by modernity's abandonment of hope in progress and faith in human reason.

To deliver on its promise, Rossellini's new art of enlightenment would need to be disseminated through a means that reflected the legacy of invention and the faith in technology that he saw missing in modernism. Cinema seemed, for Rossellini, to have abdicated its responsibility, not because of any inherent shortcomings in the medium itself but rather because it limited itself to cultural functions that he saw as disengaged and useless, offering only escapism or "cruelty"; it no longer seemed a fertile terrain to "organize a system," as Grierson had. Rossellini's desire both to achieve a synthesis of sundered activities or functions (posited as unified in a historical Enlightenment that had passed and could return) and to find an open cultural space upon which such a synthesis could be carried out, one not yet fully formed and twisted into the service of a bad modernity, found an ideal response in television. Television, that "art without traditions," represented for him the potential technology of enlightenment, equipped to redeem a failed modernity. It was free of the taint of modernism and, to some extent, of the influence of the culture industry that marked existing cultural institutions (museums, the cinema), and it was not yet, at least in Italy, given over to the interests of commercial producers but rather was still in the hands of the state (or, more specifically, those of the Christian Democracy Party). It was not subject to the same set of rules that governed the film industry. Even though he at times bemoans the difficulties of television bureaucracy, Rossellini insists that, in contrast to cinema, "television, meanwhile, is much freer because it is new and such rigid structures [as one finds in cinema] have not yet formed, it is still a more flexible means of experimentation."[37] While Rossellini seemed to value television first and foremost because of what it had *not* done, because of its lack of a fixed character, I would also connect television's suitability for the task he hoped to perform to the fact that it had already both suggested the blurring of the lines between the informational and the aesthetic and enacted a broader transformation in which fragmentation or separation gave way to a new unity. Even if this latter was often used to promote a consumerist ideology that Rossellini rejected, it suggested its "purer" double.

Furthermore, television's institutional structures offered Rossellini the chance to pursue projects that a market-based art cinema would prohibit, thanks to its continuing adherence to an idea of public service, a model that he found superior to private television, insofar as it was required to fulfill certain cultural obligations.[38] "With the feature film," he explained, "you have really no freedom. . . . The Italian television, the French television have a certain kind of social duty. And you can convince them to do a certain kind of work."[39] Rossellini's ideas about "social duty," of course, meshed well with the educational aspirations of RAI head Ettore Bernabei, discussed in chapter 1. Rossellini's project was not, furthermore, completely out of sync with favored programming; as Bourdon notes, public service channels granted a privileged position to historical material, before its telling decline in popularity during the 1970s.[40] Rossellini exploited state television's need for educational programs perhaps more than any other filmmaker, identifying it, in both conceptual and practical terms, as a site that would allow him to move beyond the constraints of cinema.

AUTOPSIA AND KNOWLEDGE

While the "what" of Rossellini's television project—a clear historical narrative that would illuminate the path to a utopian future—is clear enough, the "how" is considerably more obscure. He imagined that his

programs could serve a new cultural function: just as the identity of pedagogue for him succeeded that of artist, so would a new practice, *diffusione
di conoscenza* (diffusion of knowledge), succeed the existing practice of
education.[41] Three years later, he would suggest another alternative name
for his practice, *préparation à la pensée* (preparation for thought), which
emphasizes the teaching of a way to think rather than the transmission of
knowledge itself. Any new form of education, Rossellini argues, should
not be specialized or utilitarian but "integral," allowing us to "synthesize
a large number of determinations upon which we depend."[42] Echoing
his desire for a practice irreducible to either information or art, Rossellini longs for the nonspecialized man: given an economic system (and
corresponding educational system) that prohibits a genuinely synthetic
worldview, he argues, individuals are prevented from gaining the breadth
of knowledge that would permit them to solve major social problems.[43]
To this "specialized man," incapable of grasping the world holistically,
Rossellini opposes the ideal of the Renaissance man. The pedagogues
of the early Renaissance (Guarino, Vittorino, Alberti), he reminds us,
"were concerned not with conditioning the student and qualifying him
in a trade, but with preparing him for life and making him carry out
'one single occupation, that of man.'"[44] A holistic education, then, must
be lifelong: "it must no longer be considered preparation for life, but
rather as a permanent component of it."[45] Most importantly, education
should not be carried out under the assumption that differences in intelligence exist, as such beliefs would only serve to propagate a model of
social hierarchy in which some are regarded as natural slaves.[46] Rossellini's propositions were largely modeled on nineteenth-century efforts at
popular education, which he briefly describes in *Utopia autopsia 10¹⁰* and
in his second book (published in French), *Un esprit libre ne doit rien apprendre en esclave.*[47] He sees these efforts, however, as deeply flawed: "like
all other forms of education, popular education tends to domesticate the
masses in order to insert them into existing cultural, economic, and social
structures, and to adapt them to these."[48] Any truly emancipatory form of
education would, he argues, be free of any such social conditioning and
seek solely to develop the pupil's own capacity for critical thought and
responsibility.[49]

Rossellini believed that such a form of education was indeed possible, and he insisted on the existence of pure knowledge, free from any ideological conditioning. As he stated to *Cahiers du cinéma* in 1966, "I believe we must know things outside of any ideology. Every ideology is a prism."[50] Truth, he argues, is not relative but singular: "There exists only one; there are not several truths. It is a whole that can perhaps not be completely absorbed, but to which one can certainly draw near."[51] This pure form of knowledge, Rossellini argues, is more accessible now than ever before, given the developments of modern science: "Scientific development, which has prodigiously increased over the course of the last quarter century... demonstrates to us that what the thinkers of the Middle Ages called 'gnosis,' the supreme Knowledge, is now possible; for this to happen, society only need prepare itself for it."[52] This firm belief in "supreme Knowledge" is the guiding force of Rossellini's project. It allows him both to project a practically realizable enlightened utopia and to insist on the possibility of a pure, true image that transmits only pure knowledge, free of any ideological filters.

Rossellini's version of enlightenment is rooted in an assumption that the image can in some way be identified with pure information, so long as it is isolated from the contaminating elements that threaten to swallow it up in television practice. Vision thus becomes the central trope in his discussion of education, and he often uses vision-related language to describe the full attainment of knowledge. "It is clear," he writes, "that when everyone will have the possibility to see clearly and directly the extraordinary coherence of that which exists, many of the arguments that now afflict us will disappear. The complexity of the universe of which we are part disturbs us; when all can see it as it is, all will suddenly appear comprehensible, even linear, almost simple."[53] This notion is referenced in the title of *Utopia autopsia 10¹⁰*: in the utopia that will come about when we all see with our own eyes, seeing *is* knowing. Rossellini's use of the word *autopsia,* as well as the philosophical grounding for his vision-centered pedagogy, was drawn from the works of the seventeenth-century Moravian pedagogue John Comenius (in Czech, Jan Komenský). Comenius, Rossellini explains, was a proponent of *autopsia* as pedagogical method. Translating the term as "direct vision," Rossellini cites Comenius's argument that the difficulty of teaching overly elaborate texts could be remedied though "*autopsia,* that is, with the direct presence to the senses: visible things [present] to sight, flavors to taste, tangible things to touch."[54] Whereas in Comenius's time, available images were limited to paintings, drawings, and sculptures, Rossellini adds, we can now benefit from photographic and cinematic images.[55]

While he locates a clear historical precedent for an education through images in the figure of Comenius (who had also given way to a whole tradition of picture-based learning of which Rossellini seems unaware), Rossellini's manner of conceptualizing the image and its affinity with information also suggests a deep debt to discourses surrounding television and its supposed capacities. The purity characterizing the kind of information he believes television allows us to access and the possibility of clear vision both appeal to television's supposed informational capacities. The idea of purity corresponds well to the wave–screen dichotomy discussed in the previous chapter, insofar as one might see the movement of the image from one state to the other as a process through which intangible information is somehow "incarnated" in the television image. The idea of a pure gaze itself, of course, had earlier been used to characterize cinema and was often linked with an epistemological, if not necessarily "informational," function. Examples of such characterizations can be found in the theoretical writings of André Bazin, who likened the objective, machine-created image's disclosures of the world to a kind of spiritual revelation.[56] Although Rossellini occasionally spoke in spiritual or theological terms (despite being at this point in his life an avowed atheist), we might say that he secularizes this vein of thinking, bringing it into harmony with a medium more closely aligned with information (rather than with the "revelation," spiritual or not, offered by cinema), cutting-edge technology, and futurity. Here, again, we find an example of how cultural needs migrate between media, which can themselves differently inflect the way that need is conceived of or responded to.

Rossellini's adherence to an idealized view of the image as (at least potentially) purely informational clearly owes something to a certain way of conceptualizing the properties of film, but his rhetoric also suggests that these properties could be more fully developed on television than in the cinema: "the human eye has been equipped," he writes, "thanks to the modern camera, with a gaze that allows it, for the first time in the history of the world, to surpass its own finitude to meet up with reality in all its aspects."[57] Here the automatism and superhuman power of the camera are linked with the Vertovian dream of a total visibility, now achievable through television. Rossellini believed that this could not be accomplished, however, without an overhaul of audiovisual language, which had been shaped by both modernist art and the culture industry. It would thus need to be purified, stripped of all that prevented it from being "noninformational," of any qualities that seemed to him to be, as I will discuss in more detail later, "aesthetic" or "spectacular" in character. Any concession to aesthetics, for Rossellini, could only counteract the informational effect he hoped to produce; of his own *Louis XIV*, he remarked, "There are too many beautiful shots for it to be a successful film."[58] This process of purification, particularly when articulated as a need to get rid of any sort of "seductive" beauty, recalls early television's efforts to prevent contamination between information and its others and is ultimately subject to the same ideological lures of purity, neutrality, and objectivity; in both cases we find a denial of the deep implications of the collapsing of information and its others that television had carried out and thus an ultimately futile attempt to halt or reverse a process that had already been set into motion.

FORM AND FUNCTION

Rossellini's claims concerning the singularity of knowledge and the possibility of accessing it through "direct vision" seem, in many respects, to be the apotheosis of what political modernist theories would have called the "ideology of the visible," that is, the belief that cinema offers a transparent and direct connection to knowledge and to the real. Rossellini seems to believe in the myth of neutrality cited by Williams as the motivation behind television's fear of mixing registers, without recognizing the fact that a seemingly "neutral" informationality is always dependent on formal and discursive constructions (the shapes programs take, the assumptions advanced by television institutions, etc.) and a facade behind which lies the collapse of registers, of information and its others, upon which the medium truly relies. This is perhaps the case to a large extent, but this acceptance of television's "neutral" character does not simply lead Rossellini to duplicate existing television programs for several reasons: whereas television relies on advancing a seeming separation between information and its others while rendering them indistinguishable in practice, Rossellini (at least in theory) seeks to hunt down and eradicate all difference, reducing the audiovisual message to a univocal, unified form in which no such tensions can be identified, bypassing all ideological "prisms." His practice, on the other hand, ends up undercutting this idea of purity and objectivity: in his discourse, he fully subscribes to a belief in total visibility and the association of vision with knowledge, yet his television films demonstrate the untenability of those ideas and their undoing, as though the truth of television—that information is always mediated and mixed with its others, to the point of becoming indistinguishable from them—were ultimately revealed despite his effort to push back against it. Rossellini's television works, by almost all accounts, fail at facilitating an effective pedagogy based on "direct vision"; instead, they develop a form of pedagogy that differs from their stated mode of operation and offers an alternative to the predominant models of art's usefulness associated with Rancière's representational and aesthetic regimes. Their form and execution thus deserve further consideration here, before we proceed to a more historically minded reflection on the implications of Rossellini's interventions.

The formal attributes of the television programs can be most productively evaluated not as essences with invariable meaning, defined in terms of what they are or are not (illusionistic or not, dramatic or not, even art or not), but rather according to why they are present and what purpose they serve in relation to the didactic aims and effects of the project. While we can initially identify their functional motivation by appealing to Rossellini's conceptualization of the project, they often seem to contradict his stated intentions, creating a system in which information is in fact never immediately present and can only be reached through the mediation of a number of heterogeneous fragments. The clearest example of how an effort to accommodate information through a modification of film form leads not to "direct vision" but to further mediation can be found in the films' narrational strategies. Only in one of the films (perhaps not coincidentally the most well regarded), *The Taking of Power by Louis XIV,* is Rossellini able to carry out his informational intentions through a conventional narrative. This is largely because the central ideas the film conveys are easily articulated through narrative (Louis's creation of a new political order with himself at center) and are highly representable in visual terms (the political use of spectacle, the role of fashion). In no other instance do narrative and idea cohere so seamlessly; instead, Rossellini must continually explicate or comment upon the information he presents through a number of narrational strategies that call attention to themselves, creating a multilayered text employing multiple different levels of discourse. As a result, the text never feels unified, as though information or knowledge were present and self-evident at the level of the image; instead, it must constantly search for the proper assemblage of fragments to convey what it wishes to.

Perhaps the most obvious of these strategies is Rossellini's use of "guide" figures, which appear near the beginning of many of the television films. Here one character (the guide) will convey contextualizing information to another (the visitor, essentially a proxy for the viewer). The most notable among these are the Greek scribe (and slave) Aristarco in *Acts of the Apostles,* who explains at length the political, religious, and cultural peculiarities of Jerusalem and the Jews to a visiting Roman magistrate, and Totto Macchiavelli, who introduces the English merchant Wadding to Florence in *The Age of the Medici* (Figure 2). These sorts of guides and tours strongly recall similar narrational techniques in the utopian genre, although their function here is motivated by a need to solve a specific formal problem. They allow Rossellini to interpret and augment the visual information he presents with verbal language, at once showing and telling the viewer by reassigning the function that might otherwise be carried out by voice-over narration to a character within the diegesis; this method doubles the function of the guide in utopian narratives, allowing the television films to give us a glimpse into the minutiae of daily life without integrating them into a more focused narrative. Once this information has been established, the visitor–guide duos are cast aside, as though they

FIGURE 2. The English merchant Wadding gets a guided tour of Florence in *The Age of the Medici* (1972), thus allowing the viewer to learn about the city.

had exhausted their usefulness; they are only needed to convey bits of information that cannot be integrated into more conventionally dramatic dialogues or individual monologues or purely on the visual level. While we can explain the idiosyncrasies of Rossellini's strategies in terms of the aims of the project, however, they nonetheless seem to contradict his aspirations to reduce the image to something like pure information. Image demands a supplement, an explicator; an ensemble of techniques and modes of communication must be drawn on to convey information to the spectator, and the films' oscillation between them creates a sense that it is never present in one single form.

Another narrational strategy that "splits" or mediates information in a similar way entails the explication of visual information after its initial presentation, when it is no longer visible. Unlike the simultaneous "show and tell" of the tour structure, this strategy enacts a greater degree of rupture between the two functions and, as a result, creates two clearly distinguishable modes of narration, challenging the supposed unity strived for by "direct vision" and efforts to make the image self-sufficiently com-municative. Two examples should suffice to illustrate this strategy. In *Socrates,* the Athenian rebels' assault on Phyle serves as the sole dramatized scene of Thrasybulus's overthrow of the Thirty Tyrants of Athens. This scene metonymically represents the overthrow of Socrates's former student and current nemesis, Critias. In itself, however, it carries no indication of this significance, which only becomes clear in a subsequent conversation between Athenians that occurs after Critias's death and the overthrow of his government. This conversation resembles nothing so much as the description of an off-stage battle in a Shakespearean play, with the cru-cial difference that here the described action has been presented, albeit elliptically, as a kind of descriptive fragment. A similar scene in *Medici* situates the explanation of the descriptive fragment before its depiction but still retains a clear demarcation between explication and event. Here the discovery of a betrayal of the Florentine clothmakers' guild's secrets is followed by a scene of the murder of the traitor. Such descriptive frag-ments, however, are almost entirely absent from some of the later films, particularly those that focus on philosophical argument, such as *Blaise Pascal* and *Cartesius.* This change is most likely due to these films' interest in abstract concepts that cannot be concretely illustrated; in these cases, the words do most of the work, although as Rancière notes, the images serve to "inscribe [the philosopher's] thought in a material universe, to make it arise from this universe, as a way of interpreting it and acting within it."[59] We might go further here and say that the films insist on the inextricability of thought and knowledge from the material world, again showing how information can never exist in any fully abstract or pure form. In *The Messiah,* in contrast, the explicative half of the showing and telling dyad is often eliminated entirely, and Rossellini moves closer to his early neorealist style, showing far more than he tells. This refusal of explication most likely occurs as a result of his assumptions concerning the viewer's familiarity with the story of the Gospels, as evidenced by the film's elliptical depiction of the massacre of the innocents. Unlike the events in *The Age of the Medici* or *Socrates,* what happens on-screen here needs little explanation, so the explicative narrational function can be dispensed with. The variability of structure between the films indicates that information must be presented in multiple forms, and the suitability of one over the other depends on the type of information to be conveyed.

While the visitor–guide structure and the clear division between showing and telling functions are some of the most apparent narrational strategies Rossellini employs, he makes use of a number of subtler and less obtrusive ones. The main thematic and narrative arcs of the films constitute a primary "channel" of information (as in *Louis XIV*'s illustration of the manipulation of spectacle for political ends or *Blaise Pascal*'s struggle to reconcile faith and science). These primary channels, however, generally convey information of a broad thematic nature and are not in themselves equipped to accommodate what we might call secondary information, those ethnographic and material details of daily life and labor that Rossellini insists on presenting. Such material is presented in three main ways. In the first, the secondary material arises, as though incidentally and organically, from the presentation of the primary: Socrates's trial, for example, allows for a detailed illustration of the Athenian justice system, while Mazarin's and Pascal's illnesses provide a context for the depiction of medical practices (Figure 3). In the second, it is almost relegated to the background, as with the baking of bread in the first episode of *Acts of the Apostles* or the preparation of writing tablets in the opening of the second. Although these details are essentially treated as background material and therefore not as closely attached to narrative as those in the first category, Rossellini devotes more attention to them than their slight relevance to the narrative might lead us to expect, indicating that their presentation is motivated by a desire to illustrate the material foundations of daily life in the depicted time. Also in the second category are instances in which the primary material is conveyed by the sound track while the secondary is conveyed by the image track, as when Paul and a weaver discuss differing opinions about Christ among the Jews as they work at the loom in *Acts of the Apostles* or in the instances in *The Messiah* in which Christ practices his trade as carpenter while preaching; this differs from the sound–image interaction described earlier insofar as here, one level is not called on to explain another, but rather, each conveys a different idea independently of the other. In the third mode of presentation found in the television films, what I have been referring to as secondary information becomes

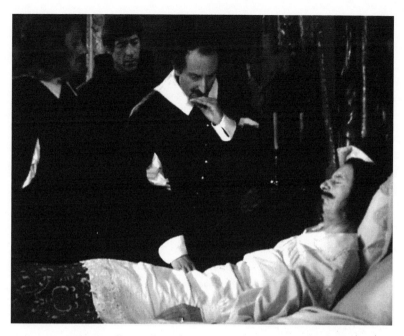

FIGURE 3. Mazarin's illness allows for an illustration of medical practices in *The Taking of Power by Louis XIV* (1966).

primary but still retains its materialist or ethnographic character. These cases, most common in *Man's Struggle for Survival* and *The Iron Age*, but also occasionally occurring in the shorter films, involve either the presentation of ethnographic information as pure spectacle (as in the fertility dance in the first episode of *Struggle* or the Etruscan funeral ceremony in the first episode of *The Iron Age*) or the direct demonstration of a particular technique or machine: this can be carried out either in a purely presentational manner (simply showing a machine or workers engaged in some kind of craft as the primary subject of the scene) or with a proxy standing in for the spectator as the audience of a demonstration.

Rossellini's approach to acting, like his narrational technique, diverges from conventional cinema in a way that can best be understood in terms of the television films' intended function. The acting style is decidedly nonnaturalistic: characters read lengthy expository texts from off-camera prompt cards, with the estranging result that they rarely look each other in the eye or show much regard for naturalistic conventions. Rossellini also imposed very specific gestures and postures upon his actors, as a description of his direction by Pierre Arditi (who played Pascal) explains: "I never had any power over what I was doing. . . . My hand had to drop like this, and then my head like that, and then I had to collapse because I had finally had the revelation of God" (Figure 4).[60] Rossellini's desire to bypass the conventional mechanisms of acting, whether by dictatorially controlling gesture or by refusing to allow actors to become familiar with their lines, might be ascribed to a depriviliging of the actor: we are not intended to see him as a believable character but rather to attend to the substance of his words and the meaning of his demonstrative gestures. In practice, this creates something like a "third-person" acting technique, one that we might link to Brechtian theater. Though this does not seem to be the intended effect, this approach ultimately foregrounds the extent to which the information we see is mediated: the actor is a kind of placeholder, a vehicle for speech and affect, rather than its source; as Adriano Aprà puts it, the actors "do not give us the illusion that they incarnate Louis XIV, Pascal or Descartes. Rather, they 'stand for' these characters, as if they were walking around with placards with their names written on them."[61] While the actors are not easily identified with the figures they portray, I would argue that the concept of "incarnation," defined in a way that diverges from Aprà's usage here, may in fact be a useful way to describe this gap. Actors are, we might say, the sites in which *information* is incarnated, as though it both needed a body and resisted total identification with that body. Bellour describes the effect as follows: "it is necessary that the actor be present, involved in the moment, the more or less tragic power of the event, but only up to the point where he opens up for the word a space of its own."[62] The actor thus refers us to something else—speech is always quotation and the body can only stand in for the source of that quotation—but it is nonetheless implied that this mediation can move us toward the ultimate referent rather than negating the possibility of accessing it.

The films' visual style also situates information as fragmentary and mediated: they rely heavily on long single takes, and camera movements are complemented by the use of Rossellini's remote-controlled zooms. Editing within scenes is thus minimal; they forgo almost entirely the

FIGURE 4. Pascal receiving the "revelation of God" in *Blaise Pascal* (1972).

standard technique of intercutting between speaking characters. While the long takes and lack of conventional editing give the sense of unified, unfragmented spaces, Rossellini conveys the idea of fragmentation on a visual level through his mise-en-scène: he frequently makes strategic use of in-depth staging in which different layers of depth correspond to different subjects or ideas. Each plane begins to appear as a separate "channel" of information, a single discrete component of a larger assemblage, as in the sound and image division discussed earlier. This sort of division is often thematically expressive, accomplishing a kind of montage-in-the-shot, as when Pascal sits sick in bed in the background while his scientific instruments sit on a table in the foreground, or as in *Cartesius,* when a doctor dissects a rabbit in the foreground while Descartes speaks of the fallibility of perception in the background (Figure 5). This technique encourages speculation about the connection between the different actions taking place but once again belies the notion that information can be concentrated and located in a single source: instead, it is polyphonic

FIGURE 5. A doctor dissects a rabbit while Descartes (center) philosophizes in the background, an example of Rossellini's multilayered compositions, in *Cartesius* (1974).

and incomplete, inviting the viewer to build toward full knowledge by beginning to put the provided fragments together.

We find this same implication—that knowledge is never fully present but must be (re)constructed from the information that the spectator is given—in another visual element of the films, namely, the frequent use of the Schüfftan process to depict buildings too large or elaborate to be constructed as sets (prominent examples include the images of Florence from afar in *Medici* and the Acropolis in *Socrates*) (Figure 6). The Schüfftan process, named for cinematographer Eugen Schüfftan, involves shooting through a partially mirrored piece of glass that reflects a painting that is positioned behind the camera.[63] Rossellini's use of such "mirror shots" has been cited as evidence of his supposed Brechtian tendencies, as though their clearly artificial nature were meant to undermine any claims to the transparent representation of historical reality.[64] While the shots are hardly convincing, it is difficult to square Rossellini's efforts to use

FIGURE 6. An image of the Athenian Acropolis created with the Schüfftan process in *Socrates* (1971).

the most realistic sets possible (in *Acts of the Apostles* above all) and his avoidance of studios with a supposed desire to undercut his films' realism. While they do not by any means abandon all effort to visually reconstruct their referent, neither does their use indicate an unwavering commitment to the greatest possible degree of illusion. The clearest reading of this odd dynamic has been provided by Àngel Quintana, who argues that "Rossellini's concern is not to reveal the mechanisms of representation to the spectator, but to find the best form to draw closer to a truth."[65] Knowledge is thus neither in nor opposed to the image; it is not accessible in some pure form, as Rossellini's statements might suggest, but rather through mediation. It is precisely such strategies that allow Rossellini to evade television's "ideology of the visible" and replace it with other, more mediated conceptions of how one learns through words and images.

The plurality of modes in which informational material is presented throughout the television project indicates how much the films diverge from what Rossellini's statements about "direct vision" would lead us to expect and suggests that no particular audiovisual language is uniquely qualified to convey information. "Informationality" thus begins to appear more as an "effect" generated by an assemblage of heterogeneous discourses than as something that inheres in the clear-eyed gaze of the film camera or in Rossellini's purgation of nonessential, nonfunctional elements of the image. The actual logic of the programs, as suggested at the outset of this section, is thus far closer to the "truth" of television, in which different discourses, functions, and forms of apprehension overlap and work together to the point that different identities can no longer be assigned to them. Such divergences from the essentialist approach articulated in Rossellini's theory suggest the possibility of retrieving a more sophisticated model of the moving image's usefulness and informing capacity and more subtle conceptualizations of the ways of knowing that it allows, ones that would leave behind the notions of transparency characteristic of a Socialist Realist or Sartrean model and hence exit the pedagogical logic of Rancière's representational regime, opting instead for a pedagogy in which knowledge is perpetually absent and deferred.

A PEDAGOGY OF DEFERRAL

As should be clear by this point, the audiovisual language of Rossellini's television films is motivated above all by the efficient transmission of information, even if that information is frequently conveyed in a way that contradicts his own theoretical starting points. It does not, meanwhile, as I will consider in more depth shortly, consider the aesthetic to be in any way connected with the kinds of knowledge that it seeks to engender. Formal strategies are not taken to be meaningful or valuable for their own sake and do not seem to be intended to produce alienation, shock, joy, or any other form of spectatorial response. Even so, such responses can hardly be ruled out; Rossellini's films, in their very effort to distance themselves from the trappings of art and the aesthetic, cannot help but in some sense aestheticize themselves, if only through mere difference. The vast difference between the experience of watching a historical fiction spectacle and watching Rossellini's television films nearly ensures that the viewer will experience them as part of a unique sensorium. To watch

Cartesius or *Acts of the Apostles* is to turn away from the breakneck pace of the thirty-minute television program or the ninety-minute feature film, opting instead to immerse oneself in a strange, "unnatural" filmic world where nothing much happens and in which words—usually the extremely dense thoughts of philosophers—often take priority over images. As a result, another revealing problem arises: Rossellini does, in the forbidding, idiosyncratic form of his films, end up producing something not unlike the "formal resistance" which for Adorno constitutes the primary virtue of art, marking his work off as part of an altogether different sensorium than that of the usual television show (or of the culture industry's aestheticization of daily life more broadly). The films' concern with information and function, however, contradicts this "resistance." This contradiction may prove productive, however, if we can find ways to cast the films' informing function as something other than a mere effort to graft ideas onto a "resistant" aesthetic form at the expense of both information and aesthetics.

The pedagogical paradigm that I would propose arises from Rossellini's system draws on two central concepts: first, that a pedagogical audiovisual practice need not make its own processes of representation its primary focus (as in so much political modernist cinema), and second, that the value of the informational text derives not from the knowledge or information it or its author possesses, nor from the transmission of this knowledge to the spectator, but rather through the way in which it propels the pupil/spectator beyond or outside of the text, forcing her to undertake the search for knowledge elsewhere. The presence and function of these concepts in Rossellini's work may be illuminated by reading them as closely related to that group of films that Peter Wollen refers to as post-Brechtian materialist texts.[66] In contrasting the post-Brechtian text with other currents of cinematic materialism more concerned with nonrepresentational forms, Wollen makes the essential observation that,

for Brecht, of course, the point of the *Verfremdung*-effect was not simply to break the spectator's involvement and empathy in order to draw attention to the artifice of art, an art-centered model, but in order to demonstrate the workings of society, a reality obscured by habitual norms of perception, by habitual modes of identification with "human problems."[67]

This view of Brecht acts as a corrective to one that would see the Brechtian alienation effect in cinema as primarily a matter of "revealing the device," whether through displaying the work's processes of production or through constantly reminding the viewer of the representation's artificiality. Wollen continues: "This 'post-Brechtian aesthetic' is not postulated on the search for an ontology, albeit a materialist ontology. It has to be approached from the side of language, here dialectic."[68] Rossellini's films, like the post-Brechtian aesthetic Wollen describes here, are not about ontology: they do not in practice, as both the director's theoretical framework and a reading that sees them as adhering to the "ideology of the visible" might lead us to believe, claim to offer up the full presence of knowledge or truth by showing us the real, nor does Rossellini feel compelled to remind the viewer that what she is watching is only a representation. The representational status of the films is a given, as demonstrated by Rossellini's lack of concern for the artificiality of his sets (the mirrors) or actors. The signs of mediation or constructedness that he displays are not foregrounded or privileged, not because he is attempting to dupe the spectator (or himself) into believing in their transparency or ontological status as real and true, but because revealing their nature as such is not part of the pedagogical operation he is carrying out. The representation is acknowledged as such, and then the question of its ontological status is simply bracketed. The signifying materials of the films are not treated with the constant anxiety that they might be false or deceptive but rather are taken as a set of components that make up a collection of what Wollen would call "linguistic" elements. They do not attempt to negate meaning, nor do they seem to possess it in themselves in their pure presence, in the immanent fashion that Rossellini's writings suggest.

Another recurring motif in Rossellini's comments about the television project, namely, his own ignorance, may offer a way to interpret his strategies in a different way than the bulk of his discourse encourages. In an interview conducted in conjunction with the broadcast of *Socrates*, Rossellini states, "I am an ignorant person, and I chose to tell about things that I don't know, those that make me curious and excite me, in the hopes that they might interest and be of use to so many other ignorant people like me."[69] Taking a cue from Rossellini's self-proclaimed status as *ignorante,* we might ask if his role as author could be recast as a kind of collector and arranger of texts. Looking at the films as the product of this kind of authorship, they begin to more closely resemble texts-before-meaning, assemblages of fragments of diverse origin that do not propose to hold any single or unified meaning. As in the post-Brechtian text that Wollen describes, "first-order signifiers remain, but they are no longer the sovereign product of the intentional act of a subject, a transcendental ego, the generator of thought that finds embodiment in language as an instrument necessary for the communication and exchange of ideas between equivalent subjects, alternating as source and receiver."[70] Following this line of thought, we could say that Rossellini's pedagogical films confront the spectator/pupil not as authoritative, self-effacing (and production–concealing) works of pure knowledge but rather as the textual manifestation of the author's own nascent learning process and research. While they still insist that pure, objective meaning does indeed exist, they do not claim to offer it: their first-order signifiers do not communicate some final meaning, nor even Rossellini's own thought, but rather act as the material counterparts, the figural translations, of the fragments of texts gathered by the director. They represent not an end point, a culmination, or an answer but only the fragmentary beginnings of the question and the ways in which one might go about answering it.

For all of his talk about remaining objective, Rossellini was in fact quite comfortable casting his films as little more than documents of his own learning process: "As this program was useful to me in putting my ideas in order," he said of *The Iron Age,* "it may be of use to others. This is what my system of pedagogy amounts to. I don't put myself on the outside or go and think about things in an abstract way. I just recount the experiences I have had."[71] This statement may seem a mere dodge on Rossellini's part, an attempt to disavow the truth claims he makes elsewhere. If we place the films alongside the kind of post-Brechtian texts that Wollen describes, however, it takes on a different meaning. Rossellini does not refuse authorship or control over the text, but he also does not take his control as author as a platform from which he imparts its final meaning or truth; he himself is not capable of delivering this meaning. Indeed, as Michèle Lagny notes, his insistences that he "knew nothing" about the subjects of his films align him with the "Ignorant Schoolmaster" described by Rancière, one who teaches by leading the pupil to learn for himself rather than assuming he has any knowledge to transmit.[72] The equal relation between author and spectator, between teacher and pupil, that Rossellini, like Rancière, idealizes begins to appear tenable when the films are read in this way. They are not vessels of knowledge handed down from on high but simply the investigations of a fellow ignorant, a curious person with a desire to learn. The teacher and pupil find themselves as equals not before a shared text that they approach together, as in Rancière's model, but rather before a larger, more distant body of knowledge. The text here becomes not the ground on which the two meet but rather a collection of materials handed from teacher to pupil in unexplicated form with the expectation that the latter will use them to draw closer to knowledge than the former yet has.

A NEW AVANT-GARDE?

Even if we do assume that Rossellini's films were—or at least could be—pedagogically successful in the terms discussed earlier, it does not by any means follow from this that his utopian plan was a tenable one. A seemingly unbridgeable gap remains between the effects of any individual film and the project's considerably more ambitious framework, yet Rossellini consistently prioritizes the latter dimension, invoking it in the title of his book and frequently reminding his readers and interlocutors of his project's lofty goals. Rossellini's commitment to using his works to achieve utopian ends has a rather anachronistic flavor, evoking not so much the art of the 1960s as that of the 1910s and 1920s, particularly in its Futurist and Constructivist strains. Though we certainly find utopian elements in the art of the 1960s, Rossellini's project, with its emphasis on technology and productive power, has considerably more affinity with these earlier movements. The possible connection between Rossellini's pedagogical films and such earlier schools or currents has not gone unnoticed but has been largely limited to comparisons with the Soviet directors of the 1920s. Raymond Bellour, for example, suggests that Rossellini's project should be situated alongside the works of Eisenstein and Vertov, while noting its difference from them insofar as it distances itself from any particular ideology.[73] Such comparisons, as justified as they may be, remain at a very superficial level. They see isolated similarities (the embrace of technology, the desire to make a "useful" cinema) but fail to take the more productive step of reading Rossellini's films not as latter-day counterparts of those of Vertov but as works that share with them a certain historically determined conception of art and its potential functions, one that diverges from the mass culture–high art dichotomy that dominates postwar European thinking about art and that presumes that a synthesis between informational and formally minded (or "aesthetic," if we bracket the fact that neither director would approve of the term) audiovisual practices is possible.

This alignment or affinity suggests the usefulness of looking to the art of the 1920s as a possible forerunner of or inspiration for Rossellini's pedagogical project. Rossellini's films can be fruitfully read as resurrecting and reconfiguring ideas that derive not from postwar modernism but rather from those currents of early-twentieth-century art that Peter Bürger, in his *Theory of the Avant-Garde,* has collectively termed the "historical avant-garde." Rossellini himself suggests such a link in a 1963 article in which he argues that the artists of the late nineteenth and early twentieth centuries "sought to follow the evolution of the world, the investigations of scientific development, trying in some way to reveal the truth indicated by new discoveries."[74] Among these artists he includes the Impressionists, the Cubists (who "wish to represent through essential lines the permanent property of objects and their stability in space without perspective and light"), and the Italian Futurists (who "exalt the beauty of speed and movement and pose thus in a new way the problems of art, both on the level of philosophic thought and on that of scientific research").[75] Oddly enough, this was the first and only instance in which Rossellini suggested parallels between his own work and that of the "scientific" Cubists and the historical avant-garde (represented here in its Italian manifestation); perhaps he later obscured the origins of his project to claim greater originality or to avoid certain political associations.

Following Bürger's definition, the historical avant-garde opposes itself to an autonomous bourgeois art. The latter is defined by its autonomy and separateness from the "praxis of life," whereas the former seeks to overcome this autonomy, attacking "art as institution" and attempting to break down the barrier between art and life praxis. Bürger's definition and analysis of the historical avant-garde provide a suggestive set of concepts through which we may carry out an analysis of Rossellini's television films, not on a formal level, but rather as a project that aims to create a new paradigm of cultural production, seeking to redefine the function of art and destroy its status as an autonomous institution. My claim here is not that Rossellini is an avant-gardist, or even that he has the same goals as the historical avant-garde, but rather, as I suggested in chapter 1, that television played host to something like a mutation of the historical avant-garde's utopian aspirations in the decades following World War II.

Rossellini's project takes up the same aims as the historical avant-garde in a number of respects. First, it rejects the idea of art as autonomous and a view, such as Adorno's, that would find art's value and meaning precisely in its separateness and negativity, instead favoring a form of cultural production that refuses such separateness and seeks to be "useful" in a more instrumental sense. Rossellini's critique of art's autonomous status—or, in his terms, its "uselessness" and introversion—is, like that of the historical avant-garde, eventually extended to apply to art as institution. In this case, the "institution" in question is that of modernism, which is characterized by a refusal of functionality and the kind of producer-centered self-expression that could be seen as occupying the same role in the 1960s as aestheticism does in the late nineteenth century in Bürger's scheme. The status of Rossellini's project as an attack on art as institution is confirmed by his insistence on relocating it to television, as though to further demarcate it from both commercial cinema (culture industry) and art cinema (high art). It would not have been enough simply to make pedagogical films for the cinema; what was needed was a completely different system of production and distribution and a different kind of relationship between the viewer and the film, and television's status as "an art without traditions" rendered it hospitable to such differences.

As broad as Bürger's definition of the historical avant-garde's aims is, and as much as it seems in so many ways applicable to Rossellini's films, the pedagogical project clashes dramatically with it in others. It is in this clash, however, that we can begin to see more clearly both the project's deeply anachronistic character and the ways in which the very cultural paradigm that Rossellini sought to act against defines it at its core. While the project is clearly concerned with attacking and providing an alternative to art as institution, it differs from the historical avant-garde in its conception of how and why the barrier between art and the praxis of life should be broken down. Rossellini was, like many artists of the historical avant-garde, concerned with his art's usefulness, yet he downplayed the role of the aesthetic—both as a quality of art and a specific kind of experience—as a source of this usefulness; he preferred to abandon the role of the artist in favor of that of the pedagogue. At the very moment in which the full representation and comprehension of the world has become possible through scientific advances, he laments, people insist that they prefer their "aesthetic jolts" to reality.[76] The aesthetic, then, is situated as the enemy to knowledge and social usefulness, something that art can dispense with in favor of nobler aims. Rossellini does not, like the artists of the historical avant-garde, "attempt to organize a new life praxis from a basis in art."[77] He is not a creator of objects, works, or events that seek to aestheticize spheres external to art. Rather, he seeks to repurpose the space-time currently occupied by either the modernist artwork or the culture industry product, namely, domestic leisure time. "We have at our disposal twenty-four hours each day," Rossellini explains with the precision of a utopian planner. "Eight are consecrated to work and eight to rest. Eight remain, not even counting weekends, to use audiovisual media for our enrichment."[78] He retains the distinction between work and leisure time, neither attempting to aestheticize the former nor altering the latter to bring it closer to work.

Because Rossellini addressed a public whose leisure time was largely spent at home rather than at the cinema or another public place, his project took as a precondition the very kind of subject addressed by the culture industry in the television age. The project, then, as much as it was concerned with using the tools of the mass media, did not aim to create a kind of new mass culture in the way that the works of the historical avant-garde did. It was essential for Rossellini that his films be received not by the "masses" but rather by an isolated, contemplative spectator, because "in general, the public in a movie theater sees a work with a mass mentality; with television, the critical spirit of the individual is more accentuated."[79] Just as he insists on the nonautonomy of art and demands that it be useful, he inscribes in his project the very conditions that make bourgeois art a largely individual, autonomous, and domestic institution. While refusing the paradigm of the cinema as institution, he replaces it with one that turns its back on the aspects of cinema (mass character, public viewing situation, aesthetic "shock") that were once seen, most notably by Walter Benjamin, as holding the potential to subvert an older, precinematic social placement and function of the work of art.

One could easily regard these contradictions as signs of the inevitable failure of Rossellini's project or as symptomatic of any such effort's incapacity to escape its own historical determinants. Rather than reading his project as incurably "infected" by elements of mass culture and bourgeois art, though, it will perhaps be more productive to examine how those very attributes that distance it from the historical avant-garde constitute not only symptoms but also strategic efforts to avoid the avant-garde's fate. One could not successfully employ the tactics of the historical avant-garde in the 1960s, Bürger argues, for two primary reasons. First, avant-garde efforts that were once taken as attacks on art as institution have been absorbed by the institution and their oppositional quality neutralized as a result. Second, the triumph of the culture industry has transformed the nonautonomy of art into a tool of subjection rather than emancipation.[80] The merging of art and life praxis sought by the avant-garde, as well as their demand for a functional art, has been achieved by the culture industry. Any further attempts to achieve these aims risks simply duplicating the products of the culture industry rather than acting in opposition to them.

Rossellini's rejection of the aesthetic, then, might indicate an effort to avoid the co-option of the aims of the historical avant-garde by the culture industry. The aesthetic, for Rossellini, is not a form of play, a route to different kinds of knowledge, or a kind of knowledge or experience that can bring about a new world by merging with the praxis of life; instead, it is the opposite of knowledge of all kinds, providing it in an illusory, deceptive form. The aesthetic and its powers, so successfully enlisted by Louis XIV and depicted in Rossellini's film, are seen as once again in the present day entirely co-opted by existing power structures, the very ones that the director seeks to dismantle: "In the end, nothing is more dangerous than the aesthetic," he writes shortly before his death. "It is always there to lend its support to money, because it itself has need of money to flourish. It is always on the steps of the palace that the aesthetes place their camp."[81] Whereas such a rejection of art and the aesthetic could, in the context of the historical avant-garde, be read as resulting from a desirable decrease in distinction between art and other spheres, in the 1960s, it meant something else altogether. What was once art's instrumental property in creating a new utopian culture, its aesthetic dimension, had been rendered useless and subverted by the culture industry. Art's only hope in retaining usefulness, then, was to reject the aesthetic altogether. In this strategy, we find one of the movements that Rancière identifies as characteristic of the aesthetic regime of art: as "everything becomes artistic," "the sensorium of art and the sensorium of everyday life are nothing more than the eternal reproduction of the 'spectacle' in which domination is both mirrored and denied."[82] In response to this state, art seeks to further separate itself from life and "must tear itself away from the territory of aestheticized life and draw a new borderline, which cannot be crossed."[83] Art distinguishes itself from aestheticized life by deaestheticizing itself, or rather, it redefines the unique sensorium of the aesthetic by differentiating it from the aestheticized forms of life that surround it. This path, of course, leads to the contradiction that surfaces when we compare Rossellini's programs with those of more conventional television: one cannot self-consciously deaestheticize one's work without being taken as highly aesthetic. There is, of course, some potential value in what was, for Rossellini, an undesirable side effect, one that would go some way toward cancelling out his project's internalization of culture industry frameworks. As wedded as they are to a vision of utopian scheduling, the television films in fact question the temporality of the usual television show or film, suggesting new experiences of temporality through their protractedness and slow pace. Similarly, they address the spectator in a way that forces him to use powers of cognition and memory rarely called upon by even the most sophisticated artworks, forcibly leading him away from the mode of passive and unthinking experience commonly associated with the culture industry.

Yet whatever value Rossellini's descent into the "de-aestheticized" aesthetic holds, it creates conditions that seem to doom his project to failure. Unlike a product of Adornian modernism, for which such a strategy would be viable, the television films, while hoping to reach the same audience (in the same viewing situation) as the typical television program does, demand that the spectator reject the pleasures that such programs generally promise. Rossellini, to invoke Horkheimer and Adorno's image, insists not only that Odysseus remain firmly tied to the mast but that he not even hear the song of the sirens. He will not, like Horkheimer and Adorno's Enlightenment man, take their song as a mere object of contemplation, as art, nor, like the historical avant-garde, attempt to bind it to the praxis of life, harnessing its power for productive ends.[84] Rossellini internalizes the suspicion of the aesthetic that seems to forbid any neo-avant-garde yet maintains faith in a utopian form of cultural production. The coexistence of these two beliefs reflects an ahistorical conception of cultural production that detaches its function and efficacy from the historical context in which it is deployed. Rossellini does not connect, as Bürger does, the conditions under which the aesthetic can fulfill certain functions with other historical conditions that allowed for a utopian art; he assumes the former have changed, but not the latter, and does not link the viability of an avant-garde art with a corresponding political force. His project thus depends on denying that a change in historical conditions lessens the possibility of creating of a useful, utopian art and, correspondingly, on believing that the very coordinates that would make it a viable possibility still exist.

Rossellini is able to sustain a faith in what would seem to be an impossibly anachronistic utopian television by constructing two very well-defined (and opposing) conceptions of the modern. For Rossellini, it is not the case that there are bad and good aspects of modernity but rather that good and bad modernities are two completely separable and concrete sets of phenomena, both of which find representation in the television films. Bad modernity, for Rossellini, is the alienated society that believes itself to be rational when it is in fact more irrational than ever before: "We claim to be positivist and rational," he writes, sounding rather Adornian. "This is false. Never have we been so governed by ignorance and the recourse to magic."[85] For Rossellini, such irrationality finds expression in modernism, which now acts as apologist "for the obscure, the enigmatic, promoting thus the cult of the irrational."[86] More broadly, bad modernity is the world in which all production, both material and cultural, is detached from knowledge and rationality. Good modernity, meanwhile, is characterized by the emancipatory force of technology and the improvements in quality of life that it has brought about. Both modernities have their own "machines," as demonstrated in *Man's Struggle for His Survival*: Enlightenment rationality finds its material manifestation in a series of metalworking machines, depicted going about their business free of human interference, their "every movement calculated and preplanned," the realization of "the scientific organization of work." Bad modernity, meanwhile, is represented by a series of machine-like art objects located in a gallery space, as the voice-over informs us that "true popular art has been supplanted and destroyed by kitsch, that is, the culture industry." This contrast, however, underscores the fetishistic nature of Rossellini's good modernity, in which awe before sheer productive force and an aesthetic appreciation for the movements of machines (neither of which would be exceptional in the works of the historical avant-garde) overtake a supposed concern with the use-value of such technologies.

The missing link between Rossellini's good and bad modernities is of course supplied by Horkheimer and Adorno's *Dialectic of Enlightenment*, the very text that lies, albeit indirectly, at the source of his critique of the culture industry. For Horkheimer and Adorno, the aspects of modernity that Rossellini sees as a betrayal of Enlightenment values—manipulation of human beings on a massive scale or the use of technology for destruction rather than production—are in fact the outcome of these very values, which in their embrace of instrumental reason and positivism produce inequality and domination.[87] Unlike Horkheimer and Adorno, Rossellini does not identify at the root of the Enlightenment conception of reason the very inequality and manipulation that he seeks to combat: although he recognizes the enormous power and function of manipulation carried out by the culture industry, he does not link this power to the conception of instrumental reason that underlies it. He uncouples the terms of the dialectic, insisting that the good can be detached from the bad and refusing to see them as necessary parts of the same whole. His attempt to deny or repress the aesthetic as the force of unreason, meanwhile, repeats the Enlightenment effort to repress myth and superstition. Just as myth returns to Enlightenment in the form of positivism as ahistorical metaphysic, the expression of a fear of all that is unknown and unknowable, it resurfaces in Rossellini's scheme as the supposedly rational metaphysic that imagines "direct vision" at the root of all knowledge, collapsing science into theology through the convenient mediator of the clear-eyed, unbiased lens of the camera and the fetishization of precision and production, detached from any use-value. It is only in its execution that the television project avoids merely reiterating such a pure and positivist standpoint: as noted earlier, it seems as though his surface-level discourse speaks the language of the television news, imagining knowledge as easily transmissible through visual form, while his practice is more in line with the compromised or mediated forms of knowing that television actually practices. Conception and practice thus both facilitate symptomatic readings, but they reveal different things; the contradictions between these two levels, furthermore, articulate the kinds of bewilderment (and attempts to contain them) that television itself had, through the cultural transformations it had carried out, engendered.

At its broadest level, however, Rossellini's project voices a more holistic anxiety about the end of history. Both in the conception of art that underlies it and in the historical figures and events it privileges, both in its form and its content, it carries out a salvage operation. His utopia is to be built first of all by redeeming the past for the future, a truth that he perhaps unwittingly declares when he proclaims, "To put things to rights you have to put history to rights too."[88] Rossellini's rewriting of history is not a matter of presenting the facts in the hopes that they will be useful for the modern viewer but rather one of re-creating and reexperiencing history from the beginning so that it leads, if only imaginarily, to a different end. Ultimately, Rossellini's project discloses its deepest utopian aspirations not in its effort to build a more rational world through pedagogical television but rather in the desire—a desire that belongs very much to his particular historical moment—to rewrite, and thus save from preemptive completion, a historical narrative that ends badly and, indeed, to reestablish a narrative just as anything resembling one seems to be vanishing. A utopian art, in this case, is not simply one that projects the synthesis or sublation of separate practices and ways of knowing but one that first and foremost allows the future to simply be *thought* at a moment when it seems to be disappearing from view. The idea that this could be done through television suggests both the extent to which the medium (not to mention the associated mission of public service broadcasting) was powerfully associated with and oriented toward the future and its potential usefulness in addressing many of the same problems confronted by earlier twentieth-century avant-gardes.

But what of the project's success or failure? Bürger argues that all attempts at anything resembling a new avant-garde are doomed to failure, as they will inevitably be absorbed by art as institution and moved back into the safe space of autonomy. And Rossellini's project did indeed fail: it did not lead to a utopian future, nor did it inspire a new conceptualization of art and its function that would be embraced by others. Rossellini has ended up not as a pedagogue but as an *auteur* once again. His venue is not the evening television broadcast, let alone the classroom, but a rather more marginal space. His attempt to repurpose and relocate cinema, thereby redefining it as an institution, concludes with his deportation back to the world of cinephilia, the very one from which he sought to escape. The pedagogical films, Giuliana Bruno reminds us, have not been shown on American television or in classrooms but rather circulate "within a world linked to the artistic avant-gardes . . . in certain academic environments, and on the circuits of independent and experimental cinema."[89] Bruno, writing in 1987, reads this placement as positive, but one can hardly imagine Rossellini being pleased with it. These are the very places that he and his pedagogical project sought to leave behind in an effort to replace art with pedagogy, aesthetics with knowledge.

In the years that have elapsed since Bruno's comments, the films have become somewhat less marginal but have moved no closer to the kind of placement that Rossellini would have desired. Instead, as presented by Gallagher for the Criterion Collection, an American art cinema DVD line, or featured as part of a 2006 retrospective at the Museum of Modern Art, the films are pushed back into the kinds of cultural institutions from which Rossellini tried so hard to distance them. One could read the failure of Rossellini's project and its reappropriation by the world of art cinema as its ultimate validation, as a sign of its success in finding its true identity as art after its creator's death. The television project, in this light, would appear to be reconcilable with the framework of modernism after all. To see it as a belated success, however, would be to minimize its difference from the artworks against which it defined itself, to refuse to recognize its anachronistic insistence on the possibility of the impossible and the need for historical salvage and narrative continuity. Its meaning and importance cannot be revealed through its recuperation by the art cinema milieu and its post facto transformation into an auteurist oeuvre. They are fully present only in a recognition of its failures, because it is in these—its inability to stave off history's "end," its inability to alter television and its social function, and its inability to achieve fully transparent communication—that the project reveals not only the promise that television held but also the difficulty of fully detaching this promise from the conditions that gave rise to it. While such limitations are ultimately insurmountable—we cannot fully think ourselves out of the present, no matter how hard we might try—they will become less problematic in the works of Godard and Watkins, which show a greater awareness of the extent to which television had already taken steps to undercut the very informational associations upon which it so heavily relied for its identity.

3

Inform, Educate, and Aestheticize

PETER WATKINS AT THE BBC

The two television films directed by Peter Watkins for the BBC, *Culloden* (1964) and *The War Game* (1965), present staged events using an audiovisual form highly reminiscent of contemporaneous documentaries. This technique has led to their frequent identification as a point of origin for docudrama or "mockumentary," although Watkins was hardly the first to use such an approach.[1] We might look to radio programs such as Orson Welles's *The War of the Worlds* or CBS's *You Are There* (later adapted for television) as precursors; what distinguishes Watkins's approach from these, however, is not simply his use of images (already present in the television version of the latter) but rather the specifically televisual character of the models he imitates. Documentary and television, however, are also both key targets of critique in Watkins's work: far more than Rossellini, he detected the explosive contradictions behind the informational claims of both and the ways in which television had begun to remap the boundaries between the informational and other categories of text and apprehension. Both, then, were at once targets and models to be imitated: Watkins's television films attempted to develop a form of moving image practice that would challenge the very sorts of texts it took as its sources, imagining a different kind of television that would derive its power not from its supposedly neutral presentation of information or its institutional authority but rather from a redefinition of what it meant, to invoke the BBC's motto, to "inform, educate, and entertain."

Watkins's case also offers a clear demonstration of the limits of television as institution, given the often hostile response to his works and his inability to find hospitable venues: while most of his projects drew financial support from public (and, on occasion, private) television companies, they often met with rejection or marginalization by these very same companies, a point that the director has bemoaned throughout much of his career.[2] While Watkins's difficulty in having his programs produced and broadcast tellingly displays the limits of what European television would permit, my emphasis here will be not on the dynamics of his struggle with broadcasting institutions but rather on what it was that made his works so objectionable: if his films so often gave rise to resistance, this had just as much to do with their formal radicality as with their political content. Their questioning of the relationship between the categories of the aesthetic and the informational threw many of the claims made by television, not to mention the forms used to support these claims, into question. Watkins thus not only, like Rossellini, called on television to deliver on the promises that it made and had not kept but also called attention to the factors behind its failure. For Watkins, setting television on the right course did entail not an effort at purification, as we find in Rossellini, but rather the transformation of its own informational discourse into an aesthetic. The formal languages television had developed by the early 1960s constituted one of the key raw materials that Watkins's aesthetic drew on and transformed, while still maintaining fidelity to a public service mission largely in harmony with the one declared by the BBC.

Watkins also differs from Rossellini in his exploitation of television's placement in the home: whereas the medium's domestic placement led Rossellini to conceive of it in a way that brought his project in line with the terms of the culture industry (encouraging individual, atomized, and detached consumption), Watkins sees it as a virtue insofar as it allows for its own overcoming. Television, unlike the cinema, allows the director to penetrate into the most intimate spaces, catching the spectator unawares and shocking him out of complacency, and thereby transforming the depoliticized, isolated space of the television-equipped living room into a site of destabilization and subversion. Both on the level of its formal practices and in its physical placement within the home, television thus offered Watkins a set of tools through which its own dismantling could be carried out. But just as Watkins at once adopts and critiques the forms

of television's audiovisual language, he imagines the dismantling of existing television not through opposition or negation but rather through its
utopian projection and transformation, an imagining of what it could
become on the basis of what it is. He treats the raw materials provided by
television as the seeds of its utopian double, drawing on what is already
immanent in them, not only as promise, but as concrete elements capable
of fulfilling that promise.

Born in Surrey in 1935, Watkins began his artistic career as a theater
director and actor, then quickly moved on to making short films with
Canterbury's Playcraft theatrical group. Unlike Rossellini or Godard,
Watkins did not in any sense come from the commercial cinema (and
would only make one studio-produced film, 1967's *Privilege*) and remains
on its peripheries. His first films were made within the context of Britain's
burgeoning amateur film movement, and his first extant work, *The Diary
of an Unknown Soldier* (1959), received an award for best amateur film.[3]
During his amateur period, Watkins worked alongside Kevin Brownlow
(the film historian and later codirector of *It Happened Here* [1965] and
Winstanley [1976], perhaps the films most closely resembling those of
Watkins) and former John Grierson associate John Trumper at World-
Wide Pictures, a company producing sponsored documentaries. While
working at World-Wide, Watkins produced a longer amateur film, *The
Forgotten Faces* (1961), which marked the first stage in his development
of the pseudo-documentary form that will concern us here. The BBC
hired him as an assistant producer in its documentary department on
the basis of the film, whose strategies he would replicate in his first BBC
production, *Culloden,* which depicted the battle fought between British
troops and the Scottish Jacobite supporters of Prince Charles Edward
Stuart in 1746. The positive reception to *Culloden* opened the door for
Watkins to develop a still more controversial project, *The War Game,*
which attempted to realistically portray the effects of a nuclear attack
on Great Britain.

The reception of *The War Game,* however, initiated a decades-long
antagonism between Watkins and the mainstream media. The film was
notoriously banned by the BBC, which refused to show it on television on the grounds that it was, according to an official statement, "too

horrifying for the medium of broadcasting."[4] Owing to the controversy over *The War Game* and the tepid critical and commercial response to *Privilege* (1967), Watkins left the United Kingdom to develop projects in Scandinavia and the United States, both for the cinema (*The Gladiators* [1969] in Sweden and *Punishment Park* [1971] in the United States) and for television (*Edvard Munch* [1974] in Norway and *The Seventies People* [1975] in Denmark, among others). Watkins's geographical meanderings represent something like a search for fertile utopian ground, for sites in which a different television would still be possible. Indeed, Watkins often casts himself as an exile, arguing that there is simply no public or private broadcasting company left that will finance or disseminate his work. This situation, as I will return to in chapter 5, eventually leads him to a greater focus on media reform and alternative, non-television-based media models, although he has worked primarily for television.

While Watkins's self-constructed exile persona does indeed provide compelling evidence for European television's limitations, he nonetheless retained throughout most of his career a belief that television could be transformed into a positive pedagogical and political tool. The promise of television, though, seemed to him to be at odds with the censoring state apparatus that he confronted early on; public service pointed beyond itself and beyond the state, holding out a promise that could only be kept by transcending its own political situation. Watkins is thus both against and for television, decrying its negative effects while finding within it the seeds of its own transcendence. Again recalling Rossellini, Watkins tends to speak of television as a negative force on two grounds. First, it is controlled by the wrong people, "those people, in short, with a clear contempt for the rest of the world," and second, it is used to deceive and pacify its viewers: "I think mass communications is [*sic*] continually encouraging people to take the easy way out. Television in particular feeds people with illusions so continuously that you're mentally harmless the entire time. It's made increasingly easy now for us to not face what's happening, and to a really lethal degree forget the actual circumstances of our society."[5] Even so, he argues that the only means through which the damage caused by the consumer society that television promotes can be undone will be television itself: "the technology of mass communications—which ideally should self-destruct in the end—at this stage undeniably has a propensity, probably more than any other single factor in our society, for helping to . . . create a healthy environment."[6]

This possibility, he believes, lies in a commitment to a usage of media that broadly conforms to the objectives of public service, objectives that are rarely attained in practice. The central task of audiovisual media, artistic and otherwise, should be first and foremost a pedagogical one, he argues: we should be "trying to use films and television with compassion and a total lack of self-interest . . . to help broaden people's understanding of the present dilemmas of the world."[7] This task applies not only to television but to cinema as well and is ignored by both commercial and art films: "Film appears to be in the hands of a minority of people who either operate on a kind of commercial bludgeon tactic or who treat film as a kind of intellectual toy," Watkins laments, echoing Rossellini's commercial cinema–modernism dyad.[8] A "useful" media is for him opposed not only to commercialism but also to "aestheticism": "Cinema is acceptable provided it is something that can be discussed in a classroom. [Critics] handle it in a kind of aesthetic way, put it back in its tin and push it away."[9] It is not the aesthetic itself that Watkins objects to, as does Rossellini, but rather its compartmentalization, the way in which it is kept separate from any pedagogical function or engagement with issues external to itself, "in its tin."

Given their similar rejections of both commercial cinema and art cinema, we might thus expect Watkins to take a similar route to Rossellini's, treating television as a site where an informational image can counteract the allure of the aesthetic images we find in the cinema. Watkins, however, conceives of information and its transmission in a far broader way than Rossellini, appealing to sensation and emotion as forms of knowing in themselves. In short, he recognizes that the radical separation called for by Rossellini is not only impossible but also undesirable: the very sorts of contaminations between thinking and feeling, voice and body, sound and image, use-value and pleasure, aesthetic and informational discourse, that television had brought about were not to be done away with in the name of information but rather used in its service. It is by taking this approach, in which audiovisual language reaches for a form and function that transcends the usual boundaries of the *partage du sensible,* that Watkins's project begins to resemble that of John Grierson, who had attempted, as discussed in chapter 1, to rethink the relationship between aesthetics and information decades before. One of the major variables that separates the two, of course, is television, which had already radically renovated the Griersonian model. A comparison between the works of Watkins and the works of the British Documentary Film Movement, taken as applications of Grierson's ideas about information and aesthetics, will thus provide an ideal means for determining what, precisely, television had changed. What could Watkins do with television that Grierson could not with cinema, and how do their conceptualizations and deployments of aesthetic and informational elements compare? Before answering this question, however, we will need to consider in more detail how Watkins's early works function rhetorically, particularly in their use of a pedagogical or informing logic, and to more precisely characterize their relationships to the documentary and television practices that they draw on. These two issues can hardly be addressed separately, given the extent to which Watkins's rhetoric depends on the adoption and transformation of the textual forms dominant in documentary cinema and television in the early 1960s.

TELEVISION, DOCUMENTARY, AND THE "IMPRESSION OF REALITY"

The most widely commented on component of Watkins's technique is the formidable "impression of reality" that his works give to their viewers. The idea that film is the medium most capable of creating this impression, of course, goes back to its very beginnings, but television perhaps exceeds it, both in adding the possibility of "liveness" or copresence of viewer and depicted event and through an institutional promotion of itself as a more factual medium. The creation of an overwhelming, even dangerous impression of reality has been associated with Watkins's films ever since the BBC's banning of *The War Game* in 1965 and has subsequently been incorporated into most accounts of the filmmaker and his work.[10] Milton Shulman, for example, recounts an anecdote concerning his first meeting with Watkins while working as an executive at Britain's Granada Television in 1961. Watkins, Shulman explains, had shown up at his office with a copy of his film *The Forgotten Faces,* in the hope of having it screened on television.[11] The film, which depicts the Hungarian Uprising of 1956 in the pseudo-documentary style that would become Watkins's trademark, fooled Shulman completely: after viewing it, he asked Watkins how he had managed to obtain such shots of Budapest during the conflict, only to be told that the film was in fact a fabrication, filmed in Canterbury with English actors. "My first reaction," he relates, "was incredulity. The faces, which I had seen in such lingering close-ups, seemed so utterly un-English and the locale so thoroughly Balkan that I found it very difficult to accept my own self-deception."[12] Shulman proceeded to show the film to two of his colleagues at Granada, only to find that they too were fooled. One, he reports, responded that "if we show a film like that . . . no one will believe our newsreels."[13]

For Shulman, the film's effectiveness rested primarily on the impression of reality that it created and on its ability to pass itself off as an indexical record of the events that it portrayed:

> The rough camera work, the crude lighting, the texture of the celluloid, the chaotic shots of fighting, tussling men had that quality of immediacy and involvement reminiscent of the work of cameramen covering the front-line fighting during the Second World War at places like Stalingrad and Arnhem. It could have only been shot on the spot.[14]

Ultimately, the veracity of Shulman's account is of little importance. If anything, it has the flavor of myth and seems to function as an updated version of the often-cited tale of spectators' attempts to dodge the oncoming train while viewing the Lumières' *L'Arrivée d'un train à La Ciotat.* Like that myth, the anecdote affirms the filmed image's power to elicit spectatorial belief in what is, on some level, not real or true and attests to the uncanny and even frightening ability of Watkins's films to create an impression of reality that is hardly diminished by the spectator's knowledge of the film's fabricated status.

As Shulman's anecdote indicates, the impression of reality that *The Forgotten Faces* created was a result of its form—"the rough camera work, the crude lighting"—yet Watkins was clearly not seeking simply to double the forms he imitated. This was, after all, not a real newsreel but a staged fiction. How, then, might we describe the relationship between his films and the films and sources that they imitated? Shulman's account proposes a response by suggesting that a film like *The Forgotten Faces* could have two possible (and antithetical) uses, namely, deception and demystification. On one hand, it could be used to convince the spectator that something that did not happen did, as a kind of counterfeit document. On the other, it could be used to attest to the falsifiability of any such document, the untrustworthiness of the image as documentary record, and the dangers of using audiovisual media for journalistic purposes. In the first case, artfulness is reduced to mimetic deception, substituting imitation for the real thing. The second case, of course, is what Shulman's colleague has in mind when he comments that after seeing the film, no viewer could ever believe a newsreel. By showing documentary form to be constructed, codified, and carrying in itself no epistemological guarantee, Watkins intervened to alter not so much the form itself as the cultural framework in which it operated, breaking apart the connections between certain forms of visibility and knowledge that had been implemented as a "law" as part of the *partage du sensible*.

Watkins's subsequent films, of course, forbid any possibility of deception: *Culloden* depicted an event that could not possibly have been filmed (having taken place in 1746), whereas *The War Game* imagined events that could occur but had not taken place. With any possibility of fraud left far behind by his choice of subject matter, Watkins would seem in these films to be opting for the second function suggested by Shulman's anecdote, namely, revealing the fact that television's and documentary's claims to give the viewer an unmediated picture of events as they occurred are based on a mere effect, a false impression of reality generated by a set of formal techniques. It is this reading, coupled with *Culloden*'s strongly critical stance toward English nationalism and militarism, that leads Raymond Durgnat to describe it as marking "the turning point of documentary tradition, from affirmation to questioning."[15] This is not, however, the only way to interpret the films' relationship to their formal models, nor their broader pedagogical functioning; in what follows, I will argue that what makes Watkins's works so unique is precisely their difference from this familiar demystifying approach. Taking a different viewpoint, however, will necessitate a further investigation into what Watkins's models were and how they conceived of the impression of reality and the moving image's informational and aesthetic qualities. By attending more closely to the state of documentary, particularly on television, at the time Watkins made his early works, we can begin to see how they go far beyond simply undercutting the informational guarantees of existing forms of media.

Both Shulman's retrospective description of his first encounter with Watkins's work and Durgnat's identification of this work as "the turning point of documentary tradition" suggest that Watkins's films had enacted a major rupture within the history of documentary—but a rupture, we might ask, with what? Key to the consideration of this question is the role that television had already played in creating its own rupture with the documentary tradition. The word *documentary* had, by the time Watkins made *Culloden,* been in use for just under forty years but was still strongly associated, particularly in the United Kingdom, with Grierson. Since Grierson's heyday in the mid-1930s, however, the face of British documentary had dramatically changed: the 1950s witnessed what John Corner calls "the reconstitution of documentary within television as a major extension of journalism" as well as "the introduction of new, lightweight equipment which allowed for extensive location shooting."[16] This turn toward journalism marked a move away from Grierson's conception of documentary, which had in fact, as discussed in chapter 1, defined itself *against* the "purely journalistic" newsreel and other "factual" film forms. For Grierson, documentary's uniqueness was meant to derive from its combination of informational and aesthetic aims, and a belief that what he called "creative treatment" was necessary for the documentary to fulfill its informing mission. To recall a passage already cited in chapter 1, Grierson lamented that nonfiction films "describe, and even expose, but in any aesthetic sense, only rarely reveal."[17] To show or describe would simply amount to reproducing the visible, whereas for Grierson, any true understanding or knowledge required an aesthetic transformation of the material that would allow for some deeper form of revelation. By the end of the 1950s, however, documentary, both in the United Kingdom and elsewhere, had increasingly positioned itself as a superior form of journalism, one that could depict firsthand what the viewer could formerly only read about in the newspapers. In this context, Corner writes, "the lofty imperatives of Griersonianism could only survive as little more than fragments of rhetorical decoration."[18]

The forms whose transformation constituted the basis of Watkins's method, then, were those of journalistic documentary, already affected by television's associations with informationality and neutrality and more strictly demarcated from anything that could be construed as aesthetic than the films of the British Documentary Film Movement had been. S. M. J. Arrowsmith notes, "Watkins adopted narrative techniques derived in the main from the documentary tradition, as it had been mutated through its own adaptation of televisual rather than cinematic communication,"[19] while Antoine de Baecque links Watkins's work to the "new reportage" British television programs produced by the BBC's documentary division in the 1950s under the leadership of Paul Rotha.[20] This new paradigm of the "documentary report," Corner argues, adopted "journalism's concern with inquiry and analysis" as well as "vérité and direct cinema's concern with observation."[21] The documentarians of 1950s England were not so much artists as they were reporters, seeking out the unseen corners of the world and faithfully capturing them for the edification of the television audience.

Their programs, such as the popular BBC series *Special Enquiry,* which ran from 1952 to 1957, typically carried out an investigation into the lives of ordinary people, coupling documentary footage with expert opinions. In *Special Enquiry,* "documentary" material—that is, images and sounds of supposedly unstaged reality, although they look rather staged to our eyes today—is cast as evidence of or support for the overall position taken by the program. An episode on poor conditions in schools, for example, shows us the schools firsthand, as though to prove through photographic evidence the program's claims about the need for reform. Such documentary images are accompanied by voice-over but are also intercut with images of a studio commentator, who further explains their meaning. In this structure, documentary images confront us as pure, uninterpreted data, which the speaker (or the journalist) has to interpret, but they nonetheless constitute a stronger proof than any argument: one needn't simply trust that schools are in poor shape when one can see this with one's own eyes. Their status as such, however, would not be nearly as pronounced in the absence of the commentator: they are marked as real and uninterpreted precisely because the form of the program insists that they must be interpreted by something external to them. The image's capacity to inform the viewer is treated as something that stems not from its expressive quality, the aesthetic experience it provides, nor even its ability to explain the situation (why school conditions are bad), but rather from its status as something like raw data, a kind of proof of existence. Photography, in this paradigm, is thus treated as an almost scientific tool, valued for its ability to faithfully document rather than to express or explain. This characterization of photography, in turn, suggests an underlying empiricist belief that what can be directly shown and seen constitutes the baseline of knowledge, the point from which all knowing begins.

Formats like the one used by *Special Enquiry* would, by the early 1960s, give way to others in which the interpreting voice was used with increasingly less frequency and the images, as though attesting to their status as evidence, became less polished, as in the "direct cinema" of Robert Drew, Ricky Leacock, and the Maysles Brothers in the United States. In the British context (as well as in Watkins's films), and especially on television, a commentator or journalist figure usually remains (even Drew Associates's *Primary* uses some voice-over), but later programs would replace the fairly static, stagey depictions of *Special Enquiry* with the spontaneous approach permitted by the use of lighter, more portable equipment pioneered by practitioners of direct cinema like Drew and Leacock.

Watkins both adopts and subverts the journalistic, empiricist approach of the "reportage" television documentary and of direct cinema. There are thus at least two steps or moments that define his relationship to the forms he imitates: one in which the imitation itself constitutes a critique (because in this case the possibility of imitating alone is enough to suggest the epistemological unreliability of the form used) and another in which the form is assigned a new value that I will refer to here as "aesthetic," to differentiate it from the informational and to insist on its deliberate appeal to a different sensorium. What makes Watkins's works unique and most precisely characterizes their rhetorical function is the coupling of these two steps: his intervention lies not primarily in his questioning of television and documentary's neutrality and informational character but rather in the positioning of this questioning alongside a reintroduction of the aesthetic or noninformational elements that had been rejected as documentary migrated to television. This intervention proposes a new answer to the question of how the categories of the aesthetic and the informational might be synthesized or sublated into another form, but it does so by drawing on the very forms that had, in the television era, largely liquidated the former term. Watkins's method, beginning with *The Forgotten Faces* and then perfected in *Culloden* and *The War Game,* thus depends simultaneously on his works' similarity to and radical difference from other documentaries or television programs of the time; his films imitate in order to illustrate the transformation of their own models, changing the meaning of the forms they use and ensuring that the viewer is aware of this change.

The techniques used in Watkins's films clearly and openly imitate the formal language of the models they draw on, combining the report structure of a program like *Special Enquiry* with the immediacy provided by the light, mobile filming techniques of a film like *Primary. Culloden* foregrounds the fact that it is mimicking the report format and correspondingly situates the image as in need of explanation or interpretation. A reporter or journalistic narrator appears in the guise of an on-site commentator, watching the battle as it unfolds. This commentator resembles the reporters in programs like *Special Enquiry,* mediators who tell us how to understand what we are seeing but whose presence itself serves, in its status as commentary, to reinforce the neutrality and self-evidence of the image (Figure 7). Another narrator (Watkins himself, clearly "outside" the action but speaking in the present tense, as narrators of journalistic TV programs often do) describes the action to us through voice-over. Both of these narrators, the somewhat comical on-screen one and the more neutral and authoritative off-screen one, *are* in fact informative, providing us with context to understand the chaos of the battle, but their function has also changed in respect to the models being imitated:

FIGURE 7. Watkins mimics the conventions of journalistic documentary through the use of an on-screen commentator in *Culloden* (1964).

the narrators can no longer be read as in any way verifying the neutral, raw quality of the image, because we are clearly seeing a re-creation and not the 1746 battle itself.

This brings us to the second imitated element, namely, the use of direct cinema-style spontaneity on the level of sound and image. Here what would in the models being imitated serve as signs of the spontaneity and uncontrolledness of the real—those elements that seem to prove the text's status as information, as if in need of commentary—are still present but have mutated into deliberately deployed components of an aesthetic, a kind of formal vocabulary, nor can the viewer interpret them otherwise, given that we know the film to be staged. Figures overlap and are not always clearly visible, and the camera at times seems to struggle to get a clear shot of the action; it shakes frequently, as though jostled by soldiers or evading gunfire. Characters often look into the camera, suggesting not only its presence but also that of a cameraman, a witness who has allowed the images to be relayed to us. Sound, like image, is used to create a sense of messiness and spontaneity, as though the recordist, like the cameraman, had to struggle to obtain his track. While the sound quality of certain interviews is improbably clear, other instances find characters shouting over surrounding noises in order to be heard. Background noises, primarily yelling, gunfire, and cannon fire, are ubiquitous in *Culloden* and provide a sense of continuity that the editing of the image track, due to its lack of concern with spatial coherence and its rapid cutting, fails to create. These constructed signs of spontaneity function to create a sense of excess, which we might link to Roland Barthes's "reality effect": Watkins's films are full of the "structurally superfluous" descriptive details that Barthes identifies as a source of realism, which serve no narrative purpose and resist absorption to any motivation.[22] The journalistic documentary form that Watkins imitates is especially well suited to such excess, given its claims to offer unmediated access to uncodified reality by indexically reproducing it. Bill Nichols differentiates between excess in fiction and documentary, arguing that "if excess tends to be that which is beyond narrative in fiction films, excess in documentary is that which stands beyond the reach of both narrative and exposition."[23] In the case of *Culloden* and *The War Game*, the excess being imitated is of the second kind, given that Watkins is less concerned with narrative than with relating a certain set of facts and making a particular argument.

Watkins thus manages to precisely mimic all of the devices we would expect from journalistic documentary or television report, drawing on all of the tools they use to create an impression of reality, yet we can no longer read the audiovisual object before us as we would its models. Here is where we begin to see the importance of contradiction in Watkins's work, precisely as the means of creating a unique sensorium and ensuring that the viewer is pushed into a new mode of apprehension: the spectator recognizes, and even experiences, the authenticity and immediacy usually associated with documentary techniques but can no longer interpret this immediacy as a function of the reality of the images, which are clearly false by documentary standards, nor can she take these images as the empirical, evidential basis of an argument developed by the commentary.

We need to question the rhetorical functioning not merely of the simple demystifying moment, then, but also of its juxtaposition with something that still closely resembles, and even seems to exploit, the effects of the form being demystified. The impression of reality persists, a fact attested to by the BBC censors who found *The War Game* too horrifying to be broadcast—but why? Though the films may well decrease the viewer's faith in television and documentary's trustworthiness, their complexity and their utopian character depend on the fact that they make, in one single gesture, both a negational maneuver and an affirmative one, transforming what in one framework would be dismissed as pure ideology into something that becomes valuable in another: *The Forgotten Faces, Culloden,* and *The War Game* do indeed denaturalize the television documentary form they employ and call into question the effect through which it appears to us as transparently informative and real, but at the same time, they insist on the *value* of this form and this effect. If they simply led spectators to dismiss what they were seeing as false, they would convey nothing of the horrors of war and violence that Watkins seeks to express; they would lose the uncanny effect that they had upon Shulman and his colleagues. Any interpretation of the films as primarily critical has to disregard or discount the fact that a film like *Culloden* powerfully exploits the power of the image to make us feel as though we are experiencing things firsthand. The persistence of the impression of reality, despite its undercutting, is thus not meant to demonstrate the insidious power of the code and the spectator's status as dupe but is itself still viewed as a potentially valuable, knowledge-creating device.

What value, then, do television documentary form and the impression of reality that it creates have for Watkins? His description of his intentions at this point in his career suggests that he had an aim that was altogether separate from (and even in contradiction with) a desire to reveal the mythical nature of documentary's objectivity and truth, namely, "to substitute the artificiality of Hollywood and its high-key lighting, with the faces and feelings of *real people.*"[24] Whereas a demystifying procedure would take documentary and its unveiling as its object, this quest for authenticity opposes itself to Hollywood's artificiality. What is a target or object of demystification on one front thus becomes a weapon on another, as Watkins attacks Hollywood artificiality precisely by substituting for it the documentary form whose authenticity and truth value, in other terms, is being cast into doubt. Watkins's use of television documentary forms to generate a greater sense of authenticity seeks to retain their value in eliciting belief and an impression of reality before an avowedly reconstructed or mediated real while jettisoning the epistemological grounding to which they are usually linked. As such epistemologically charged forms are transformed into elements of style, becoming one possible form of discourse among many that can be used to recount fictional events, their truth claims are undermined, yet their ability to create an impression of reality and elicit a sense of belief within the realm of aesthetic experience are not. The sense of closeness to the real elicited by the journalistic television documentary forms Watkins draws on is revealed, through its demystification and subsequent redeployment, to be *not epistemological but aesthetic* in character. It is this effect of difference—this insistence that there is a value that exceeds or follows a different logic than that of the informational—that indicates the presence of another mode of expression and apprehension. Information and knowledge are not opposed to this aesthetic mode, as they were by Rossellini; rather, they are seen as functions that can blur with others and locate themselves in different places than the customary distribution of the sensible might lead us to expect.

One might well object that this reduces Watkins's films to fictions like any other: the spectator is no longer provided with any guaranteed connection with the real but simply with a compelling simulacrum, which is taken as such and apprehended differently than an audiovisual text that purports to give direct access to the real. Information and knowledge may still be present (as, say, in a conventional historical drama) but are no longer "pure," having mixed themselves with aesthetic elements that intensify our experience. If this were the case, we could liken Watkins's enlistment of televisual forms to create a sense of immediacy or impression of reality to other renewals of realism, those distortions or revivifications that Roman Jakobson sees as creating a succession of forms, each of whose claim to connect us with reality rests primarily on its difference from its predecessor, from its disruption of an existing code; interpreted thus, the films' realism would derive from Watkins dismantling the code of Hollywood film to achieve a more realistic fiction, just as when, to take Jakobson's example, Cézanne and Degas rejected the forms used by their academic predecessors and thus gave the viewers of their works a more palpable feeling of "reality."[25] It is not mere difference here, however, but the co-option of a specific code that brings along with it strong connotations of closeness to truth or reality, that secures for Watkins's films the capacity to create a strong impression of reality. Obvious parallels would be the less wholesale adoption of newsreel or documentary approaches in Italian neo-realism and American film noir or the use of verité-style camerawork in "docudramas" like Loach's *Cathy Come Home,* but what remains unique in Watkins's films is the extent to which he calls into question and undermines the claims of the form that creates such a strong impression of reality while still exploiting this impression. What is key here is the deliberate staging of a contradiction: the spectator is, on one hand, invited to experience what is on the screen as immediate and real but is, on the other, constantly reminded, unlike in most fiction films, that it cannot be taken as such, and that the usual uses of such impressions of reality are duplicitous. *Culloden* and *The War Game* are therefore unlike any of the categories of films with which they share traits: unlike the television documentary mode whose forms they adopt because they demystify these forms, unlike the Brechtian or demystifying text in that they do not undermine these forms' capacity to create an impression of reality and elicit belief, but also unlike the docudrama, which attempts to create an impression of reality without addressing the difference between epistemological and aesthetic closeness to reality or foregrounding the means by which it creates this impression.

Watkins's films can be further differentiated from other artistic renewals of realism or attempts to elicit a strong impression of reality insofar as they do not seek to create an impression of reality for its own sake, any more than they seek to completely reject any power or value that it might have. Rather, they employ the tactics they do for explicitly pedagogical reasons, maintaining the informing imperative of Griersonian documentary: they present staged action not merely to give the viewer a sense of immediacy but also to accomplish a specific rhetorical task. They maintain a grounding in historical reality, an organizational strategy that relates more to argument than to story (and in which, in accordance with Nichols's characterization of documentary, "sounds and images stand as evidence . . . rather than elements of a plot"), and, most importantly, an insistence on what Nichols calls "informing logic."[26] This insistence on a grounding in historical reality and "informing logic" is demonstrated not only by the wealth of "straight" information relayed by voice-over and written titles in Watkins's films but also by the research that underlies his visual representations, even in the case of the hypothetical *The War Game*.[27] The images used in the films thus still function in support of a larger case or argument, just like those of *Special Enquiry*, but the grounds on which they do so are no longer the same. Whereas in *Special Enquiry* (or *Primary*), the documentary image supported an overall argument thanks to its supposedly unmediated documentation of the real, its status as empirical evidence, here the support becomes one of a more properly aesthetic nature.

AESTHETICIZING INFORMATION

The modes of communication and apprehension that I refer to as aesthetic here are characterized by a rejection of the category of the informational as used by television reportage and documentary; they are not aesthetic in the sense of presenting themselves as belonging to the cultural category of art but rather in their self-presentation as offering a form of experience that is different from that of the audiovisual objects that surround them, and whose intelligibility depends on the viewer's recognition of this difference. Yet the modality of the aesthetic here is also *still* informational; it is not disinterested or noninstrumental but rather seeks to teach the viewer something. By blurring the lines between what would, in conventional television practice (both in textual forms and in generic distinctions between programs), be separate or contained categories, Watkins gestures toward ways of knowing that are different from the informational modalities of news or documentaries and toward a category of text and apprehension that ultimately challenges any demarcation between the aesthetic and the informational. This pointing to a synthesis of information and its others, along with his insistence on the potential usefulness of forms whose present usage is, for him, largely deceptive and pacifying, marks the utopian character of Watkins's practice. I realize that this may seem somewhat paradoxical or even ironic, given that many of his films (not only *The War Game* but also *The Gladiators* and *Punishment Park*) depict clearly dystopian scenarios. It is not, however, the subject that is utopian here but rather the form itself, insofar as it illustrates the possibility of another television that would be a truly effective form of communication by both transforming elements of already-existing television and recognizing the redistribution of the sensible and the leveling of categories that television seeks to obscure or contain as providing utopian raw material in their own right. While the world depicted is dystopian, the medium that depicts it is utopian, a kind of broadcast news from nowhere: the fact that so many of Watkins's works set their action in the near future allows not only the dystopian projection of the present, with existing tendencies taken to their most horrific conclusions, but also a utopian projection of the kind of media that might prevent this future. They contain within themselves both the model for a utopian future form of communication and a vision of what will befall us if our current forms do not undergo a radical transformation.

To a greater extent than *Culloden*, *The War Game* demonstrates how the utopian revalencing of television might be carried out and suggests the new forms of apprehension that it would allow. It is on one hand a film whose goal is to convey the total ill preparedness of the United Kingdom for a nuclear strike and the ridiculousness of the response plans currently in place. On the other, though, its lesson concerns the current forms of informational discourse. Through a montage technique that juxtaposes multiple distinct modes taken from television (much as a program like *Special Enquiry* alternates between "documentary" and "studio" modes), the film demonstrates their insufficiency and illustrates how they might be made to function differently. In short, the film is a kind of polemical user's manual for Watkins's method, one that both clarifies the stakes of the transformations carried out in *Culloden* and demonstrates their use-value.

To ensure that the film breaks with conventional modes of apprehension, Watkins deliberately blocks reading strategies that would attempt to discern between informative and aesthetic approaches and thwarts the ways in which we normally understand the connection between the two. The discourses that it imitates clearly belong to the informational category of television (seemingly spontaneous reportage, expert commentary), yet their transformation undercuts the tenability of this category itself. In one key sequence, actors playing notable figures from various fields engage in a Brechtian style of third-person acting, in which their lines are recited as though quoted (as they indeed are), and hold forth on the topic of nuclear war (Figure 8). These "talking head" sequences are intercut with staged scenes depicting the aftermath of a nuclear attack on Great Britain, filmed in the same pseudo-documentary style used in *Culloden*. The former sequences feel darkly satirical because of the acting style employed but are punctuated by written titles that assure us that the absurd statements pronounced (for example, that there will be ample time and resources to prepare for subsequent world wars after an initial nuclear attack) were in fact actually made by clergymen and scientists (Figure 8b). The latter continue the use of feigned spontaneity found in *Culloden* but amplify its brutality, depicting images of a post-bombing firestorm (based on what occurred in Dresden in World War II) and the execution of civilians by military police. The juxtaposition of these two modes, itself something like an exaggeration of the raw image–commentary model favored by television, creates an effect in which what we might call a hierarchy of truths is turned on its head, insofar as statements that are in fact documented—that come from a specified source of information outside of the text itself, as the film insists—are delivered in such a way as to make them seem less real than the invented elements.

Although this technique might be read as an ironic rhetorical strategy—that is, merely a form of argument rather than an aesthetic device—it also creates a deeply unsettling and paradoxical experience for the spectator, one that seriously upsets the reading strategies that we normally use to discern between informational and aesthetic discourse. On one hand, it calls on the viewer to question the connection to reality contained in the less seemingly artificial segments (the staged nuclear war sequences). On the other hand, it strengthens them through contrast: the actors' statements, though "true" in the sense that they are documented, are meant to be examples of ridiculous positions or arguments

FIGURE 8. "Talking heads" provide ridiculous, but documented, opinions in *The War Game* (1965).

and are therefore depicted in an exaggerated, unnaturalistic fashion. The documented reality of the statements is thus rendered false, while the hypothetical events of the staged sequences appear coded as true in terms of the transparent language of television documentary, all the while undercutting this very truth through a foregrounding of their construct-edness. The force of this contradiction is further strengthened through the quick alternation between modes: the viewer has no time to get her bearings or to adjust her mode of reading. Even if the rhetorical effect of the sequence is very clear and intelligible, the means through which it is created are quite jarring: the usual connection between transparency, truth, and a certain set of formal techniques is severed, yet without presum-ing that this forbids the communication of any information whatsoever. Any information delivered to the spectator here, however, is hardly factual or empirical in character and indeed undermines the idea that one could possibly apprehend anything worth knowing through mere facts, at least as far as nuclear war is concerned.

Instead, the viewer must be shocked. The violence that occurs in *The War Game* is not merely represented on-screen but also enacted upon the spectator's senses and available codes for reading and experiencing filmic texts. She will learn something, and indeed be informed, but in a way that reconfigures what counts as information. This sort of shock is taken to its extreme in the scenes in which the conditional tense of the voice-over clashes with the immediacy of the image.[28] As we see a raging firestorm, the voice-over informs us, "This is the phenomenon which could happen in Britain following a nuclear strike." The contradiction between the conditional tense of the verb "could happen" and the pres-ent tense image is further stressed by the verb "is," rendering ambiguous the ontological status of the image: what could happen, *is.* The image's undermining as indexical or documentary record is already present in its status as hypothetical, so one might ask why Watkins further insists upon this by adding the conditional tense voice-over. This undermining is further complicated by the later dropping of the conditional tense from the sequence altogether, when the voice-over states, "This is what is tech-nically known as a firestorm." I would posit two possible motives behind these strategies, both of which seek to create a sustained contradiction.

First, the apparent contradiction of tenses between the voice-over and the image ("could happen") is a means of short-circuiting the viewer's habitual categories of perception and is intended first and foremost to be jarring and upsetting. Second, by foregrounding the hypothetical and fabricated nature of the image through the conditional tense while still cultivating an impression of reality, Watkins insists on the exemption of the experience of watching his film from the epistemological expectations that would normally be applied to a documentary. A viewer of this film will indeed be informed, but in a considerably different way than she would be by a conventional documentary, insofar as knowledge is no longer gained primarily through sober, rationalistic means.

Watkins also insists on noninformational forms of knowledge in his consistent appeal to embodied spectatorship. This strategy differs from the ones described earlier insofar as it does not rely on specific formal procedures meant to subvert conventional ways of knowing but, like them, insists that the spectator's comprehension of the film has little to do with what is normally defined as informational and that our modes of understanding can hardly be limited to logical, or even conceptual, thought. Whereas the "experts" depicted in the sequence discussed earlier lead us to suspect that one can learn little about nuclear war from reading or writing about it, the references to the effects of violence upon the body contained in both *Culloden* and *The War Game* suggest that a form of imaginative embodiment may be the most effective way to do so, not to mention the most important way to get us to resist war and the large-scale militarization of society characteristic of the Cold War. Watkins thus exploits the spectator's status as what Vivian Sobchack calls a "cinesthetic subject," whose understanding of a filmic text relies on both "embodied vision" and an ability to experience it, by way of a kind of sensory rerouting, through senses beyond sight and vision.[29] As Sobchack puts it, "we do not experience any movie only through our eyes. We see and comprehend and feel films with our entire bodily being, informed by the full history and carnal knowledge of our acculturated sensorium."[30]

At several points in *Culloden* and *The War Game,* the voice-over describes injuries, while the image track depicts them. On one hand, the effect here is to mark the image as the location of excess: the suffering we are seeing can never be contained in discourse, but the very plenitude or impression of reality generated by the image derives in part from this juxtaposition. On the other, this very excess, despite being acknowledged as constructed, is positioned as the only possible means through which one could approach knowledge of what it means to be injured or maimed in battle. Watkins's voice-over narration introduces the first scene of physical suffering in *Culloden* with the statement, "This is roundshot. This is what it does." Images of injured and often screaming soldiers follow, accompanied by voice-over narration describing their injuries (Figure 9). The "cold" objective descriptions in the voice-over contrast with the visceral impact of the image, as though to illustrate the extent to which images are capable of providing us with far more embodied sensations than verbal language. We find similar techniques in *The War Game,* as when a sober, informational voice-over describes the capacity of a nuclear explosion to "cause melting of the upturned eyeball" and we see two figures who may have experienced just that clutching their faces and moaning. What Watkins exploits here is cinema's capacity, as described by Sobchack, to delocalize sensation from either the represented body or the spectator's body, instead blurring the boundaries between the two.[31] The fact that Watkins relies so extensively on the spectator's capacity for embodied vision takes on a further significance in light of early television's resistance to depictions of the body: as discussed in chapter 1, it treated the body as a site of noninformationality and as a threat to television's status as a useful medium. His focus on the body thus not only offers the spectator an important alternative to informational modes of apprehension but also serves as an implicit critique of television's efforts to contain it, revealing them not only to be untenable but also to *prevent* the effective communication of information.

The experience that Watkins offers us does not consider itself to be opposed to the true (as it would be in Rossellini's antiaesthetic system, in his theory if not in his practice), nor does it purport to allow us to access it directly (as in the journalistic television documentary), but nonetheless, it provides us, through images and the way that they affect us on a psychological and embodied level, with an effective means of arriving at truths about the historical (as opposed to fictional) world. This position,

FIGURE 9. One of the many appeals to the "cinesthetic subject" in *Culloden* (1964): an image of a young boy wounded during battle.

however, needs to be historically situated for its meaning to fully emerge. It is not merely a philosophical stance but rather represents a way of dealing with images, aesthetics, and information that is symptomatic of a more widespread cultural logic. It anticipates the turn away from Manichean dualities of true and false, representation and reality, that would later take place in film studies (and in the humanities more broadly). It is not an autonomous insight on the part of Watkins but rather a symptom of a cultural paradigm in which all information or knowledge is experienced as mediated or reached indirectly, very often through images, and often through what feels very much like an aesthetic experience (while the separateness of this category itself becomes increasingly untenable). This paradigm, I would argue, is one advanced by television itself. Watkins thus not only creates an exemplary testament to the way we perceive and know in the television age but also reveals the way television really works, behind its claims of separation.

Recent accounts of Watkins's works have focused on their "prophetic" qualities, "the uncanny way his films ... presage the contemporary cultural and political landscape—from Fox News to *The Daily Show,* from reality TV to the coverage of the Iraq war."[32] What these accounts miss, though, is the fact that his prescience lies not so much in his prediction of the prominence of media in all aspects of our culture and the advent of "reality television" as in his anticipation of a cultural logic largely undetected and little understood in the 1960s but now clearly visible, a logic that Watkins chooses to exploit rather than to negate. Already, for Watkins, the image need not be "real" to be "true"; it need not be "factual" to inform. The boundaries between aesthetic experience and rational apprehension seem to be irrelevant in practice. While this might seem a commonplace at this point, what is essential to note here is the fact that this insight seems, in Watkins's case, to be generated and then expressed specifically by television: television fails in its claims to direct knowledge, yet this failure itself suggests that all forms of knowledge or information will be equally mediated—and that this is not necessarily a bad (or even avoidable) thing in itself.

TRANSFORMING THE GRIERSONIAN MODEL

Watkins's insistence on facilitating nonempirical, nonconceptual ways of knowing that both critique and exploit the power of the informational models they draw on recalls Grierson's avowed practice of "using the aesthetes" in the service of a didactic cinema. Indeed, Watkins's approach, in its rejection of a formula that would equate journalism with documentary, and empiricism and the "ideology of the visible" with knowledge, is far closer to that of the British Documentary Film Movement's films of the 1930s than to the television documentaries that arose in the 1950s. A more concrete illustration of the kinds of aestheticization present in the films Grierson produced, and the ways in which they take an antiempiricist and "impure" approach to informing, will allow us to compare them to Watkins's works in order to gain a better sense of the historical transformations—many due to television itself—that had occurred between the 1930s and the 1960s.

Of course, there is an extremely large amount of diversity in the films of the British Documentary Film Movement, nor do all of them by any means share a unified idea of how the aesthetic might be defined, what it does, and how it is to be used. I will focus here on two examples that employ aesthetic strategies in different ways, both of which display fundamental similarities to and differences from Watkins's later approach. In the first case, the aesthetic serves to convey something that cannot be represented directly. *The Coming of the Dial* (1933), produced by Grierson and directed by Stuart Legg, depicts and explains the new dial-based telephone and the telephone communications infrastructure of London. It opens, however, not with an image of the telephone but with an abstract, rotating sculpture (the *Light-Space Modulator*) designed by Hungarian artist László Moholy-Nagy (Figure 10). While telephones and wires do eventually appear, they are hardly less abstract than Moholy-Nagy's sculpture, portrayed in a fashion that emphasizes their visual form (intersecting horizontals and verticals, their serial or repetitive quality, their apparently unending extension into space) over their recognizable identity as physical objects (Figure 10). Grierson and Legg's decision to begin the film with Moholy-Nagy's sculpture suggests a strongly antiempiricist position in which one can only hope to understand the technological sublime of London's new telephone network by bypassing its direct depiction, looking instead to aesthetic strategies that can better convey its essence. To see telephones being operated, in other words, would convey little or nothing about them, let alone about the age of technical modernity that the film wishes to herald, whereas Moholy-Nagy's sculpture and Legg's depiction of technological components convey abstract ideas through concrete images. The film thus demonstrates the logic behind Grierson's rejection of the newsreel and his insistence on aesthetic treatment. The newsreel, he writes, "has gone dithering on mistaking the phenomenon for the thing in itself."[33] In other words, its journalistic mentality assumes that what needs to be conveyed is somehow present in "the phenomenon," but the "thing in itself"—a more abstract idea—cannot be accessed through it. The aesthetic, then, is essential in the documentary's informing mission, insofar as it constitutes a way of knowing that

FIGURE 10. A sculpture by László Moholy-Nagy stands in for the unrepresent-
able concepts dealt with in Legg's *The Coming of the Dial* (1933), while a shot of
communications cables depicts them as though they were an abstract sculpture.

provides access to phenomena and ideas that cannot be directly represented or expressed.

In a less radical usage, the aesthetic is called on to transform the "raw material" of the image, imbuing it with an affect and meaning that an approach grounded in empirical precision and fidelity would be entirely incapable of conveying. We see such a strategy at work in Alberto Cavalcanti's 1935 *Coal Face,* which couples footage of coal miners with music by Benjamin Britten and a text by W. H. Auden. Auden's words are chanted, nearly unintelligible, as though to emphasize their sonorous and rhythmic qualities over their semantic meaning, while Britten's score is dissonant and percussive in an unmistakably modernist fashion. Placed against images of miners, this sound track functions as both a kind of artistic translation of the rhythms of their work and an ennobling or cultural "raising" of the image, as though to suggest that the labor being depicted deserves the same reverence and respect as any modernist artwork. While Cavalcanti's approach is quite different from Legg's, the philosophical underpinnings and the formal and rhetorical operation of both of these two Grierson-produced films could hardly be more at odds with those of *Special Enquiry* and its direct cinema–influenced offspring: there is no need here to insist on the unmediated or unfiltered quality of the image, because any such "raw" image would serve little instructive purpose, and it is only through a process of aesthetic transformation that the image can express anything at all. Meaning, as understood by the later journalistic model, arises through a process of the interpretation of visible evidence: a commentator tells us what images mean, while his conclusions are supported by the supposed integrity and rawness of those images. In these two examples, though, meaning arises through a defamiliarization or abstraction of raw material, as though the visible and empirically accessible could only yield it when its appearance were somehow bypassed or transcended.

The conceptualizations and usages of the aesthetic that we find in the Grierson films can also be located in those of Watkins: in both *Culloden* and *The War Game,* he seeks to express the horror of war not by convincing us that he is delivering it to us directly, through "true" images, but rather through a calculated aesthetic effect. If the viewer experiences war, it is not because it is empirically accessible in the images that we see, as firsthand evidence, but rather because the images function as its distillation or indirect expression. Watkins's films convey the idea of war through the direct representation of battle, just as *Coal Face* does indeed depict coal miners, but in both cases the meaning and argument arise through formal construction, not through the supposed properties of the image itself, as in *Special Enquiry* or a direct cinema film like *Primary*. At other moments, though, Watkins opts for a kind of formal "translation" like the one we saw in *The Coming of the Dial* (in the sculpture) and *Coal Face* (in the sound track): just as, in the former, the abstract form of Moholy-Nagy's sculpture stood in for an idea, both *Culloden* and *The War Game* translate the violence of war into their very form, through their disruption of the stable empirically grounded image and the contradictory effects they create, which in turn force the spectator into an unfamiliar and precarious viewing position.

While there are some key affinities between the deployment of the aesthetic in the Grierson films and in Watkins's, the latter are considerably more complex in their operation and employ a new strategy specific to their later historical context. In the case of Grierson's films, the aesthetic, conceived of as a means of expressing abstract concepts or of providing raw material with a certain affect or meaning, draws on recognizable forms of modernist art. Watkins's aesthetic material, conversely—the formal language he relies on to provide the viewer with an aesthetic experience—is that of a "non-art," namely, journalistic documentary. Watkins thus engages in an operation of transformation that we do not find in Grierson's films: a sculpture by Moholy-Nagy or music by Benjamin Britten is immediately legible as art, as something other than what we might call informing discourse, whereas Watkins's intervention entails transforming the informing discourse itself into aesthetic material.

This difference—between an approach in which art is easily identifiable as separate from merely informational discourse and one in which it is a transformed, epistemologically drained version of that informational discourse itself—suggests that Watkins's intervention does not simply reinstate the aesthetic as a privileged but discrete kind of rhetorical tool, returning to Grierson's position, but also insists that what we normally take to be informational should, in fact, be viewed as indistinguishable from the aesthetic. The aesthetic for Watkins, then, is not just a source of meaning but a way to critique the empirically grounded approach that had eclipsed an artistic one. For Grierson, an appeal to the aesthetic was necessary due to his belief that pure information both was incapable of grasping "the thing in itself" and did a poor job of conveying it. For Watkins, an appeal to the aesthetic is a means of critiquing the idea that there ever could be such a thing as purely informational discourse to begin with and hence is a critique of the dominant form of television documentary—a critique that Grierson never had to make. In neither case, however, is the fact that aesthetic strategies are more effective than informational ones used to cast doubt on the veracity of the ideas that they convey. Watkins's grounding in Grierson's ideal of documentary filmmaking as civically engaged, educational, and informative keeps him from descending into a position of total relativism and cynicism: as *The War Game* proves, he does not take the fact that there can be no such thing as purely informational discourse as an ominous sign that film or television cannot communicate anything at all, nor that it should not be engaged in pedagogical practice.

TELEVISION AS WEAPON

Watkins's films are more jarring and unpleasant than anything that Grierson and his colleagues would ever have attempted. They are far more critical, not merely enlisting the aesthetic in the service of pedagogy but offering a form of spectatorial experience that challenges and upsets more conventional ones. The strategies described herein—Watkins's reference to and repurposing of existing forms, his undermining of existing forms of apprehension and their separation, and his appeal to embodied spectatorship—explain how such an operation is carried out on the level of the text but leave open the question of how this formal work might be integrated into a more holistic rhetorical process that will lead to new knowledge on the part of the spectator. A new element introduces itself when we begin to consider the spectator, namely, the idea that he may "resist" or react hostilely toward the very aggressive rhetorical operations of the text. It is this subjective factor, in addition to the magnitude of the kinds of events that Watkins seeks to depict—the effects of violence upon the body, the possible consequences of nuclear war—that requires any effective communication to move from the informational to the aesthetic level. Watkins not only attempts to illuminate the potential value of the new "postinformational" mode of apprehension engendered by television but demonstrates why it is in fact the only one that can successfully move the spectator. A sequence from *The War Game* implies such an argument in its attack on the sorts of dry, informational print media that existed at the time for educating the public about nuclear war: a solider hands out copies of a pamphlet (which is not Watkins's creation but an actually existing text) regarding the measures to take in case of nuclear attack (Figure 11). The soldier is confronted by an off-screen voice, that of Watkins, asking why they were not given out sooner and responds that they were previously only offered for sale and no one bought them. The implications here seem to be double. On one hand, conventional forms of information simply fail to reach their target, unlike the television, which is already in the home (a matter whose implications I will return to shortly); furthermore, television is a public service available to anyone who pays the license fee, whereas the booklet in question had to be purchased. On the other, a more conventional form of text, situated within the context of Watkins's film, appears feeble, if not ludicrous, in its lack of impact. If one aims to teach about the damage inflicted on the body by war, or the destructive power of nuclear weapons, other tools will be necessary. Pedagogy here becomes aesthetic, and the pedagogue by necessity an artist, insofar as the subjects about which he wishes to teach can only be conveyed by means of an exceptional modality of experience.

What sets Watkins's aesthetic modality apart from both the informational and older forms of aesthetic pedagogy like that of Grierson (or, for that matter, Brecht) is not merely the way it allows one to know and understand but also the degree to which a kind of violence must be carried out upon the spectator for this understanding to occur. This is not merely a question of temperament or political orientation, which would allow one to explain the difference by appealing to Grierson's willingness to compromise or his liberalism (as opposed to Watkins's intransigence

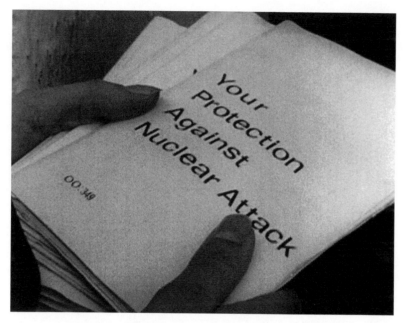

FIGURE 11. Pamphlets on how to prepare for nuclear attack suggest the uselessness of conventional forms of information in *The War Game* (1965).

and radicalism), but rather a difference motivated by historical context: as a pedagogue and artist who sends his sounds and images into the undifferentiated flow of the television age, Watkins had to compete with far more sources of information and an addressee hailed by a far more sophisticated media apparatus. The subject who had been, at least in part, interpellated and constructed through this media apparatus would need to be "undone," forced to confront truths about himself and the world that he might prefer to leave unexamined.

Before considering how this process might work in further detail, we should also note the extent to which it exploits the television medium by repurposing its associations with domesticity and intimacy. For some of its early commentators, such as Bazin, television's "domesticity" was a virtue insofar as it allowed for a relaxed, informal kind of attention but, above all, in that it promoted an intimacy between the spectator and those on the screen:

It is easy to experience the imaginary reciprocity of the television image. Frequently it happens that on the street or at a reception I approach someone I think I know, or I pull back my offer of an inopportune handshake at the last minute, finding myself in the presence of people I have never seen except on television. The mental illusion is particular to television; it doesn't exist in cinema.[34]

Watkins exploits the viewer's comfort and intimacy with the television image to catch her off-guard: in his hands, the television is transformed from a friendly, if somewhat detached, companion into an uninvited visitor bearing bad tidings and unleashing a sensory assault on the unsuspecting spectator. If shown on TV, *The War Game* need not be sought out; rather, it may appear as the viewer switches on the television, expecting something else entirely. This possibility itself, in fact, was part of the justification for the BBC's refusal to broadcast the film on television while allowing it to play in cinemas.[35] The delivery method here, then, is key, as the film's potential impact greatly depends on it.

Television, as an "intimate" device, seemed to offer a greater degree of access to the spectator's mind and body than cinema had. A historical comparison may be useful to ascertain how television might have altered the way in which the filmmaker conceptualized his action upon those minds and bodies. In a 1973 interview in which Watkins discusses political violence, he declares that "the only effective bomb is a coming to consciousness."[36] This statement suggests at once his concern with an alteration of individual subjectivity as the foundation of any effective action and a vision of this alteration as something of a weapon in itself. The former point, of course, explains why pedagogy is for Watkins of such great importance in any kind of social change, but it is the bellicose metaphor, and how it might take on particular characteristics when viewed in relation to television, that I would like to draw attention to here. Joseph Gomez compares Watkins's attitude toward the spectator with that of Sergei Eisenstein, referring to the Soviet director's statement that a film should "furnish the audience with cartridges, not dissipate the energies that it brought into the theatre."[37] I would go further, however, and suggest that the audience, for Eisenstein and Watkins alike, could possess neither a bomb nor cartridges until it had been attacked by the filmmaker. Both view the spectator as material to be worked upon by the text: I have in mind here Eisenstein's assertion (formulated in relation to theater and later applied to cinema) that "theatre's basic material derives from the audience: the molding of the audience in a desired direction (or mood) is the task of every utilitarian theatre."[38] Watkins's assaults work in a manner similar to Eisenstein's "attractions," insofar as they are "aggressive moments" that "produce specific emotional shocks in the spectator," "influencing this audience in the desired directions through a series of calculated pressures on its psyche."[39] The pedagogical process, for Watkins as for Eisenstein, entails the infliction of "a series of blows to the consciousness and emotions of the audience"—and here we might also note Sobchack's acknowledgment of Eisenstein as one of the first practitioners of film to be interested in its "somatic effects."[40] The film or television program itself, then, is a weapon, one directed not only at the society it critiques but at a spectator who is complicit with that society. The only way to undo this complicity and to begin the pedagogical process is to launch a kind of aesthetic bomb at the viewer.

By the 1960s, this bomb was no longer directed, as it was for Eisenstein, toward a public space, be it theater or cinema. Instead, television's potential to force viewers to see something they did not want to see, and to bring the most terrifying images into their homes (as Watkins literally does in *The Journey* [1987], showing families' photographs of victims of the American atomic attacks on Japan), offered the most powerful possible resource. Of *The War Game,* Watkins remarks, "I feel that people should almost be made to see this film even if they don't want to," a possibility that was certainly greater on television than in the cinema. A work that fails to upset the viewer and destabilize the domestic sphere, meanwhile, has failed: *Culloden,* Watkins laments, "sits at the edge of the definition where a white, middle-class liberal . . . can sort of indulge in the cathartic exercise of looking at something, getting a kick out of it, washing his guilt off, and then getting on with the dishes afterwards."[41] This description echoes a common view of television as something that offers too much

security or comfort to the viewer precisely because of its domestic placement (one can turn away more quickly, and get on with the dishes), yet
it is also this placement that suggests the possibility of a surprise attack.
This attack is intended to counteract an overly protective and shel-
tering media and educational system. Educators, Watkins argues, ex-
hibit a kind of "aggressive protectiveness," handling their students "on a
downward-looking, derogatory basis."[42] Any effort to remedy this situation
must by necessity be painful, insofar as it involves confronting things,
either about the world or about ourselves, that have been disavowed for
our own protection. This idea of education as pain appeared early on in
comments about Watkins's work, as in Kenneth Tynan's remark that in
refusing to show *The War Game,* "the BBC is like a doctor withholding
the truth from a patient who is suffering from a potentially fatal disease;
silence may preclude pain, but also precludes cure."[43] The therapeutic
metaphor, meanwhile, is taken up by Watkins himself when he compares
the effect of watching one of his films to undergoing psychotherapy: "The
closest analysis I can place on my work is that it provides the same sort of
bleak, rather unpleasant, and to some degree often shattering experience
one has when one goes to a psychiatrist for therapy for the first time."[44]
While adhering to Eisenstein's strategies of using aesthetic stimuli as
"a series of blows to the consciousness and emotions of the audience,"
Watkins situated these blows as part of a more drawn-out psychoanalytic
process and, in so doing, distanced himself from the sort of mechanical
behaviorism we find in Eisenstein in favor of an acknowledgment of the
spectator as a subject-in-process. This tactical shift emphasizes the importance of experience over any particular lessons to be learned: after *The
War Game,* which had already begun to develop an experiential pedagogy,
Watkins moved increasingly toward an approach that sought to create
conflict in the psyche of the spectator as a way of forcing her to reevaluate
her political positioning and agency rather than simply encouraging her
to draw certain conclusions about political issues.

TRANSGRESSION AND RESISTANCE

Experience and its pedagogical capacity, rather than any given message or
political line, is foregrounded in Watkins's post-BBC works of the 1970s,

such as the 1971 film *Punishment Park,* set in a near, dystopian future. As the film begins, we are informed via a voice-over (spoken by Watkins himself) that the McCarran Act has been used to allow the president of the United States to declare a state of internal emergency and to set up detention camps for suspected subversives, who may be imprisoned even before they commit any crimes. These prisoners are sent to the titular parks, in which they are tried without a jury before a tribunal and then given the choice to accept a prison term or a shorter trial in "Punishment Park." If they opt for the second (as they all do), they will be given the opportunity to avoid prison by undertaking a grueling sixteen-mile trek through the desert, attempting to reach their goal (marked by an American flag) before being apprehended by police officers. The film is edited so as to alternate between two main threads, one depicting the trial of subversives before the tribunal, the other the attempt of a previously sentenced group to reach the flag. The latter group, however, discovers that the game is fixed: it is almost impossible to survive the trek in the desert, and even those who nearly reach the flag are murdered by the officers who pursue them.

To a far greater extent than *The War Game,* the film's pedagogical approach moves away from conveying a clear message to the viewer, as would a work operating according to the logic of Rancière's representational regime. Here the gap between "message" and "knowledge" already detectable in *The War Game* grows even wider, as though to suggest that our habituation to the informational discourses of television necessitated a further distancing from them. As in the earlier work, a sensory violence directed toward the viewer pervades the film, which employs a very rapid pace of cutting both within and between scenes: very short shots and jarring edits are used, and no sense of spatial coherence is established. In short, there is no secure "place" for the spectator, who seems instead to be dragged around by the camera. Individual shots are almost invariably mobile: the film was shot with a handheld 16mm camera, which director of photography Joan Churchill frantically moves to follow the action, zooming when not actually in motion. The sound mix is equally volatile, as diegetic sound from one of the film's two main threads is consistently overlapped upon the other, sometimes replacing it completely. As the film progresses, shouting and gunshots are more or less omnipresent. Violence—both in form and content—in fact prevents the apprehension of any clear message. As Gomez writes, "there are no lulls, no diversions, no opportunities to pause and consider the validity of arguments. The tensions of an omnipresent confrontation are constantly reinforced through both the form and the content of the film, and these tensions are quickly transferred to the audience."[45] On the formal level, this aggressive editing strategy seems to reflect a desire to keep the viewer overwhelmed, precisely to avoid the kind of rational or detached reflection that many of Watkins's critics call for. Its lack of a clear political argument has been cited as the film's greatest failing, yet it is in this lack that the rationale behind Watkins's approach becomes clear. A 1972 review complains that the young radicals in *Punishment Park,* "instead of articulating their case with some semblance of rationality . . . fall into frustrated frenzies. . . . Any intention that the film might have had of informing us politically disintegrates."[46] What the review fails to consider is the possibility that for Watkins's pedagogy to be effective, the need to inform must not be opposed to, but rather coupled with, the need to provoke: a "frustrated frenzy" may in fact be the only way to break through to an audience accustomed to setting up barriers or to immediately "tuning out" when anything resembling a didactic message begins to be transmitted. One does not destabilize subject positions through informative and rational arguments. Watkins seems to acknowledge this shift to a form of pedagogy that offers no answers, only destabilization, when he notes in an interview given the year of the film's release,

> There is no such thing as a "truth" and there is no such thing as a predictable way in which the individual reading that input will respond. So to some my films may be a statement and to others they may be a catalyst. But I hope—I'd like to believe—that my work does not, more overtly than I would ever hope necessary, suggest answers or courses of action to any problems which my films echo or raise.[47]

Rather than works attempting to express a clear message, Watkins characterizes his films as "trying to help develop a philosophy of self-

examination."[48] The sorts of "frenzies" that some spectators found objectionable in the film, we might extrapolate from his comments, were
precisely the sorts of states he sought to induce in his spectators.

Other critiques of *Punishment Park* are symptomatic of the impermis-
sibility of Watkins's revival of the Griersonian integration of information and its others. The angry responses to the film (which was not, like
most of Watkins's works, made for television, but which uses the same
pseudo-documentary techniques as the BBC films, unlike his previous
theatrical features, *Privilege* and *The Gladiators*) attest to the extent to
which this combination was felt to violate certain rules of separation or
containment; it is in their violation, furthermore, that the existence of
such boundaries becomes particularly evident. As Steven Kramer and
James Welsh note, a common objection to *Punishment Park* was that "the
documentary approach treating a fantasized situation in overly realistic
terms was manipulative, misleading, and false—that the director had no
business imposing his fantasies on an unsuspecting audience."[49] Critic
George Melly, for example, objects that "the documentary realism . . . far
from helping us to accept Watkins's metaphor, tends to make us resist it.
Filmed as straight fiction we wouldn't get the feeling that Watkins was
trying to trick us into believing what he has, after all, invented."[50] These
critiques almost exactly double the common objection noted by Raymond
Williams, as discussed in chapter 1, that television engenders "confusion
between reality and fiction."[51] Despite the fact that *Punishment Park* is
not a television film, it demonstrates, like *Culloden* and *The War Game*
before it, that audiovisual messages in the television age at once disavow
and rely upon such a confusion, but that its full exposure results in strong
resistance from the spectator.

The hostile responses to Watkins's films express a disavowal and refusal
of the broader cultural logic they reveal, acting as a defense against that
psychoanalytic "shattering" they seek to carry out. While one component of these responses, namely, that Watkins was unfairly "imposing his
fantasies," simply reflects an objection to mixing affective and embodied
ways of knowing with an informational form, one also suspects that the
accusations of trickery attest to a resentment of a clearly fictional film's
ability to elicit belief and its capacity to agitate. There can be no question

of trickery here, insofar as we can assume that all but the most naive viewer would be conscious of the constructed nature of the text. The effect in question is precisely that of the perceptual disorientation or dissonance created by *The War Game*: the viewer realizes that the action he is seeing is not real, yet it affects him as such. This leads to a resentment of the director who is "forcing" such responses, and this resentment itself may well be intended as part of the pedagogical process. Knowledge here has become not something easily communicable and verbalized, to be neutrally transmitted, nor simply a kind of experience detached from the realm of quotidian meaning, but rather a psychic upheaval that transforms the spectator's orientation toward himself and the world. This strategy suggests, much like Watkins's disclosure of the indistinguishability between informational and aesthetic modes of discourse and experience, his intuition of a profound shift in cultural logic. It assumes that television has irrevocably altered not only the way we categorize and "channel" modes of discourse and apprehension but also the very ways that audiovisual experiences work upon us: they do not, as in Adorno's analyses of mass culture, contain layered "messages" that manipulate us through their advancement of an ideological agenda but rather transform us through their formal texture itself, reshaping our minds and bodies in ways that we are not even remotely aware of. Watkins recognizes and exploits a cultural situation in which knowledge as category has been radically redefined, presuming that we, the spectator, have been "taught" by the medium and that only the same tools can "un-teach" us.

If Watkins uses the same kinds of sensory violence and aesthetic "messaging" through which television itself (albeit never so openly and consciously) operates, the question arises as to whether the remedy is ultimately any different from the disease. Like Eisenstein, Watkins takes the horrific eye-gouging spectacle of the Grand Guignol as model, yet one could easily argue that such shocking imagery had, by the 1960s, been fully appropriated by commercial cinema and the culture industry more broadly; indeed, one could argue that his films find their closest parallels, rhetorically and aesthetically speaking, in violent or gory exploitation cinema, a parallel that certainly resonates if we think of his films in terms of Sobchack's phenomenological approach. We might even place them among what Carol Clover and Linda Williams have called "body genres," not simply in their address to the embodied spectator but also in their tendency to be experienced, as Williams notes of body genres, as manipulative and thus resented.[52] Just as his films call on the aesthetic as an extrarational form of experience, so does the equally aestheticized commercial film (albeit for different ends). As I will return to in chapter 5, Watkins himself will in fact later reach a similar conclusion, arguing that all forms of audiovisual media are equally under the sway of the uniform language system he calls the "Monoform": "We can no longer separate or differentiate films in terms of being artistic, pleasurable, aesthetic vs. those we consider as rubbish."[53]

Potential drawbacks to Watkins's methods thus arise. Their instrumentalization of the aesthetic, particularly in associating it with visceral "shock" effects, renders them closer in kind than they wish to be to that which they oppose. More broadly, and perhaps more fatally, they face the historical dissolution of any specifically aesthetic form or apprehension into the fabric of everyday life: if all forms of rhetoric (advertising, media, etc.) are now aestheticized, there may no longer be any specific modality of the aesthetic that falls outside of them, offering an altogether different experience. One can hardly imagine *The War Game* working as well today, given most spectators' habituation to all sorts of violent imagery and, more importantly, abrasive or aggressive audiovisual forms. What makes Watkins's works different, however, is their insistence on using noninformational ways of knowing not simply to make information more forceful or effective but also to engender radical displeasure and psychic destabilization; for Watkins, aesthetic experience is a powerful means of education, but it is not a pleasant one, far from the means of seduction it represented for Rossellini. At the cinema, one would need to choose to subject oneself to such an unpleasant experience, and as we have seen, Watkins's spectators were often less than willing. By choosing to work predominantly for television, Watkins instead smuggled the power of the aesthetic into the most banal and yet sacred of spaces, the domestic living room. In doing so, he struck at the core of complacency and stability, as the BBC's ban on broadcast, but not cinematic exhibition, of *The War Game* shows.

While his works from the 1980s onward, as we will see in chapter 5, decisively reject the concept, their earlier counterparts perhaps teach us their most valuable lesson in their illumination of mediation as a defining characteristic of contemporary modes of apprehension. For much of the 1960s and 1970s, and even today, the idea of mediated knowledge or experience was dismissed as inauthentic, contaminated, or somehow tyrannical. For Watkins, though, the notion that knowledge and experience are always impure, mediated, subjective, and affective is taken as simple fact—one disclosed by television itself—which leads to startling insights about both actual and potential uses of the image. These insights, furthermore, have only become more relevant since the 1960s: the myth of informational television, I think, still persists, although the informational has now of course come to be more closely associated with computers and other digital media—if anything, these reinforce ideas about how information (now often equated with binary code) can be clearly separated from its others and give a new lease on life to the idea that one could "purify" information (what could be purer than a world like that of *The Matrix*?). Watkins's use of television, however, also offers concepts and methods that could be productively applied to the present, and to new media in particular: these include an insistence on adopting and transforming existing codes rather than simply negating or opting out of them as well as a use of communications media to forcibly smuggle messages and experiences to those who are not necessarily seeking them. Equally important is Watkins's insistence that the ways in which we experience and know through any media are prone to ideological petrification and a corresponding lack of effectiveness; their utopian potential depends on rerouting or exploding the circuits along which they usually travel, not to mention the ones that exist inside our own minds. It is precisely such a rerouting, as we will now see, that serves as the basis for Jean-Luc Godard's notion of communication, a concept whose formulation owed much to television and whose successful accomplishment could be best imagined through it.

4

Radical Communications

JEAN-LUC GODARD ON AND AROUND TELEVISION

Jean-Luc Godard's engagement with television as a specific form of audiovisual practice was not as sustained as that of Rossellini or Watkins;
although Godard continued to make films and essays for television after
the 1970s, it was during this decade that he undertook his most clearly
televisual works, most importantly his two long-form, multiepisode TV
series *Six fois deux: sur et sous la communication* (1976) and *France tour
détour deux enfants* (1977), both coauthored with Anne-Marie Miéville.
Godard's interest in television, however, was not confined to works produced specifically for the small screen: television plays a significant role
in his other 1970s films as well, such as *Tout va bien* (in which Yves
Montand portrays a director of television commercials), *Ici et ailleurs,
Numéro deux,* and *Comment ça va?* Each of these films focuses at length
on informational and communicational processes, particularly in their
press and televisual forms; Godard's interest in these issues also animated
his collaborations with leftist print journals and, later, the government
of the newly independent state of Mozambique, where he was invited to
develop a state television network. Despite the centrality of television in
his work during the 1970s, however, Godard is most often characterized
as an antitelevision partisan of cinema. This characterization—largely
encouraged by Godard himself—obscures the extent to which so many
of the central concepts in his work from the 1970s onward were informed by his theoretical and practical work on television. While I will
turn in chapter 5 to the particulars of Godard's overwhelmingly negative subsequent treatment of television, here I will argue that it was in
fact in television that he found solutions to many of the problems that

he initially posed within the framework of cinema, particularly in the "countercinema" he developed with the Dziga Vertov Group in the late 1960s and early 1970s. As Godard left the Dziga Vertov Group behind and began collaborating with Miéville, his work began to rely more and more heavily on concepts and practices drawn from television, while still posing implicit and explicit critiques of the medium. In short, as in the case of Watkins, we find in Godard a willingness to treat existing television simultaneously as an object of critique and as the raw material for a utopian projection: he draws on the possibilities it has only suggested, revalences its current practices, and uses them to imagine new forms of mass communication that radically redefine the term *communication* itself.

Godard's first television commission, to produce an adaptation of Rousseau's *Émile* for the ORTF, arrived in 1967, while he was still active in commercial cinema. This was not, however, to be his television debut, as the program was ultimately rejected by the network (largely for political reasons) and released later in cinemas as *Le Gai Savoir.*[1] This experience was followed, beginning in 1969, by a sustained engagement with television during the Dziga Vertov Group period. Television was not at the conceptual center of the Dziga Vertov Group films but rather provided them with financing and a potential venue for broadcast. Even in this sense, though, television was able to serve Godard as a working space (and eventually conceptual model) for a form of audiovisual practice that would come *after* cinema and leave the identity of the *auteur* behind. All of this occurred, of course, in a highly politicized context: it is hardly incidental that what I am here calling Godard's televisual period (roughly 1969–79) corresponds with his so-called radical or Maoist period, during which he frequently sought to create works that would contribute to revolutionary political struggle, and which were thus unlikely to receive financing from commercial film producers. The televisual period, then, is one that was resolutely non- or even postcinematic, marked by a need to move beyond cinema as medium and institution in the name of political practice and theoretical inquiry. While Godard's move to television was hardly as categorical and decisive as that of Rossellini, it was part of a larger and more gradual distancing from cinema that allowed him, I will argue here, to develop a mode of postcinematic or televisual thinking, albeit one he would not abandon when he returned to the world of commercial cinema in 1980.[2]

AFTER CINEMA, BEFORE TELEVISION

While television may not have been at the conceptual heart of the Dziga Vertov Group films, the idea of an informational and pedagogical use of the moving image most certainly was. *British Sounds,* the first film (retroactively) attributed to the group, and made by Godard in collaboration with Jean-Henri Roger for London Weekend Television (an ITV franchise, hence private) in 1969, sets the tone for what would follow, declaring in a voice-over (in English),

> During the projection of an imperialist film, the screen sells the voice of the boss to the viewer. The voice caresses and beats into submission. During the projection of a revisionist film, the screen is the loudspeaker for a voice delegated by the people, which is no longer the voice of the people. In silence, people see their own disfigured face. During the projection of a militant film, the screen is no more than a blackboard, the wall of a school offering concrete analysis of a concrete situation. In front of that screen, the living soul of Marxism, the students criticize, struggle, and transform.

This formulation serves as a clear expression of Godard's conviction, after his break with commercial filmmaking in 1968, that a militant cinema had to be an informational and pedagogical cinema. As Serge Daney puts it, "Godard and [Jean-Pierre] Gorin transformed the screening space [*le cube scénographique*] into a classroom."[3] This description, however, tells us more about the sorts of viewing conditions that Godard and his colleagues were imagining than about what was to be taught or how this new mode of audiovisual practice might have defined its function in relation to existing forms of informational and pedagogical practice (journalism, militant pamphlets and posters, the teaching of Marxist theory and practice within an academic setting, etc.). The way that this relationship was articulated (both in films and in interviews conducted during this period) suggests that Godard conceived of his projects as falling into at least two separate categories, one that I will call "counter-information" and one that I will call, following Peter Wollen, "counter-cinema."[4]

The lines between counter-information and counter-cinema are not by any means self-evident, but their placement will illustrate the very kinds of boundaries between practices and modes of apprehension that Godard's later televisual work would call into question. These boundaries appear blurry at first, as in the case of Godard's 1968 ciné-tracts. The ciné-tracts were short films composed of still images that were shot by a number of filmmakers during the events of May–June 1968 to be shown during meetings and assemblies. Those by Godard, whose elements would later be incorporated into Le Gai Savoir, adopt a collage aesthetic informed by Situationist détournement rather than seeking to convey easily intelligible and useful messages. Their quick fabrication and local distribution, however, gave them the character of an alternative media form, a character that Godard clearly recognized: "[Their fabrication] has a local interest that allows for working together and discussing ... and then their distribution can take place in apartments or meetings."[5] While one might place the ciné-tracts in the categories of both counter-information and counter-cinema, a more clearly journalistic approach followed shortly afterward in December, as Godard attempted to create a program on a miners' strike for a local television network in Quebec. The director and the miners imagined replacing conventional broadcasts with their own militant programming, but Godard abruptly left Quebec before the project got under way.[6] In contrast to these two instances, both of which were elicited by and responded to specific situations, the Dziga Vertov Group project adopted a somewhat more detached approach. While some have argued that this was a function of political limitations—an unfortunate result of the dwindling number of radicals still active a year after the May events—it seems to me that the Dziga Vertov Group project was in fact Godard's way of designating certain works as something other than counter-information.[7] This idea of a separation between forms and functions is borne out by the fact that Godard continued to work in left-wing journalism well into the 1970s. These activities were separate from his filmmaking, and his films themselves did not aspire to act as an adjunct or replacement for them.[8] Even when they were carried out via audiovisual means, Godard's counter-informational projects remained distinct in form, function, and placement from the Dziga Vertov Group films: some examples include his attempt to develop a video news service for l'Agence de presse Libération (later to become the daily *Libération*) or the videotaped mock news broadcasts made with Gorin and shown in François Maspero's bookstore.[9]

The counter-cinema of the Dziga Vertov Group distinguishes itself from a counter-informational practice in several ways. First, it insists that questions of production take precedence over those of distribution; it is the *research* that counts most of all, because it is the solving of theoretical problems and not the conveying of a simple and discrete quantity of information that is aspired to.[10] In a counter-informational project, we would expect to see the opposite, with importance placed on competing with conventional media outlets and spreading useful information to the largest possible number of people. Second, the Dziga Vertov Group's works tend to focus on questions of form and aesthetics. As David Faroult puts it, "the maturity that [Godard] had acquired through his questionings of an aesthetic order, his interest in Brecht and in his enterprise of subverting fiction, led him to avoid ceding to the spontaneous and spontaneist temptation, which had carried away many other filmmakers, of putting himself 'simply' at the service of 'revolutionary counter-information.'"[11] Godard and the Dziga Vertov Group's counter-cinema, then, was not necessarily opposed to a counter-informational project but also had distinct aims and a distinct form that differentiated it from one.

The Godard of the late 1960s and early 1970s thus found himself attempting to balance multiple different imperatives and ideas about what, precisely, the political role of the filmmaker was or could be. The works of this period are not utopian ones, at least not according to the definition I have been using here, but rather a kind of ground-clearing or attempt to, as Godard puts it in *Le Gai Savoir,* "return to zero." They provide an exit from cinema as it exists and develop a series of conceptual innovations that lay the groundwork for a subsequent entry into a new form of noncinematic production synthesizing aesthetic and informational practices. The process of ground-clearing, or starting from zero, carried out through the establishment of the Dziga Vertov Group contains at least three discrete components: first, it is an abandonment of authorship and the role of the art cinema *auteur*; second, it is a symbolic gesture of "linking up" with a historical lineage of leftist cinema (and, indeed, a utopian and televisual one, although this aspect of Vertov's work will initially be of little importance to Godard and Gorin); and third, it represents a shift to new methods of financing, production, and distribution, in which television plays a central role.

After the events of May, Godard began to withdraw from cinema. This change came about as a result of his attempt to distance himself from the high-culture trappings that had brought him insults from the Situationists and other militants and from his desire to "become unknown."[12] He no longer wished to be perceived as France's premier *auteur*. Speaking of his experience of the events of 1968 ten years later, he explains, "I felt challenged; it did me good. I felt—in my case I was a little afraid also, I said to myself, 'All right, this may be the end.'"[13] For an artist of Godard's stature, however, becoming unknown and returning to obscurity were all but impossible. Yet it is as an expression of his desire to disavow his old identity that one may interpret his choice to submit himself to others, to work collaboratively, and to begin signing his films collectively (or not at all). To make a film not like the others (to play on the title of his 1968 film *Un Film comme les autres*), Godard ceased to be an *auteur*, turning his back on the very status that he and his colleagues at *Cahiers du cinéma* had won for the film director. He strove, he declared, "to abandon the notion of the *auteur*, such as it is ... the notion of the *auteur* is completely reactionary."[14] As Godard's first partner in collective filmmaking, Jean-Henri Roger, notes, "these films were obviously Godard's, by Godard in discussion with others. Which is not to say that the Dziga Vertov Group appellation was only a kind of camouflage. It was his manner of marking the radicality of the change, to take into account all of these discussions on cinema and politics."[15] Here we see, albeit for different reasons, the same rejection of art-as-institution, and of cinema in particular, that we find in Rossellini, along with the corresponding rejection of the "reactionary" auteur. Godard in some sense, then, doubled or followed Rossellini's gesture, perhaps appropriate given his assertion, in 1959, that "the place where others will not arrive for twenty years, [Rossellini] has already left."[16]

Like the rejection of *auteur* status and the turn to signing films collectively, the name of the group signaled the creation of a new space, clearly outside of 1960s European art cinema but nonetheless connected to the history of cinema (or its utopian successor, as projected by Vertov) more broadly. The name first appeared in September 1969, in a short article on *British Sounds* printed in *Cinéthique*, no. 5 and signed "Jean-Luc Godard pour le Groupe Dziga Vertov."[17] The group's public debut, meanwhile, took place at the Musée d'Art Moderne de la Ville de Paris in February 1970, where *British Sounds* and *Pravda* were screened with Godard, Roger, and Gorin in attendance.[18] All three, when subsequently asked about the significance of the group's name, have given differing and even contradictory answers, but these can be reduced to four key points. First, Vertov represented a filmmaker who put politics in command of his filmmaking practice, just as Godard and his colleagues did.[19] Second, the name signaled the group's adherence to Vertov's theories about the need for montage at every level of filmmaking; as Colin MacCabe notes, "for Vertov montage was a principle which had primacy in every moment of filming—the Dziga Vertov Group formulated this principle in the slogan: Montage before shooting, montage during shooting, and montage after shooting."[20] Third, it referred to an opposition between two kinds of political cinema, or even two different relationships between politics and cinema, one represented by Vertov and the other by Eisenstein. In this opposition, Eisenstein is variously described as either a bourgeois or revisionist filmmaker, whereas Vertov is a true Bolshevik (i.e., the one who fights against revisionism and bourgeois ideology, a role in which the French Maoists cast themselves); the former sticks to the "novelistic representation of struggles," as Roger puts it, whereas the latter rejects them.[21] Eisenstein, furthermore, turned to the past at the very moment when Vertov was creating a new vision of the Soviet present. Fourth, and most important, invoking Vertov's name signified an effort, Godard states, to situate the group's work within the history of cinema: "In short, it was necessary for us as filmmakers to situate ourselves historically, not just in any history, but most of all that of cinema. From which comes the oriflamme of Vertov, 'kino-pravda,' the Bolshevik cinema. And it is that cinema which is our true birthdate."[22] The revolutionary cinema, following this explanation, was born not with the works of the Dziga Vertov Group but with the works of Dziga Vertov himself. The legacy of Vertov that Godard and his colleagues had in mind at this point was thus at once a formal, political, and historical one. While the group did not make note of Vertov's interest in television and in transcending the existing boundaries between different media and functions more broadly, its name nonetheless suggested a movement beyond cinema as a commercial institution, a politically located practice, and a form of audiovisual text.

We begin to see this movement in the Dziga Vertov Group's reliance on television, both public and private, for funding and dissemination. While television funding was certainly valuable insofar as it allowed the group to make films that would have never been considered as viable theatrical releases, the small screen was hardly hospitable. Following the abortive attempts of *Le Gai Savoir* and 1968's *One A.M.,* a program commissioned by the American Public Broadcasting Laboratory (a New York–based public network), Godard's first television work was the aforementioned *British Sounds. British Sounds* was commissioned by Kestrel Productions, a company run by Irving Teitelbaum and Tony Garnett (producer of the BBC's Wednesday Play series and, later, Ken Loach's *Kes*) for London Weekend Television (ITV), which refused to air the film and only showed a few brief excerpts.[23] *Pravda* (1969), although largely financed by the American publisher Grove Press (another major source of funding during this period), was initiated by an invitation to Godard from Czechoslovakian television but was also never broadcast.[24] Godard and Gorin's *Lotte in Italia* (1970) met a similar fate, being first commissioned and then rejected by Italy's RAI.[25] The duo's subsequent and last television commission, *Vladimir and Rosa* (1971, also cofinanced by Grove), produced for West German regional public channel Munich Tele-pool, was likewise refused.[26] These refusals demonstrate the limits of what European networks were willing to broadcast, but we also might see them as part of the impetus behind Godard's later efforts to imagine what his version of television might look like. Overall, the Dziga Vertov Group's interactions with television seem to be something of a missed encounter, albeit one that is later recognized as holding the key to the very sorts of problems that their films were articulating.

IMAGE, SOUND, AND MEANING IN THE FILMS
OF THE DZIGA VERTOV GROUP

We might divide the primary questions or problems posed by the Dziga Vertov Group works into two categories: first, there are those, as we have seen, that concern a search for a new space beyond the cinema for audio-visual practice, a new identity for its practitioner, and a new cultural and political function. Second, there are questions more explicitly related to form: how could one make sounds and images communicate, and what could they "say" or "do," beyond the framework of existing modes of cinema, even the envelope-pushing and experimental work *(La Chinoise, Weekend)* that Godard had recently undertaken? Here, too, the question of the practitioner's role emerges, less as a matter of identity and more as one of intervention or agency: if images (and sounds) do indeed signify, what is the filmmaker's role in constructing or facilitating the emergence of meaning?

The first major mode of dealing with image, sound, and meaning we find in the Dziga Vertov Group works predominates in *British Sounds* and *Pravda* and is rooted in an attitude that associates the image with falsity. The position broadly taken by these films is that the image cannot convey or produce knowledge, a characterization that MacCabe ascribes to the Dziga Vertov Group's work as a whole: "All the films are in some simple sense unwatchable—the premise of each is that the image is unable to provide the knowledge it claims."[27] Both films turn the gaze of the camera on the world outside, both in the sense that they were shot on location, beyond the controlled comfort of the studio, and in that they were shot outside of France, the first in England and the second in Czechoslovakia. The images that dominate each film, furthermore, are largely unstaged and unconstructed and thus almost "documentary" in character. To use the terminology later adopted by the Dziga Vertov Group, both films are composed largely of "fetched" images rather than "built" ones.[28] The documentary tendency that animates both films (both codirected and written with Roger), although never referred to as such by Godard, could well be seen as their most Vertovian element.

British Sounds, as the title suggests, works on the principle that true meaning and knowledge are not found in images but can nonetheless be produced through the confrontation of image and sound. The film, clearly divided into discrete episodes, consists of two main types of sequences: in the first type, a single scene or motif (a car factory assembly line, a nude woman in her home, a newscaster speaking on television) is paired with a sound track that creates a meaning not found in the image alone. In the second type, sound and image are joined in a more conventional, even documentary manner, but a voice-over continues to intervene. The voice-over passage concerning the blackboard quoted earlier, for example, is spoken over a scene of students at the University of Essex rewriting Beatles songs with political lyrics. Through these juxtapositions of sound and image, the viewer theoretically comes to realize how much the meaning of any image is determined by its entry into relationship with other elements and the extent to which that meaning can be manipulated. As the voice-over tells us, "there are neither self-evident images, nor images that speak for themselves in the way that the Russian revisionist films and the mass circulation magazines in the West pretend." *British Sounds,* unlike these other cultural objects, demonstrates how finding the correct meaning of an image, and hence creating knowledge rather than illusion (as the images on their own would), depends on finding a sound that reveals it.

An image's true or "correct" meaning, then, is found not in the image itself but in its "correction" by sound: the falsity of the image and its status as vehicle for the "ideology of the visible" are countered through the truth of the word. Knowledge is not, contrary to Godard's statement about a dialectical relationship between sound and image, created through the collision of the two elements. There is simply a negation, as word rebuts image. Furthermore, this verbal truth stands as an unquestioned discourse: we do not see its production, nor are its sources made known to us. A further problem is apparent in the film's tendency to equate images and their referents, as though an image of something "bad" (revisionist, counterrevolutionary, etc.) could do no more than double what it represents: the image not only stands in for a particular referent (an assembly line, a newscaster, a workers' meeting) but is treated as though it *were* that referent, without any reflection on its construction or the process of transformation carried out by the filmmaker. This problem, present in *Pravda* as well, is acutely expressed by an equivalent elision carried out on the verbal level. The opening statement of *British Sounds,* spoken as a fist punches through the Union Jack, is as follows: "In a word, the bourgeoisie creates a world in its image. Comrades, we must destroy that image." The formulation is indebted to Marx and Engels (its first clause a paraphrase of *The Communist Manifesto*), but when applied to a film, to a discourse that thinks about and in actual images, it becomes frustratingly ambiguous. It suggests, on one hand, that the world *is* an image, constructed by the bourgeoisie (a notion that recalls Debord's spectacle).[29] On the other, it could be taken to express the idea that representations of the world show that world illusorily, distorted by bourgeois ideology. While both readings make sense in isolation, the slippage between the two results in confusion, in which no distinction is made between the world and its photographic image, referred to in the film as a tool of the bourgeoisie used to "disguise reality from the masses." This results in what is, paradoxically, a total adherence to the equivalence between image and thing, a lack of reflection on the image as produced, and thus a sort of faith in the image—not as right or good but as fundamentally neutral or merely reproductive—that one would expect Godard to fight against.

Like that of *British Sounds, Pravda*'s method entails revealing the true meaning of various images by passing beyond their phenomenal surface and adding different sounds to them. The film begins with images of post–Prague Spring Czechoslovakia, which show it to be what the voice-over calls a "sick country," claiming to be Socialist but laden with signs of Western consumer capitalism, such as advertisements for Western companies and young people with long hair who listen to the Beatles. These initial images and the verbal analysis that accompanies them are subsequently dismissed by the voice-over as inadequate: "Only travelers' impressions, memories like those of Delacroix in Algeria or Chris Marker at Rhodiaceta. It's what the *New York Times* and *Le Monde* call information." Correct information, meanwhile, is not to be found in the image itself, and once again, montage is called on to generate it: "We need to use montage; we will organize images and sounds differently . . . we will treat these images and these sounds according to an anti-revisionist line, trying to establish a new contradictory relationship between them." Applying the methods of montage to the lesson at hand, the second section of the film shows images of Czechoslovakia accompanied by a voice-over that diagnoses the country's malady, interpreting the various phenomena it depicts as signs of revisionism. The third section, which begins to propose solutions to the problem, describes its operation as putting "a correct sound [*un son juste*] with a false image in order to then find a correct image." The sounds, Godard explains in the notes distributed at a Paris screening of the film, are "already correct because they come from revolutionary struggle. The images, still false, because they are produced in the camp of imperialist ideology."[30] As in *British Sounds,* images can only be false, and this falsity is opposed by the truth of words, here again presented as authoritative. *Pravda's* montage of sound and image is neither dialectical nor contradictory: as the Groupe Lou Sin writes in *Cahiers du cinéma,* "the film claims to pass from sensory knowledge of the Czech situation to rational knowledge of it, but the categories of Marxism, Leninism, and Mao Tse-Tung thought are dogmatically stuck onto the same 'false' images."[31]

While the theoretical premise articulated by *British Sounds* and *Pravda* may be a highly problematic one, it nonetheless contains symptomatic value insofar as its rejection of the visible as false suggests a point of view that treats the visible world as though it had been irreversibly infected by ideology. Behind this refusal lies the idea, to recall Adorno, that "the more completely the world becomes appearance, the more imperviously the appearance becomes ideology."[32] In other words, the clearly ideological function of the world-as-image, which reaches its apotheosis in television, gives rise to a situation in which both image and world seem like nothing more than pure ideology, hence purely negative; if the filmmaker deals with the visible, he can only recapitulate this negativity and ideology, hence Godard and Roger's recourse to the word as corrective. The clear connection between Adorno's comments on television and Godard and Roger's characterization of the image suggests that the first two Dziga Vertov Group films are in some sense an "antitelevision": the images they rebel against are not those of the fiction film (as will be the case in *Vent d'est* [1970]) but rather the images of the world-as-fact that populate television broadcasts. Godard and Roger's attempt to critique these images' claims to transparency and informationality, however, can only create their mirror image: in place of television, we have the "pure word" of radio, a medium not incidentally already figuratively invoked as a transmitter of truthful messages in *La Chinoise* and *Le Gai Savoir*.[33] More abstractly, though, we find a repetition of that attempt at containment present in William Haley's refusal of television (as opposed to radio) news broadcasts, the fear that the visible can only ever detract from accurate information or even metaphysical truth. *British Sounds* and *Pravda* are thus highly informed by television and the conceptual oppositions it encourages, but they attempt to settle or contain these oppositions through a simple switching of the valorized term (sounds instead of images, word instead of appearance, truth instead of falsity) rather than through a dialectical overcoming or revalencing of television as it exists. They create an antitelevision that is little more than television's double, responding to visibility with its prohibition. They show little concern with how or what images signify but instead take a stance characteristic of what Rancière calls the "ethical regime," in which "there is properly speaking no art as such but instead images that are judged in terms of their intrinsic truth and of their impact on the ways of being of individuals and of the collectivity."[34] Here there can be neither art nor information on the level of the visible: the first is simply not a recognized or acknowledged category, and the second is incommensurable with any images whatsoever, which have been rejected en bloc as "sick" and false.

As Gorin replaced Roger as Godard's primary collaborator, however, the Dziga Vertov Group moved away from the equation of image and referent and the total rejection of image as site of knowledge. Their first collaboration, 1970's *Vent d'est,* demonstrates how the image, being a codified form of expression, can comment on the codes through which it communicates and, correspondingly, can transform its referent rather than simply transparently rendering it. This shift may simply have been the product of circumstance: as originally conceived, *Vent d'est* was to be Godard's return to a more conventional mode of fiction filmmaking, a collaboration with May student leader Daniel Cohn-Bendit on a "leftist spaghetti western."[35] It was thus the terms of the production itself that obligated Godard to abandon the "fetched" images of the previous two films and instead to "build" images resembling those from the world of fiction (or, more specifically, the Western), all the while taking these images as objects of critique. Compelled to investigate the images of fiction film, the filmmakers ended up not simply criticizing them but also discovering ways in which their material character and status as elements of a code predisposed them to creating new meanings.

A fortuitous escape from the confusions between images and things that troubled the documentary-style films is thus offered by the turn to fiction. In *Vent d'est,* the image is acknowledged as inevitably "built" rather than "fetched," having been created by the filmmakers themselves. It cannot therefore be elided with its referent, nor in turn rejected as patently false because of its belonging to that "fallen" world the previous two films depicted. The questions of metaphysical and political "justness" or truthfulness are hence off the table at the outset. This shift can be summed up in the film's most famous declaration: "It's not a just image, it's just an image." Although, in the context of the film, this line applies to an image of repression (a drawing of Stalin), it might also be taken as signaling an acceptance of the fact that images are nothing but images and therefore cannot be conflated with their referents or declared to be, in themselves, unequivocally true or false.

In contrast to the almost exclusive reliance on image–sound confrontation in the previous two films, here we find multiple strategies; some still maintain the primacy of the word, while others rely more on the image. The concept of the illusory and ideological nature of bourgeois cinema, for example, finds multiple modes of expression in addition to its statement by the voice-over. First, it is articulated through the dismantling of synchronous and falsely naturalistic sound–image relationships and the large-scale fracturing and fragmenting of the film text. This dismantling of sound–image relationships, furthermore, leads to the recognition of the image's polyvalence, as when the voice-over variously describes the same image of a bourgeois woman as depicting multiple counterrevolutionary figures. In other instances, the true ideological character of bourgeois cinema is expressed through allegorical representations that make use of the Western genre figures that populate the narrative: as the Cavalryman, on horseback, drags an Indian at the end of a rope, the former repeatedly declares his identity as "General Motor," while the Indian replies, "I am black! I am Palestinian! I am an Indian!" The spectacle of the bourgeois cinema, which passes itself off as mere entertainment, in fact both depicts and enacts the ideological repression of the masses by the bourgeoisie (embodied here in "General Motor," the punning representative of the military–industrial complex). In a variation on this method, a figure who is not part of the Western iconography addresses the audience directly, demonstrating the false seductions of the bourgeois cinema by inviting the spectator to come into the film with him. As the voice-over in the film puts it, "he is a Western character from a psychological drama, a thriller, a historical film. It doesn't make any difference. In fact, he's always the seducer."

An open disruption of conventional film form, allegory, and other transformations of the referent are thus acknowledged as means for producing knowledge. While couched in an ideological approach specific to post-1968 political culture, the knowledge conveyed might be read as a critique of the pedagogies of the representational regime: whereas Rousseau cast doubt on the theater's ability to alter behavior, however, Godard and Gorin presume the need to deactivate cinema's ability to do so. This is accomplished through a distance taken from the codes presented in the film: a cowboy who would be "false" in a Western (as a representative of an incorrect political position and as a vehicle of ideology more broadly) is revalenced as "true" here simply by naming him "General Motor," thus revealing his true nature. There is no need to seek the *juste image,* and indeed there is no such thing (although there may be, for certain occasions, an *image juste,* as there is a *mot juste*). An image is *juste une image,* a conclusion that expresses not a lament but rather an acknowledgment that images cannot be subject to political and epistemological judgment in any idealist, essentialist fashion.

If, in *Vent d'est,* it is the representational regime that is critiqued, what takes its place? The film offers a system in which information is usually (although not always, because the "correct" voice-over still reemerges at times) mediated in a way that recalls Watkins's repurposing of television documentary codes. Whereas in *British Sounds* and *Pravda,* the informational "correct line" was clearly in the word (a response to the sound–image opposition that resolved it rather than questioning it), here it is nowhere in particular. As in Watkins, it emerges through a conflict between codes rather than their negation or attempts to "purify" them, as was the case in the previous Dziga Vertov Group films. In some sense, then, if the thinking behind the previous films was pretelevisual (even as they were antitelevisual), here the insights of television itself are brought to bear. There is no particular reason to attribute these insights to television, but the analogies we can draw between Godard's original position (the essentialist commitment to the voice, perhaps a relic of the radio age) and objections to the image-as-information on television, and between the position espoused in *Vent d'est* and the approach taken by Watkins, suggest a possible connection, at least on the level of a shift between two broad positions that replays one of the central cultural transformations carried out by television. There can no longer be clear lines drawn between "pure" and mediated knowledge, nor can spectacle and information be fully separated from one another. While the role of television will become clearer in later works, the cultural logic that it facilitates is nonetheless detectable in *Vent d'est* and remains so even if television was in no way an immediate factor in the film's conception.

Also transformed by *Vent d'est* is the role of the audiovisual practitioner, who here becomes less a figure who must, through the "correct sound," negate the meanings of images and more one who rearranges and alters the meaning of various codes or discourses. Despite the appeal to the importance of montage in Godard's discussion of the earlier films, then, it is truly only here that montage becomes a key operation. The Dziga Vertov Group's subsequent film, however, demonstrates how an overly rigid conception of montage can lead to an undesirable imposition of meaning upon the image; I pause over this problem here because it will be one of the central ones to be addressed (and, in part, resolved by concepts taken from television) in Godard's later work with Miéville. *Lotte in Italia*, commissioned by Italy's RAI state television network and filmed mostly in Paris in early 1970, treats shots as neutral signifying units whose meaning is fully dependent on montage. Meaning, then, is in syntax rather than in the image itself, as representation. The film's theoretical lesson is based on an early, unpublished draft of Louis Althusser's semi-nal "Ideology and Ideological State Apparatuses" essay and hinges on its argument that "ideology represents the imaginary relationship of individuals to their real conditions of existence."[36] The militant specta-tor finds her counterpart in the film's protagonist, Paola, a young Italian student and militant with the left-wing group Lotta Continua. Like *Pravda*, the film is divided into sections that correspond to steps taken toward the acquisition of knowledge—both by Paola and by the viewer. In the first section, we see her carrying out a series of quotidian activities: going to lectures at the university, eating dinner at home, giving lessons to a worker, and selling papers for Lotta Continua. The simple images, invariably static, are punctuated with flashes of an entirely black screen, whose significance will only emerge later on. At the conclusion of this section, the voice-over addresses not the spectator but Paola, pointing out the ways in which, despite her proclaimed militancy, her behavior remains bourgeois and idealist. She conceives of her life, the voice explains, as an imaginary whole: "This imaginary, your real conditions of existence; their relations, what does that mean?" As images from the first section are repeated, again punctuated by the black screen, the voice explains that the relationship between her and the black spaces is, in fact, ideology: the black spaces, we might say, represent ideologically produced "blind spots," an incapacity to understand the relations that comprise her "real conditions of existence." As the film continues, we see changes in Paola's behavior as she tries to amend her bourgeois tendencies. Eventually, im-ages of industrial production appear where the black screen once was, representing Paola's emergence from ideology and realization of her true place within the relations of production. The situations from the first part of the film are played again, only this time alongside images of industrial production and interpreted by her voice-over in terms of her place in the relations of production. A heterogeneous element, however, remains, as a solid red square takes the place of the black one, perhaps representing a further level of knowledge—the Communist ideal or the instantiation of Communism—yet to be obtained.

This rather literal approach to montage indicates a problematic return to a conflation of the image and the thing it represents. Once meaning is located on the level of montage rather than in the image itself, the latter tends to be treated as a neutral unit, as though it could be deprived of all connotation and polyvalence. This results in what Gerard Leblanc describes as a "liquidation of struggle at the level of certain non-specific codes": as Vertov might put it, the importance of montage-within-the-shot is denied and, along with it, the status of the image as itself the product of codes.[37] Marc Cerisuelo similarly notes the way in which the concepts the film deals with tend to be condensed into signs ("health, for example, is visualized by tea and medicines placed on a table") (Figure 12).[38] As a result, there is once again no meaning in the image, or at least, there is no meaning particular to it. It is not an element that produces something but rather a form of encoding, a way of providing an image equivalent to a word or fixed concept. Verbal language remains the master category, a kind of fixed schema the image is now not expelled from, as in *British Sounds* and *Pravda,* but rather fully determined by.

One of the central problems that remains unresolved by the Dziga Vertov Group films, then, is how, if one is to look to the image as a source of information or knowledge, this knowledge can be found in or with it, both without assuming that the meaning is identical to that of the referent (as in *British Sounds* and *Pravda*) and without imposing it from outside (as in *Lotte*). This problem itself is encompassed by a larger, more global one: is there any way in which the audiovisual practitioner can provide information in a unique or specific way, one that cannot be reduced to the verbal? In the first two films, the verbal simply negates, while in the second two, another "code" provides for the restructuring and revalencing of the image. Even in the case of *Vent d'est,* which is far less schematic than *Lotte,* the image is more a site to be used against itself, as its own undermining, rather than one from which new meaning may emerge. This problem will preoccupy Godard for the rest of his career; ideally, as Michael Witt puts it, he believes that "meaning should emanate directly from the combination of images and sounds rather than from an explanatory or interpretative text written about or imposed on them."[39]

While Godard will only begin to reconceptualize these problems relating to image and meaning in terms of television after the dissolution of the Dziga Vertov Group, the group's films nonetheless offer a few

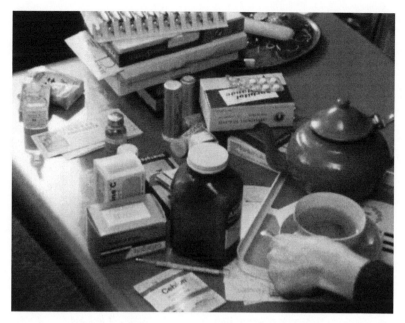

FIGURE 12. An example of an image used as a sign for a concept ("health, visualized by tea and medicines placed on a table") in *Lotte in Italia* (1970).

thoughts about the medium's potential usefulness. In its few mentions, television is cast as a site that can be co-opted or somehow harnessed for revolutionary purposes: at the end of *Lotte in Italia,* Paola speaks about how appearing on television—in the film we have just seen—is part of her militant practice, as she exploits the contradictions of liberal democracy by replacing the usual "voice" of the state with her own, as small as the period in which she is able to do so might be:

> Who does Italian television belong to? Italian television belongs to the state. . . . Every day a delegate of the state speaks to the Italian people. Speaks against workers, peasants, and their allies who organize themselves in struggle, to respond to the daily violence that is imposed upon them. To destroy and change that is to make revolution, to think otherwise, to make revolution. For me, to take a step forward is to speak today on Italian television for two or three minutes in a different way. They told

me that I had the right, in between a variety show, a drama, and a journalistic program, to tell my story, because we are a democracy. Because
we are humanist, liberal, and objective, I could tell my story.

A liberal commitment to democracy is positioned as one of the key values
of state television, and thus it remains a privileged site for the expression
of minority views, even those that challenge the institution itself. Yet there
is also a clearly dialectical view of television at work here: it is because
television still prides itself on a certain commitment to democracy that
it can be destroyed from within. Even before he begins to consider the
implications of television in relation to questions of form and meaning,
Godard thus spots its utopian potential as an institution.

A similar conception of TV as something to be "hijacked" or subverted appears in *Vladimir and Rosa,* in which it is cast as a stage for
subversives. Informed by the tactics of Abbie Hoffman and the Yippies, the film stages a burlesque of the Chicago Seven trial. In one scene
depicting a press conference held by the radicals (itself already a way
to subvert television's demand for spectacle), Godard and Gorin mime
shooting two CBS cameramen in the head and then take control of the
cameras themselves (Figure 13), as the voice-over speaks of the need to
fight against "imperialist television" and the "cameras of the enemy": "If
we fight all day against police, one must also fight against police information. Logical." News cameras stop being the tools of the enemy and
give radicals a chance to convey their message. Television thus is cast as
potentially valuable precisely because, as the Chicago demonstrators had
declared, "the whole world is watching": in its commitment to depict
the visible, television could also host disruptions of that visible, pushing
protest to take on more spectacular forms. The tactics of Hoffman and
the Yippies, referred to here, allowed the "out of order" speaker—in this
case, the defendants themselves—to speak from within the televised news
broadcast; the object becomes subject, reversing the power dynamic of
informational discourse and its objectifying tendencies.

This valorization of television, however, has little to say about the
role of the audiovisual practitioner, the possible usefulness of any specific
textual attributes of television form, or its functions beyond the news

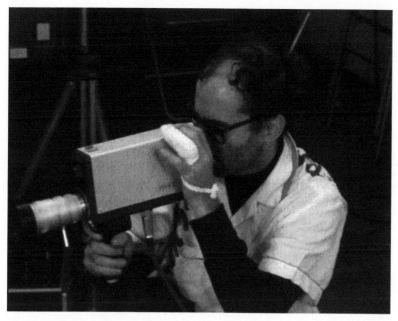

FIGURE 13. Godard commandeers a CBS news camera and puts it to revolutionary use in *Vladimir and Rosa* (1971).

broadcast. Godard and Gorin's use of television as a site of funding and exhibition does indeed double the acts of subversion depicted in their films, insofar as they exploit television's commitment to cultural and informational programming, not to mention its large audience, to deliver a subversive message (or at least to attempt its delivery). This remains, however, an approach that values television as venue rather than as cultural form; TV still sits on the side of counterinformation, divided from whatever we choose to call Godard's formally minded practice. It remains a kind of vessel or space rather than a set of textual practices and cultural operations; if one can hijack it, it is because it is basically empty—one simply steals the stage. Any other usage of television, meanwhile, appears suspect, as in Godard and Gorin's *Tout va bien,* in which Yves Montand portrays a former filmmaker now making absurd television commercials. Here television plays a familiar role as a site of decadence, commercialism (in many ways the equivalent of the American film industry in *Contempt*

[1963], as represented by Jack Palance's Jeremy Prokosh), and loss of political hope.

Tout va bien, released in 1972, marked Godard and Gorin's final collaboration. The shift between the Dziga Vertov Group work and Godard's later collaborations with Anne-Marie Miéville would lead to a deeper consideration of television, but this consideration itself is perhaps best situated as part of a broader historical shift, a kind of reorientation that allowed for the particular sort of utopian thinking that would follow. *Tout va bien,* after all, is set in 1972, a year that, as Alain Badiou reminds us, "without the slightest doubt initiated the fold of the wave of mass revolts for which the syntagm 'May 68' has become the indicator.... It is unquestionable that from the beginning of 1972 a great fatigue was felt on the part of the mass of young militants."[40] At this moment, the historical narrative invoked by the Dziga Vertov Group's name—one that could imagine Gorin and Godard as the modern-day heirs to Vertov—seems to collapse, as though the past of leftism had revealed itself powerless to confront the present. The matter, of course, is hardly so simple, but the projection of a narrative concerned primarily with fidelity to the revolutionary past falls apart along with the Dziga Vertov Group. Yet this narrative gives way to another, one that is concerned not so much with a linear historical process and political self-identification as it is with the unexplored promises and utopian thrust of figures like Vertov. As we will see, Godard's clearest turn to the utopian elements in Vertov lies in a new fascination with technology and a move even further away from the cinema as medium. The return to the utopian treatment of technology characteristic of Vertov (and the historical avant-garde more broadly), however, in a fashion not unlike what we see in Rossellini, intersects with a reorientation that might initially seem far from utopian: the losing wager to insert oneself and one's art into a historical narrative gives way to a turn inward, toward both an examination of the self and political questions concerned more with the home and the family, the site of television itself. The "exit from history" that we might connect not only with television and the domestic but also with the collapse of post-1968 movements more broadly turns out to be nothing of the sort. Rather, it allows for Godard to conceive of his place in history in a different way;

his work over the next five years, as Brecht might put it, "is not linked to the good old days but to the bad new ones."[41] What seems a step back is in fact necessary to take two steps forward, as it is precisely within the world of new consumer technology and domestic comfort that Godard will find the keys to the problems his previous works left unsolved.

ON COMMUNICATION

The Dziga Vertov Group period, though in many senses deeply engaged with television as cultural force, left open two fundamental problems that would find productive development only after Godard's turn to a deeper consideration of the televisual: first, how to make meaning come from or through images, rather than imposing it, and second, how to *use* television, not just as a site of counter-information or cooption, but as something that could be taken as formal raw material or otherwise inspire new thinking about the uses of sound and image. Both problems are dramatically reframed in Godard's work with Anne-Marie Miéville by looking more closely at the form and function of television, news media, and the field of mass communications more broadly; as Godard notes of this work, "for us television was a much more interesting way of thinking about cinema differently."[42] The films and television series that Godard carried out in collaboration with Miéville, from 1974's *Ici et ailleurs* (Here and elsewhere) (a film that draws on footage shot several years earlier by Godard and Gorin in Palestine) to 1977's *France tour détour deux enfants,* yielded two major new theoretical approaches informed by television: first, there was a shift away from the "classroom" model of the Dziga Vertov Group films, in which one (the spectator) watches and listens while the other (the filmmaker) shows and tells, to a conception of communication as a complex and embodied circuit, in which the placement of any sound or image (and the placement of the image-maker and the spectator)—not within a single text, as in *Lotte in Italia,* but within what we might call a more holistic "ecology"—is just as or more important than what appears in the image itself. This notion is closely related to television insofar as the image is characterized more by mobility and circulation than by a permanent or fixed state (a notion we might associate both with the cinema screen and with a conception of montage as cementing images into their "correct" place). This new conception of communication applies both to audiovisual texts and to the spectator, who is (anticipating Deleuze) also treated as an "image" in the larger chain of communication. Second, new forms of thinking about montage emerge, ones that are informed and enabled by the display of multiple images at once, either as monitors or as projected slides, and by the use of video techniques, such as the superimposition of multiple images and writing or drawing on images. Although these techniques are often identified with Godard's turn to video in the mid-1970s, I will contend that they also draw heavily on forms and concepts derived from television that do not necessarily relate to or necessitate the use of video technology.

In the 1974–77 works with Miéville, the concern with form developed in the Dziga Vertov Group works was merged with a theoretical conception of information that they lacked. Michael Witt has noted the importance of Claude Shannon's information theory for Godard during this period, and indeed, Shannon's work is mentioned in *Comment ça va?* (in passing) and *Six fois deux*, both from 1976.[43] Though Witt notes several ways in which information theory broadly speaking was useful to Godard and Miéville (as a means of "scrutinizing a wide range of communication processes," "to isolate and analyse points of blockage," and "to theorize their own lacunary essayistic practices"), it is unclear to what extent Shannon's ideas specifically inform Godard's works, for reasons I will return to in a moment.[44] However loosely they were adapted, communications and information theory clearly provide a general field or set of terms with which the 1970s works operate. Godard was explicit about his interest in information and explained that he and Miéville's new production company, Sonimage, was

an information company. On our stationary, we put at the top "Information, calculation, writing"; we replaced an information technology [*informatique*] store that was called "Information Technology, Calculation, Writing." We changed the sign that said "information technology" into "information." And in information, there is calculation and writing.

The goal is to make information in a broad sense, moving more towards fiction than documentary.[45]

The questions of what precisely constitutes information and why existing forms of mass communication seem to do anything *but* communicate are the central subjects of the 1974–77 works, both as topics for essayistic analysis (as in the films *Ici et ailleurs, Numéro deux,* and *Comment ça va?*) and as the starting point for imagining alternative media forms (as in the television series *Six fois deux* and, to a lesser extent, *France tour*).

"Cinema," Godard remarks in 1975, "is the need to communicate with people that one doesn't see. Cinema is no more than that, a means of communication."[46] While one could certainly argue that communication was an essential concern in the Dziga Vertov Group films—and even prior, when Godard imagined in the late 1960s a multiauthor, twenty-four-hour-long project titled *Communications*—here it takes on a rather different form.[47] Communication is no longer, as it was in the past films, an idea to be transmitted to the viewer or a theoretical meditation; rather, it is a kind of movement, more process than content: "Communication," Godard states simply, "is what moves."[48] Effective communication can thus be seen not as a successfully delivered message but as a displacement, both of the existing means of communication and of the sender and receiver who use them. This idea seems in fact to challenge the linear model proposed by Shannon and William Weaver in the 1940s, in which the message itself exists independently of and prior to its transmission. For Shannon and Weaver, "information was detached from qualitative considerations of meaning and rendered as a calculus of signal load,"[49] whereas Godard's model challenges this abstraction and more closely aligns with constitutive models of communication that had begun to be developed in the 1970s, in which "information is not an ontological function with an absolute content or quantity, but is relative to the predispositions of the observer that constitutes it and that observer's position along the total channel through which communications must proceed."[50] For Godard, MacCabe notes, communication is only possible "at the moment where everywhere changes place," as though all of the boundaries that govern both our perceptions of the world around us and the way we speak to each other have been broken down and restructured in a single gesture, in something like a *repartage du sensible*.[51] For cinema (or video or television) to carry out this action, the image will need to be reconconceptualized as something other than a blackboard. Godard himself offers a fitting replacement: "Making cinema or television, technically, is sending twenty-five postcards per second to millions of people."[52] Unlike a blackboard, a postcard is characterized by its mobility. It is at once a discrete physical object, an image, and a message—like television itself. It is not, furthermore, a true or false representation of a good or bad object but simply one image-object that populates a world full of others and that sometimes elicits the circulation of another in return. Finally, it is addressed not, like a lesson on a blackboard, to a group of pupils in the classroom but to an individual, most often at home. Godard's cinema and television works of this period are postcards, printed and written upon in the Sonimage studio in Grenoble, where he had relocated with Miéville, and sent through time and space to the individual spectator, whether at home or in the cinema.

The basic terms of the inquiry into information, communications, and media that Godard and Miéville would pursue over the following years are clearly formulated in 1974's *Ici et ailleurs* (released in 1976) and 1976's *Comment ça va?* (released in 1978). The first introduces the essential concept of the image as "what moves," and this concept is explicitly grounded in television itself, as something that "delivers" and "circulates" images in a different way than cinema. *Ici et ailleurs* combines footage shot by Godard and Gorin for their uncompleted Palestinian film with new footage shot in France. Its title evokes both the postcard and the television, suggesting a space or distance (between "here" and "there") but also the simultaneity ("*et*") of multiple positions, and it is television that serves as the film's central visual motif. Much of the new footage shot by Godard and Miéville depicts a French family watching television (usually advertisements, but sometimes, through point-of-view cuts, the Palestinian images, which are never shown in situ on their television screen) (Figure 14). The television, like the postcard, functions as a means of transmitting a message but is also both an object and a boundary,

FIGURE 14. A television set serves as both the boundary and the connection between "here" and "elsewhere" in *Ici et ailleurs* (1976).

that which both links and separates our "here" from "elsewhere"; it is an object that becomes movement and a message that becomes object. This characterization recalls David Joselit's emphasis on the object–movement dichotomy as one of the most significant characteristics of television as a medium. Adopting Paul Virilio's use of the term "trajective," Joselit argues that the trajective or nonobject state of images or commodities stands as a potentially liberating antidote to their reified stability.[53] Godard, however, seems to consider the two aspects of the television image—its mobility and its fixed location on the television screen—as superimposed or complementary rather than antagonistic or dialectical, although he shares Joselit's belief in the importance of tracing new trajectories and displacing existing images. The fact, however, that both arrive at such a similar characterization of the image suggests the extent to which television itself promotes it; the entire concept of communication that will so deeply inform Godard's subsequent thought about the image would be almost unthinkable without television and suggests the broader ways in which television had profoundly altered cinematic conceptions of the image.

The idea of the image not as a discrete bit of information but as a form of motion or displacement leads in turn to the insight that every image exists and derives its meaning from a larger placement, not in the "text," as in older conceptions of montage, but in what we would now call a "media ecology." With television (and, later, other forms of video displays), *where* an image is begins to be as important as *what* it is. The image in *Ici et ailleurs* never stands in isolation or as a fixed surface to be gazed upon, as in the Dziga Vertov Group films, but is always part of both a circuit and an image-environment and takes on meaning only within the context of a totality, a linking of "here and there": as Godard puts it, "if one doesn't link here and there, one limits the movement to its point of departure and arrival . . . there is no fixation [in the film] on the departure or the arrival, but only on movement, on relations, on comings and goings."[54] In practice, this means that any informational or communicative practice will deal less with making an image "say" something and more with displacing it and its spectator, with a broader rerouting of the circuits of communication. The television practice pursued by Godard and Miéville will not seek to convey information as some sort of translatable quantity (as it would be both in a journalistic model and in artworks operating according to the logic of Rancière's representational regime) but rather find its informational quality on the level of form itself, further blurring distinctions between informational and aesthetic practice. Communication, in turn, takes place when information is successfully displaced and displacing.

Godard and Miéville's new approach is also televisual insofar as it conceives of the circuit of images itself as a homogenizing grid or schema. The grid is not, however, necessarily an unequivocally negative levelling force or a kind of ideological regimentation; rather, it is precisely the existence of a grid that allows for communication to take place. If there is no initial "placement," there can be no disruption or destabilization of image and meaning. Every image, Godard laments at the end of *Ici et ailleurs,* is "in its place, like each of us in our place, in the chain of events, over which we have lost all power." This state of things is not eternal and essential but rather represents a changeable condition, one that offers hidden benefits. Godard and Miéville's televisual art will concern itself not, as the Dziga Vertov Group films did, with expressing a fixed, essential meaning (as actually existing television would, keeping things "in their place") but with taking things (and people) out of their "correct places," imagining a television in which the grid never quite fixes itself and in which the homogenization it might impose is deferred.

The idea of communication as movement through a circuit and a set of places leads, in turn, to a new concept of how images might be made to signify. This involves not only displacement, as a kind of literal *détournement,* but also the creation, through a practice that will remain central to Godard's practice for the rest of his career, of new connections. Both *Ici et ailleurs* and *Comment ça va?* juxtapose this displacement and creation of new connections to their opposite, a practice in which the image would fail to signify and keep everything "in its place." In the former, this negative opposite is located in the films of the Dziga Vertov Group. Both metaphorically and literally expressing his and Gorin's failure to observe, to be spoken to by the images they filmed, Godard explains, "We took some images, and we put the sound too loud, with no matter what image." As he lists a litany of places, many in which the group's films sought to intervene (Prague, France, Italy), the image track depicts a hand raising and lowering the volume on a stereo playing "The Internationale." The meaning is clear: abstraction and the desire for revolution led to a failure simply to see, to observe the world without imposing already-drawn conclusions upon it. The sequence also suggests a disavowal of the privileging of the voice over the image, which in practice amounted to a privileging of the abstract over the concrete, the rational over the sensory—an attempt at total containment or purification, an "antitelevision." Sound and image thus seem to have changed places in a hierarchy of value: one should no longer speak or listen to find the truth but simply look, as though truth were contained or could be reached through the image. This reversal points to what MacCabe sees as "a new and hesitant faith in the image" arising in this film, but this faith may well be arrived at all too hastily.[55] It seems to reflect a kind of knee-jerk reaction, a desire to compensate for past errors by reversing one's position, particularly given the fact that it is not clear here what precisely images can tell us and whether whatever truth they hold is self-evident.

This "hesitant faith" in the image, however, is balanced by a skepticism about the possibility of the image's ability to communicate; it cannot do so on its own, in some self-evident and transparent way, but requires the intervention of the filmmaker. To avoid clichéd and noncommunicative images, the filmmaker must, on one hand, avoid the imposition of any preexisting schema and, on the other, overcome the tyranny of the single image; as Godard often puts it, to see one needs two. Three possibilities for how the filmmaker might facilitate communication are posed by *Ici et ailleurs,* and lay the groundwork for the strategies used in *Six fois deux.* First, the filmmaker can attempt to clear away whatever obscures the image by turning the sound down, metaphorically speaking. Second, the filmmaker can disrupt the chain of images by altering what we might call apparatuses of visibility. To do so, he will need to intervene not on the level of individual images but rather on that of the structures through which they appear to us. It is on this level that video technology becomes an instrumental part of Godard's work: the turn to video offers a different kind of visibility to images, as they can be superimposed upon each other, written on, broken down and combined, in short manipulated in ways that film would not permit. Video, furthermore, allows for the presentation of multiple still or moving images at once: the film strip, in which one image chases away the one before it (as represented in *Ici et ailleurs* by a scene in which people enact this process, each holding a single image), can be replaced by multiple "channels," as when Godard films two or more video monitors at a time. Finally, the filmmaker can combine images, either within such video apparatuses or within a filmic chain, in unexpected ways. In this case, communication results not from any work on the single image or its support (film, video, filmed monitor, etc.) but rather from the creation of what Deleuze calls a new "interstice," a notion I will return to later. Although the first two operations are perhaps more easily grasped and might seem to be more novel approaches, it is in fact this third one that will be most powerfully mobilized by Godard's subsequent work, as we will see when we turn to *Six fois deux*.

Godard and Miéville's *Comment ça va?*, made two years later, develops these latter two operations—altering apparatuses of visibility and creating new links or interstices—while also venturing to carry out the first, namely, teaching us how to see images without imposing anything upon them. Indeed, the film responds to the demand posed near the end of *Ici et ailleurs*: "Learn to see here, in order to hear elsewhere." *Comment ça va?* deals explicitly with media and information: the minimal narrative concerns a Communist who is making a video documentary about a Communist newspaper and the shortcomings that his secretary Odette (played by Miéville) finds in his work. Journalism, the film argues, is among the forms of ostensible communication that in fact hide exactly what they purport to show, both by obscuring the place from which they speak and by drowning information and images with false objectivity and cliché. This narrative framework signals that Godard and Miéville's work is not simply a research into images and communications for their own sake but rather one that does indeed imagine the reform or transformation of the informational apparatuses that currently exist. This goal is further underscored by the fact that the "scene of pedagogy" depicted in the film is a dramatization or mise-en-scène of an actual lesson carried out prior to the shooting of the film by Godard himself. As reported by *Libération,* the director visited the newspaper's offices in September 1975 to speak to its editors about the text–image juxtaposition in an article about the post–Carnation Revolution conflicts in Portugal. Godard displayed two images to the editors, the very same images whose juxtaposition would constitute a major component of *Comment ça va?*: one from Portugal that had been previously printed by the newspaper and one taken during a French strike in 1972.[56] The film's genesis out of this incident attests to Godard's continuing commitment to a counter-informational or counter-journalistic practice but also raises the question as to what a film might offer that the presentation to *Libération*'s editors could not. *Comment ça va?* thus provides an exemplary case to examine how Godard and Miéville conceptualize the specific communicative capacities of audiovisual media and see them as going beyond informational practice as it currently exists.

Godard's presentation to the *Libération* journalists finds its way into the film as Odette objects to the in-film documentary's portrayal of a caption being written to go alongside the image of the demonstrators in Portugal. The caption, she suggests, obscures rather than illuminates the image. To demonstrate why this might be the case, she asks her boss to read it. As he does so, we see his eyes scan back and forth, as though mimicking the mechanical motions of a typewriter. The same action, Odette argues, is repeated when he looks at an image: "When you look at something, for example, this image of Portugal, you skim it with your eyes.... You are trained by the movement of your hands, which the typewriter has put into you, and you forget what you have seen." A practice of "reading" the image rather than seeing it generates a caption that imposes a preexisting idea upon it and dictates our perception of it. Once again, metaphorically speaking, the sound is too loud, drowning out the image and preventing us from truly seeing or communicating with it.

Odette suggests two ways to better see (and make seen) the image: first, she creates alternate footage for the documentary that simply consists of people's subjective reactions to the photo, replacing the sourceless and clichéd voice of authority present in the caption by unguided, autonomous gazes and spontaneous verbal responses. Second, she juxtaposes, like Godard in his presentation to *Libération,* the Portuguese image with one from the Joint factory strike in France. This combination elicits, both from the individuals whose reactions Odette records and from her boss, a realization of how the image of what is happening in Portugal might relate to a viewer in France and thus begins to narrow the distance between here and there. It is in this juxtaposition that we begin to see the Deleuzian creation of interstices, in which the frontier between images becomes not a gap but a site at which new visibilities and new thoughts are created. "I began to see why she insisted on putting these two images together," the narrator recounts. "Simply to think."

Odette, however, is not the only one putting together images in *Comment ça va?* Though it is she whose voice we hear, and who takes the role of pedagogue in the fictional world of the film, the transformation of apparatuses of visibility is reserved for Godard and Miéville as directors. While Odette can, within the diegesis, propose a "lowering of the sound"

and a juxtaposition of two images, it is only the filmmakers who can manipulate them, superimposing them upon one another, wiping them, and
flashing back and forth between them. It is these techniques that allow
us to see the "thinking" that the narrator speaks of, as Philippe Dubois
notes: "Because seeing (with video) is thinking (live, with the image)."[57]
In *Comment ça va?*, then, we are given an explicit demonstration (indeed,
one framed as such) of how the restructuring of the visible can lead to the
creation of new meanings or interstices: it is because of the restructuring
of apparatuses of visibility (video superimposition, wipes) that a new kind
of juxtaposition (no longer montage as succession of images but the visibility of multiple images at once) is possible. The interstice opened up
by this juxtaposition allows for a fuller vision of the image of Portugal
and elicits the viewer's consciousness of his own position.

Comment ça va? both illustrates the theoretical and practical underpinnings of Godard and Miéville's theory of communication and gestures
toward the way in which their communication, the practice resulting from
that theory, aspires to be a replacement for that of the mainstream media.
Even here, though, there is an undercurrent of impossibility, as though to
insist on the utopian, rather than realizable, value of the project. Although
Odette's boss decides to accept her recommendations and proposes to his
colleagues that their documentary be altered accordingly, she predicts that
the changes will be rejected by the higher-ups in the party, as indeed they
are. The film concludes with the narrator describing how he wanted to
fight this decision and work further with Odette, only to have her disappear forever after a winter vacation. While this ending has the positive
valence of suggesting the filmmaker's autonomy from an authoritative
discourse and his successful absorption of Odette's lesson, it can likewise
be read as an expression of his project's futility. Even if a new method of
communication can be developed, that method's deployment will, at least
on the level of mass communications, be prohibited by existing institutions. Communication and vision, even if we know how they could be
achieved, will ultimately be prohibited by the powers that be. They may
be demonstrated under controlled conditions as an experiment but will
never succeed in the outside world. To imagine the redistribution of the
sensible does not allow one to enact it. Communication, then, would be

a lost cause, not because it cannot be taught, or because the filmmaker is incapable of teaching it, but rather because political and media institutions will simply not permit it.

AN IMPOSSIBLE TELEVISION

This sense of impossibility carries over into *Six fois deux: sur et sous la communication* (Six times two: on and under communication), the long-form television series that represents Godard and Miéville's fullest vision of what a utopian television might look like. The series positions itself as a kind of revisioning or transformation of existing television; as Jerry White puts it, Godard and Miéville's television "does not exist in opposition to mainstream forms, but instead exists alongside" them.[58] They do not take television as a simple means of distribution, nor as a kind of formal tabula rasa; rather, as David Sterritt puts it, they aim "to radicalize popular attitudes toward TV by pushing to the limit the elements and capabilities that [Godard] finds most potentially valuable within it."[59] What we find here is thus an exemplary use of Jameson's utopian method, as what currently exists is used to imagine its utopian double through both a process of exaggeration (drawing out or more fully developing immanent characteristics) and one of revalencing (illustrating how what might now seem negative could, within a different context, turn into a positive). In the same spirit, the move to television in *Six fois deux* is not so much a critique or "correction" of an object held at a distance (as in *Ici et ailleurs* and *Comment ça va?*, not to mention many of the Dziga Vertov Group projects) as it is an occasion to imagine its replacement, a replacement only gestured toward in *Comment ça va?* As Godard states while discussing *Comment ça va?* in 1978, "I did some experiments and then I stopped; I'm trying to apply them."[60] Producing material for television allows Godard and Miéville to "apply" their previous theorizations, to work from within the apparatus of mass communication that the earlier films had critiqued from outside. Their imagining of a replacement, however, is never as systematic as the one we find in Rossellini but rather more aware of its provisional and imaginary, or even impossible, character. It posits an ideal, but treats it as one whose conditions need to be meditated upon and interrogated rather than hastily and quixotically implemented, and whose viewer remains in many senses an ideal or future one. It recognizes (unlike Rossellini, to a large extent, and unlike the late Watkins, as we will see in the next chapter) that a utopian anticipatory projection is just that: it can show us where we might go or how we might imagine the future, but it does not get us there. Indeed, one of its most valuable functions lies in its ability to let us see and imagine the overcoming of the distance between here and elsewhere, what is and what could be.

Six fois deux also displays an attitude toward technology that characterizes Godard's 1970s works more broadly: it adopts technology not only as a tool but also as a kind of symbol for the utopian imagination, a Vertovian transcendence of man and machine that would also lead to the creation of a new form of cultural practice. This vision is perhaps most succinctly conveyed in *Numéro deux,* in which we find multiple shots of Godard sitting among and manipulating an array of machines (Figure 15). This array suggests the idea of Godard's Grenoble studios as a kind of technology laboratory, one that, as Michael Witt notes, "might be seen as the belated realization of the cinematic research laboratory dreamt of by Vertov."[61] This man–machine fusion suggests one of the potential displacing capacities of television and video technology: it obscures the boundaries of individual subjectivity, in remapping (or effacing) the boundaries both between human and nonhuman and between human subjects, as they are linked into a circuit mediated by cables and monitors. For Godard, this technology remains fully artisanal, a means of independence from that which exists rather than a sign of subjection to it; new technology here both is (in its undetermined quality) and allows for the personal building of a utopian enclave. As Godard explains to MacCabe, "you have a theatre which is the TV set. You have a laboratory which is the tape-recorder. At any time you can always make a picture.... You just need small money, you don't have to beg from a banker. So at least I feel secure."[62] Echoing Rossellini's comments about television as an "art without traditions," Godard declares, responding to a question about his taste for using new technologies, "There is not less law, but it hasn't been made, it isn't written down.... You have no rules so you have something to live with, you have to invent some rules and to communicate with other people."[63] Godard and Miéville's television work would seek to do

FIGURE 15. Godard in the "belated realization of the cinematic research laboratory dreamt of by Vertov" in *Numéro deux* (1975).

simply that, inserting itself into people's daily lives in order to speak to and with them.

Finally, *Six fois deux* represents the belated return to the forms of local television that Godard had flirted with in Quebec and a fulfillment of the "missed encounters" with the medium that occurred during the Dziga Vertov Group period. It was precisely the independence that technology allowed Godard—the ownership of the means of production—that allowed his and Miéville's utopian television to take shape, as a sort of peripheral alternative (Grenoble, not Paris) to conventional television, instantiating a "decentralized television practice" and "a deliberate assault on the monolith from the margins," as Witt puts it.[64] At the same time, however, the project assumes a national audience, in the way that only a program broadcast by state television can; even if it might be marginal in character, it does not speak to any specific demographic, as the Dziga Vertov Group films often had. As MacCabe argues, "the burden of the argument of *Ici et ailleurs* had been the necessity to focus on the domestic audience for television, and it was this audience that Sonimage tried to address with *Six fois deux...* and *France tour détour deux enfants.*"[65] *Six fois deux* would represent Godard and Miéville's chance not only to imagine a different kind of television but also to speak to a much wider audience, in a very different context, than any of the films they or the Dziga Vertov Group had released in the preceding years.

France's national television company ORTF was broken up, as part of a series of reforms and restructurings, into several smaller entities in 1974. One of these, the Institut National de l'Audiovisuel (INA), decided after seeing the video-dominated *Numéro deux* that Godard would be well suited to make a television series and offered him the chance to produce material to fill six one-hundred-minute slots on FR3, the third public channel. Originally, Godard was offered one of these slots, but he insisted, to the astonishment of the INA executives, on producing material for all six, perhaps a sign of his desire to produce programming that would function as a true series, as an example of an alternative form of television, as opposed to a self-contained and more conventionally delimited work:

> There was a contract to make [FR3] one hour per year. I told them no, two months for an hour is not enough time, because an hour is enormous and I need time to do it.... But when we learned that they had six hours, we said to them: maybe six hours, we could do that for you in three months. Because at that point you conceive it completely differently.... Because if you have to say everything in an hour it may not be enough. You panic completely... but suddenly, with six hours, you say to yourself: "Well, at least I can do a frank and honest conversation, at least I can do what is never done on television, which is not to cut, not even after ten minutes."[66]

Scale here provides not only a way to imagine audiovisual communication in a different temporal framework but also another hint as to the project's utopian aspirations, its status as system (if only an imaginary one) rather than simply a one-off project.

Finally, *Six fois deux* represents a change in venue, from the cinema to the home. The placement of Godard and Miéville's work in the home rather than in the *art et essai* cinema meshes well with their concern with domestic matters (first voiced in *Ici et ailleurs* and then, more prominently, in *Numéro deux*) and creates a new intimacy between filmmaker and spectator. Rather than being spoken to by the otherworldly, Olympian voices of the Dziga Vertov Group, the spectator is addressed as one domestic subject by another. Godard, it would seem, agrees with and seeks to promote Bazin's convictions that "intimacy is the privileged style of television" and that "before being a spectacle, television is a conversation."[67] For Godard, as for Rossellini, the television spectator is addressed as an individual, although one who is connected, through the very act of viewing, with others: "in a cinema people are many (together) to be alone in front of the screen. In an apartment linked to a TV aerial people are alone to be many (together) in front of the screen."[68] This focus on the domestic as both viewing location and as subject, furthermore, is for Godard a political one. As he tells an amateur cinema magazine in 1973, "the real 'political' film I'd like to end up making would be a film about me that would show my wife and my daughter [i.e., Miéville and her daughter] what I am, in other words, a family film."[69] It is the home movie, after all, he notes, that represents the true "popular cinema."[70] The home is not, however, a safe or cloistered space, and television is a kind of membrane or boundary between the home and the world: "Television isn't the factory, it isn't the home," *Six fois deux* reminds us. "It's between the factory and the home."

The utopian transformation or revalencing of television that takes place throughout *Six fois deux* appears, at its broadest level, in the overall structure of the series itself. As the title indicates, the series is divided into six episodes (each filling one of the one-hundred-minute television slots), but each of these six episodes is divided into two fully independent subsections. The division and subdivision into episodes both emulates and defies television convention, insofar as the concept of television programs as existing "in series" is appealed to, but the logic governing that series is an unexpected and rather obscure one. There is no sense of progression or advancement (narrative or otherwise) between episodes, and each installment is differentiated from the others not as part of an ordered whole with its own specific place but as treating a specific subject or employing a specific formal strategy. Furthermore, as Witt notes, the usual linear development of television programs is challenged here "by including references backwards and forwards between the various episodes."[71] The two segments of each episode, meanwhile, follow a repeating pattern. The first segment is generally an "essay" on a single topic (unemployment, the relationship between words and things, photojournalism), while the second is a lengthy interview, usually with a single subject. Though this division is somewhat obscured by the fact that interviews often occur in the first segment as well, it appears to replicate, as MacCabe argues, the structure of French school lessons: "In *Six fois deux,* the divisions of the programmes are taken from the divisions of French primary education in which there are two types of lesson—lessons about things, in which the child engages with the world, and lessons about words, in which the child learns about language."[72] This parallel suggests an affinity between televisual and pedagogical forms, in which a news report would constitute a lesson about things, or *leçon des choses,* and an interview a lesson about words. In keeping with their overall strategy of using existing television conventions in unexpected ways, Godard and Miéville do not invent a parallelism but rather illuminate and exaggerate a latent one.

Existing television also serves as a template for the series's capaciousness and variety: over its duration, *Six fois deux* touches on almost every subject imaginable, although several characteristic Godardian preoccupations predominate. Deleuze, who offers a brilliantly concise and comprehensive reading of the series, singles out two ideas or lines of questioning as primary. The first concerns work and the sale of labor, and asks, "What is it, in fact, that is bought, and what is sold? What is it that some people are prepared to buy and others to sell, and that is not necessarily the same thing?"[73] The second concerns language and information, examines the nature of communicative exchanges, and argues that "language is a system of orders, not a medium of communication"; this use of language is, of course, the opposite of what Godard and Miéville wish to pursue.[74] It is this second concern I will privilege here. While we might expect *Six fois deux* to continue the valuation of images over words initiated in

Ici et ailleurs and *Comment ça va?*, it is in fact a highly verbal program, much of whose running time is filled up with long monologues or interviews. This, too, constitutes a mirroring and transformation of television: in Godard and Miéville's television, a French farmer can speak at length without fear of interruption rather than being reduced to a sound bite. The verbal element I would like to stress most here, however, is the way in which the interviews Godard carries out in the series in many ways double, in another form, the actions carried out by the play with images. It is communicative exchanges more broadly that are the subject of the series, not simply images. This fact both indicates the overcoming of the earlier overvaluations of sound or image (the first in the Dziga Vertov Group films, the second in *Ici et ailleurs*) and suggests that the two can be conceptualized in a nonoppositional manner. It is in parallels that arise here between image and language, without one dominating the other, that we can see the hints of a utopian form of communication in which the two would no longer be discernible from one another.

Both image and speech are subject in *Six fois deux* to a displacement from their usual contexts and functions. While several sections of the program (for example, episode 3A, "Photos et cie.," in which we see a black-and-white photo of an execution carried out in Dhaka, Bangladesh, as its photographer explains its conditions of production) continue the critique of the media's use of images and their failure to communicate initiated in *Comment ça va?*, much of its running time is spent demonstrating instead how communicative power might be restored to images and words. In the case of images, we see more conventional efforts to decontextualize or defamiliarize them as well as their "activation" through the creation of new interstices. An example of the former appears in episode 2A, titled "Leçons des choses," which begins with a demonstration of how communicative power relies in large part on the defamiliarization achieved through metaphor but also how different types of metaphor generate different types of visibility and meaning. Over a shot of two coffee cups and the hands holding them, Godard and another man begin to discuss images just moments before they are revealed. Godard remarks, "There's a baby"; the voice of his companion declares, "No, it's a prisoner of war," and then the picture of the baby appears on-screen. The conversation continues to develop this metaphor, as a fence that appears in an image of children in a schoolyard is described as the fence of a prison that the baby will soon find itself trapped behind. The initial metaphor thus serves as a kind of generative matrix, allowing not only for the first image to be seen in a new way but also for its extension to a larger semantic field (childhood). The same technique is repeated over a shot of a river (this time seen as it is commented on rather than afterward): Godard remarks, "Oh, a river," only to have his companion reply, "No, it's a long story." Although the technique may be the same, the result is different: nothing is revealed about the river, as though unveiling its true character. Rather, a link is drawn between two very different phenomena without one being interpreted in terms of the other. Keeping in mind this distinction, both of these metaphors are nevertheless alike insofar as they instantiate a new way of seeing.

This "new way of seeing" alone, however, would seem rather banal, simply a new way of carrying out one of the most commonly agreed-on functions of art. Godard and Miéville are concerned with going further, and this is accomplished by a move from interpretative metaphor into what Deleuze calls the creation of the interstice, which may or may not entail the use of metaphor. The second example here, that of the river, taken in opposition to the first, begins to illustrate the subtle difference between the two: rather than one term of the metaphor being altered by the other (baby *becomes* prisoner of war), the two are superimposed in a way that gives neither primacy, interpretative or otherwise (river is story, story is river, both are long, flowing, etc.). What occurs is not thus an interpretation or new visibility arising from it but rather "a shifting horizon, a confusion between inside and outside, a transgression of boundary which makes it possible to be in two places or in two systems of thought at the same time."[75] One must hold the river and the story in mind at once, rather than transforming the river into a story. What occurs in this second case is not merely the imposition of one object on another but rather the greater confusion or superimposition of two discursive systems (here language or narrative and nature), no longer kept separate but joined without reducing their difference. One might argue that superimposition occurs in the first example as well, insofar as we are forced to keep two terms (one visible and one not) in mind at the same time, but this juxtaposition is still interpretative in a way that the second is not, constituting more a revelation of truth, a hermeneutic process, than a generation of new meaning.

The way in which the practice of superimposition (although it need not entail literal superimposition of images) functions as communicative act and demonstration can be further illustrated by its implementation through images alone. While the beginning of episode 2A, perhaps both acknowledging and confusing the distinction MacCabe notes between lessons about words and things in the French pedagogical tradition, sometimes juxtaposes words and images, Godard and Miéville more frequently place two images together. This variation of the "interstitial" technique, furthermore, underscores the difference between the two examples of the baby and the river. As Godard notes in episode 3A, recalling Odette's lesson in *Comment ça va?*, "you always need two photos to be able to see anything." To see with two images entails not an interpretation, which would imply a latent meaning in one image that needs to be brought out by another (as with the image of the baby whose meaning is brought out by the words "prisoner of war"), but rather the making-visible of a space between them. Meaning is not in the image, neither as an essence captured by the impassive lens nor as a secret waiting to be deciphered, but rather exists as a kind of potentiality that can only be activated through its juxtaposition with another image. Episode 3A carries out a number of these juxtapositions: after declaring that one needs two images to see, it displays several still images and asks how they are linked, editing in series an image of an assembly line at Billancourt and one of Palestinian soldiers, then one of earth from space and one of a fetus. The meaning produced *between* these images emerges not, as in Eisensteinian montage, from conflict or collision but rather through their conjunction. Deleuze makes the crucial observation that "Godard is not a dialectician. What counts with him is not two or three, or however many you like, it's AND, the conjunction AND."[76] It is this "and," Deleuze explains, that restructures the way that we group the images intellectually and perceptually in such a way that something new is produced:

In Godard's method, it is not a question of association. Given one image, another image has to be chosen that will induce an interstice between the two. This is not an operation of association, but of differentiation.... Given one potential, another one has to be chosen, not any whatever, but in such a way that a difference of potential is established between the two, which will be productive of a third or something new.[77]

That "something new" redefines both of the two initial terms while also carrying out the superimposition of discourses referred to earlier, displacing the boundaries that structure our habitual modes of thinking. The fetus becomes, the voice-over reports, as though verbalizing the result of this combination, "the first astronaut on earth," while an astronaut (not part of the image of earth that we have just seen but semantically related to it, hence suggesting the superimposition of two fields rather than simply two images) becomes "the first pedestrian in space." Here we begin to see how the concept of superimposition provides a solution to the problems about how meaning could be generated by images without imposing it upon them or looking for it within them that were raised by the Dziga Vertov Group films.

Superimpositions also occur in *Six fois deux* through writing or drawing on the image, using the screen as what Witt, evoking *British Sounds,* calls an "electronic blackboard."[78] While this technique has the same effect of creating an interstice and hence superimposing one form of discourse upon another (here quite literally), it does so through action upon a single image rather than by juxtaposing two separate images. This adds a different temporal dimension to the practice of linkage, insofar as the writing or drawing implicitly takes place after the filming of the image itself and therefore constitutes not only a comment upon it but also a returning of difference to it. What is fixed or set within one set of boundaries is displaced as a new boundary is created, as when Godard writes "faux" over the image of mathematician René Thom in response to his words in episode 5B ("René(e)s") or creates his own diagrams over the image in imitation of those that Thom draws on a blackboard. Such diagrams, usually drawn directly over an image, also appear in episode 4A

("Pas d'histoire"), when Godard demonstrates how a boundary arises between mother and child by drawing a white line between them on a magazine image and then labeling each side with a number (Figure 16). The Lacan-inspired diagram not only reenacts the separation and self-estrangement that serve as the precondition for individual subjectivity but, in separating the image from the temporally posterior writing upon it, creates yet another interstice. Godard's diagrams, then, are on one hand a kind of illustrated lecture about boundaries and subjectivity but, on the other, enact precisely what they teach, namely, that all meaning arises from the creation of an interstice, a distance.

In both cases illustrated here—either the activation of a metaphor through word applied to image or the overlapping or blurring of boundaries between discourses or semantic fields, either through a combination of word and image or through the juxtaposition of two images—we find a movement in the opposite direction from the antitelevision practiced by *British Sounds* and *Pravda.* Rather than a medium in which the visible is conflated with the real and thus must be rejected as completely ideological, television is valorized as a site upon which images and words might move out of their place. While fixing and containment may be perpetually sought by mainstream producers (either through the supposed separation of types of discourses or through the imposition of a structure that imposes order and uniformity on apparent difference), television also activates a mobility in which things that do not "belong" together (images, types of texts, discourses, cultural functions) find themselves in close proximity. It is in this sense that I think we can see the practice of superimposition itself as a form of televisual thinking, one both suggested and enabled by television. Godard and Miéville's task here is to promote and prolong television's instability, to radicalize its gestures toward displacement and the promiscuous mixing of elements, rather than counteracting these gestures through the imposition of a fixed structure or the subordination to a single logic or regime of visibility. The fact, however, that this same logic of superimposition and the displacement of boundaries is detectable even in the purely verbal exchanges that dominate *Six fois deux,* however, suggests another way in which we might read the program as a utopian revalencing of existing television practices: this logic does not merely

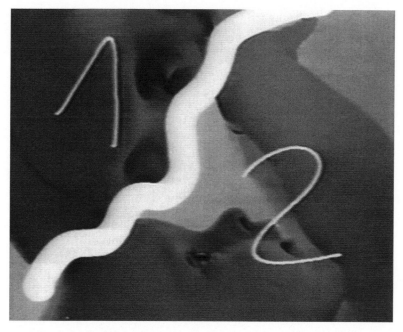

FIGURE 16. Godard uses video technology to write over an image in *Six fois deux* (1976).

provide a way out of the theoretical dead ends that Godard had earlier encountered in his efforts to determine how to generate meaning from images but also suggests a utopian state in which all forms of discourse and practice would be unified. This point of synthesis itself, however, is constantly deferred by the reintroduction of difference.

In many of the series's extensive interviews, found primarily in the "B" sections of each program but also essential to episode 1A ("Y a personne"), Godard often takes on a leading role, acting something like a Socratic schoolmaster guiding the interviewee to a certain insight. He does so not with the questions we might expect of the typical television interviewer (or the pedagogue, for that matter) but with rather strange and almost absurdly simplistic ones. This is the kind of questioning that leads Deleuze to remark on Godard's attempts at "being a foreigner in [his] own language," "Not a stammerer in speech, but a stammerer in language itself."[79] An example of such questioning takes place in episode 1A, in which Godard interviews a young unemployed welder. As he asks him about his work, Godard begins to use the word "weld" *(souder)* in unexpected ways: who, he asks, "welded" the welder to his family? He, he explains, welds as well, welding images together. Developing this metaphorical play to the point that it begins to carry out the kind of superimposition of discourses we noted previously, Godard asks the welder to demonstrate his work using the objects found on the desk in front of them. One of these is a pencil, which Godard suggests might be similar to a welding rod. Offering this cue as a way of starting the process, he then asks the welder to draw analogies between the tools used in welding and those used in writing (what, in writing, is the iron? What are the pieces to be welded? What is the paper?). As in the earlier example of the river, these questions go both ways—they do not serve to interpret writing in terms of welding, or welding in terms of writing, but rather force both activities to exist in the same space, almost magically joined in the hands of the welder wielding the pencil. Once again, two fields (writing and welding; intellectual and manual labor; cultural production and industrial production) are brought together and superimposed on each other, not only revealing unexpected similarities but also suggesting a unity or potential conjunction between all objects and all practices. This potential for all things to be connected leads to the impression that, as Deleuze puts it, "the AND is then no longer even a specific conjunction or relation, but implies all relations; there are as many relations as there are ANDs... the AND... is exactly the creative stammering, the foreign use of language, as opposed to its conforming and dominant use, based on the verb 'to be.'"[80] The act of communication demonstrated here illustrates that Godard's practice of creating "conjunctions" is by no means medium specific: conjunctions and interstices can arise between images, between words and images, or simply through a manner of speaking that transforms the objects and practices we engage in on a daily basis into something else, to make writing both writing AND welding, a pencil both a pencil AND a welding rod.

Godard's interview with mathematician René Thom in episode 5B illustrates a similar superimposition of discourses, but in a far more abstract way, forcing us to question the limits of or the potential problems that might be generated by this technique. By using both inserted images and writing on the image, Godard links the algebraic processes of "capture" and "emission" (in which two quantities become one or one becomes two, respectively) explained by Thom to political discourse: capture is related to Golda Meir's "capture" of Palestinians, while emission becomes illustrative of Mao's dictum "one becomes two." The sense of these linkages, while not merely interpretative, remains unclear: is Godard suggesting that all political phenomena have their counterparts in basic mathematical formulae, hence revealing an order underlying all things? Or perhaps he merely seeks to enliven his political discourse by defamiliarizing it with mathematics? While both plausible, neither of these options seems quite right. What occurs here is more extensive, and less based on any particular rhetorical or artistic aim, than either would suggest: as the process continues, one discourse no longer illustrates or acts on the other, so much as each becomes reducible in terms of the other. This reducibility is represented by Godard's writing of "faux" upon the screen as Thom explains that "capture is more natural than emission" (Figure 17). For Godard this statement is false not in mathematical terms but because it contradicts Mao's theory of contradiction and a dialectical view of nature in which contradictions (one becomes two, emission) and not their resolutions (two becomes one, capture) exist in all phenomena. The claim of "falsity," however, cannot be isolated to any single discourse, once multiple ones have converged. This apparent refusal to differentiate between mathematical, philosophical, and political discourse when making a true/false judgment suggests that Godard's practice of conjunction might lead into the trap of simply equating all things. The infinity of possible "ands" that Deleuze refers to begins to look like the path to the absence of any epistemology and order whatsoever, to a mode of thinking in which conjunction reveals not new ideas but simply false parallels. The danger lies in making everything the same rather than preserving the necessary distance or interstice in the act of superimposition. Yet this very danger is perhaps an intentional and inevitable part of creating conjunctions or interstices, as the potential communication opened up by their creation perpetually threatens to turn into its opposite, a fixed relationship in which terms can always be joined because they are always

FIGURE 17. Both visual and discursive superimpositions take place in *Six fois deux* (1976), as Godard dubs René Thom's lecture on mathematics "false" for political reasons.

reducible to one another. The only way to avoid this problem is to refuse any total unity or synthesis. Although *Six fois deux* imagines a state in which different forms of practice—informing, making art, making a film, welding—begin to become indiscernible, their potential for generating meaning through their increasing proximity itself depends on maintaining separation, on this convergence being provisional or incomplete, rather than a static, achieved state. Difference must be continually reinstantiated, in both language and images.

While the practices demonstrated in *Six fois deux* may seem to lie far from television as we know it, they are nonetheless firmly rooted in it: television serves as a model for the literal superimposition of text or drawing over image, which is revealed as a space of potential creation rather than a way to capture the gaze with each and every tool at one's disposal. It provides the template for the interview, a space in which speech, in Godard and Miéville's reimagining of conventional interview practices, is allowed to meander, to lose itself, and to communicate, rather than degenerating into a set of strictly delimited questions and answers. Finally, the act of superimposition so central to the demonstrations of communication in *Six fois deux* doubles television's cultural collapsing of discourses and functions: what is only virtual, however, in the flow of programming, in which one is still confined to looking at and listening to one thing at a time, is radicalized in moments of extreme convergence that nonetheless refuse to congeal into static unities. Godard and Miéville take the logic of television further than it will ever go itself but turn its status as a cultural catch-all and a repository of heterogeneous images into a generative matrix for new meanings and new ways of seeing.

The domestic spectator of television, meanwhile, is not rejected as atomized or detached from the collective, seeking refuge in the domestic, but rather revalenced as a solitary individual who enters into an intimate relationship with the practitioner, as though reading a postcard from a friend. This postcard, though, presents a challenge and asks the spectator to do the opposite of what conventional television would: not to sit still but to leave her place. The spectator is therefore a partner in the program's operation. This partnership is signaled in episode 6A, which functions as the series's conclusion, as a speaker explains, "We started out in the school of television, and then we did our homework." The homework or school-work *(devoirs)* is, of course, that carried out by the spectator at home (as well as that carried out by Godard and Miéville in their studio-home). But by consenting to this work and this new relationship to television, the spectator has also consented to be moved out of his habitual place, taking up the lesson of *Comment ça va* that one must leave one's place if one is to communicate. The speaker in episode 6A explains what the series has implied throughout, revealing that television is at least potentially an interstice that moves and redefines both of the terms between which it emerges: "Television. It is neither me nor you. You are not in your place on television, only television is in its place." What allows for television to be communicative is its capacity to function as an interstice rather than illusorily reinforcing the spectator's sense of mastery over that which he views on it, its allowing the *ailleurs* to penetrate into the *ici,* thereby displacing and transforming both. The very apparatus that Godard will spend much of the remainder of his career attacking becomes, for a moment, the interstice par excellence, its utopian potential salvaged.

The clear absence in Godard and Miéville of any final moment of synthesis, in which all difference and distinction between discourses and practices would be erased, staves off the sense of finality or death that accompanies many utopian imaginings and avoids the mistake of imagining that some final goal has been reached. It also, however, demonstrates the distance that remains, for better or worse, between what can be achieved and implemented and what exists as a speculative exercise in thought. *Six fois deux* is, as mentioned earlier, quite aware of this gap, which surfaces in the program as a pervasive pessimism and sense of failure. Much like Odette in *Comment ça va?*, Godard seems to anticipate the project's untenability just as he demonstrates its desirability and efficacy. Episode 6A, as though to indicate this unrealizability, ends mid-sentence, cutting off as the speaker imagines what television could be: "Television is always an image of something that can be . . . can show people . . ." Although one final interview follows, in which Godard speaks to two patients at a mental hospital (those who communicate differently, just as the series seeks to "do television differently"), this conclusion suggests an interruption of communication as well as the rude awakening from a utopian dream. Similarly, as Godard discusses television with the journalists from *Libération* in episode 2B, the following words, a citation of Brecht that will come up again in *Histoire(s) du cinéma*, appear on the screen: "With care, I examine my plan. It is unrealizable." If this is indeed correct, then *why* is it correct? *Six fois deux* would in fact garner Godard one of his largest audiences to date, yet even this large figure was too low to make an impact in the television ratings scale: the series had 200,000–250,000 viewers, "which means that we were below the rating indexes because we didn't have even 1% [of viewership], so we weren't noted, but there were all the same 200,000–250,000 spectators, and I have never had 250,000 spectators."[81] France 3, meanwhile, was concerned about airing the series because of its "difficulty" and prefaced it with a disclaimer noting that it did not "offer the usual technical characteristics" of their programs.[82] To lessen the damage, they broadcast the series during a low season, on

Sunday nights from July 25 to August 29, in order to, as Godard puts it, "fill the holes of a television on vacation."[83]

Despite positive press reactions from *Le Monde* and *Le Nouvel Observateur*, other publications dealing more specifically with television, as well as the Association of Journalists and News Photographers, were positively hostile to the program, objecting to the intrusion of the "cinéaste" into the living room and condemning the show as a misuse of public funds.[84] Such reactions are particularly significant in that they demonstrate that the boundaries of television as an institution had been transgressed: art and experimentation were rejected as not belonging on public television and their creator painted as a kind of public nuisance or parasite, siphoning off the hard-earned money of the viewers to support his own eccentricities. Godard's anticipation of marginalization and suppression proved, like Odette's, to be correct, as the series met with resistance in governmental (FR3), cultural (the press), and popular (low ratings) spheres. Later, Godard spoke of this failure in terms that make the program's utopian self-conception explicit. Asked by MacCabe how he would respond to charges that his television series were boring, he states, "No, the trouble is that you can't see their exhilaration—the exhilaration in all my work. They don't suit the time that you're looking at them because you're obliged to live in this society."[85] Here Godard seems to be saying that the reason the series are so difficult to appreciate is because they come from another time; these are works that imagine themselves as something like a future television, one that does not explicitly imagine some utopian condition but rather imagines what its television, its communication, would look like and transmits it to us from another world.

Despite the poor ratings figures, *Six fois deux* found its fair share of supporters, among them Marcel Jullian, the director of France's second state channel, Antenne 2.[86] Impressed with Godard and Miéville's first foray into television, Jullian proposed that they film an adaptation of *Le Tour de la France par deux enfants*, an 1877 educational book by Augustine Fouillée (pseudonymously known as "G. Bruno") about two orphans who travel through France used in Third Republic schools.[87] While Godard and Miéville would stick to the format proposed by Jullian—twelve episodes of twenty-six minutes each—they retained little else. The book details a journey across France, in which the two children learn various crafts, about the "great men" of French history, and about the moral values of the nation. Godard and Miéville dispense with these "lessons" but find the book's form, in its combination of words and pictures, to be something of a precursor to modern television, noting "the triple relation between engravings (already photographs), their legends, and the reality of the text."[88] The combination of image, written text, and speech in the television series thus mimics the book's usage of engravings, legends, and text. While the two children are retained from the book as well, the film clearly does not function as a children's primer. More importantly, it does not continue the method of *Six fois deux,* in which communication, displacement, and pedagogy comprised the moments of a single movement. While the superimposition of discourses and the overall theme of grids or schemas and the need to break free from them remains, *France tour* lacks the informational, pedagogical character of the previous program. It uses television to comment on television, but without positing the same sort of replacement or synthesis of informational and aesthetic imperatives we find in *Six fois deux.* As Philippe Dubois, who describes *Six fois deux* as Godard's "last political film," argues, *France tour* "is more the announcement of what will come at the beginning of the eighties: a writing in which one senses the dawning of a more philosophical and poetic perspective, turned rather toward artistic creation than toward a social problematic."[89]

France tour follows two children, Camille and Arnaud, as they go about the tasks of their daily lives: going to school, eating dinner, watching television, getting ready for bed, and so forth. Each of the twelve episodes follows a similar structure, usually beginning with a scene of a child engaged in some activity at home, school, or outside. This sequence is then followed by one titled "Vérité," in which Godard interviews one of the two children.[90] The interview is interrupted, and then commented upon, by two presenters, who are introduced with the title "Télévision" and who close the program with a short essay or meditation titled "Histoire." This division into parts suggests both the serial structure of many television programs and an effort to juxtapose several types of program (interview, news report, drama) within each episode. Here, even more strongly than in *Six fois deux,* Godard and Miéville mimic and distort television conventions, as though creating an alternative form of media that is all the more strange and uncanny because of its familiarity. The greater part of the series's running time, however, is devoted to Godard's interviews with the two children, who may be able to teach us about how we have become what we are: adults, called "monsters" in the series, are never spoken to but only about. The monsters, the voice-over tells us, "have invented machines that dictate a series of orders which they obey.... Other monsters fight against this system.... For eight hours [they] place themselves at the disposition of the great military-industrial complexes." While the subjects Godard discusses with the children are quite varied, ranging from the political to the existential to the grammatical, Constance Penley argues that the series's guiding argument is one about how the "monsters" reproduce themselves, submitting their children to rigid divisions of time and space and disciplining their minds and bodies.[91] Penley's interpretation tellingly suggests that *France tour,* more than *Six fois deux,* is a thematically driven argument or essay rather than a demonstration or enactment of a method of communication. Television here serves as a metonym for all of the grids that are imposed upon our perceptions and our daily lives, and the use of its forms constitutes a commentary upon these grids more broadly. While the program still creates a television that mimics and transforms the existing one, then, it does so more as critique than as the positing of an alternative or its utopian imagining.

While *France tour* abandons the direct effort at communication made by *Six fois deux,* it nonetheless enacts a displacement of conventional television structures. Television scheduling and practices represent, after all, one of the ways of dividing time that affects the lives of Godard and Miéville's subjects. By disrupting them as they examine other forms of regulation, Penley argues, Godard and Miéville aim "to intervene into both the rhythms, regulations and repetitions of television narrative as well as these same monitorings in the fiction of daily life."[92] Whereas similar displacements in *Six fois deux* seemed to demonstrate and enact how the breaking of boundaries could restructure our perceptions of and relationship with the world, here they function almost parodically: they do not constitute an effort to "move" the spectator so much as a kind of mirror-television, a form whose distortion of established conventions is meant to make a statement rather than to function instrumentally. The link between form and displacement, in short, has been broken; the circulation of images is no longer identified with information, or communication with their successful displacement. In a corresponding shift, communication no longer takes place on-screen, from one party to the other, as it did in *Six fois deux*. Despite the length of Godard's conversations with the children, one never gets the sense that he is speaking to them so much as he is using them as a kind of artistic raw material. Indeed, it is difficult to see Godard and his interviewees here as equal parties in the conversation; as Claire Strohm puts it, contrasting the series with *Six fois deux*, "how can one speak of communication or exchange when it is a matter of imposing his vision of the world, of speaking from a territory or a border about which the children and the spectator, perhaps, have not the faintest idea?"[93] Whereas Godard seemed in *Six fois deux* to genuinely displace his interlocutors, here he seems more to confuse and irritate them. The children, perhaps, are more difficult to move from the grid because they have not yet fully entered it.

The most commented-upon aspect of the program, which deserves further mention here, is its use of slow motion, a technique that would also be heavily employed in Godard's 1980 return to commercial feature filmmaking, *Sauve qui peut (la vie)*. The use of slow motion in *France tour* constitutes a variation on Godard's long-standing interest in learning how to see differently. Here vision is renewed not by doing away with the various codes that dictate our perception but rather by using technology to access phenomenal reality in a previously unavailable way. This strategy, with its suggestion of both a scientific dissection or analysis and of a superior technologically enhanced perception, recalls not only Vertov but also, as Witt notes, the precinematic experiments of Marey and Muybridge.[94] While the stopping and starting of images—such as those of Camille dressing for bed in the series's first episode—reminds us that the stream of images we see does in fact comprise a series of stills, it also reveals the number of opportunities for difference and variation contained both in those images and in the movements they register. The ability to freeze and unfreeze on any single image, using video technology, thus opens up an infinite number of variations within what might otherwise seem to be single unique images. As Godard puts it,

> as soon as one stops one image in a movement that has twenty-five of them . . . one perceives that in the shot that one filmed, depending on how one stops it, there are all of a sudden thousands of possibilities, all of the possible permutations between these twenty-five images represent thousands of possibilities.[95]

This method of decomposition and analysis leads to the revelation of a previously undetectable freedom: the slowed-down movements demonstrate the range of expressive possibilities available to the filmmaker and to our own bodies. Here Godard and Miéville no longer allow a single image to be opened up by its juxtaposition with or superimposition onto another but by finding difference already inherent within it.

This shift seems to draw Godard back toward cinema: *France tour* privileges the act of looking over that of communicating or displacing, returns the question of motion to the image itself, rather than its placement or trajectory, and recalls early praise of the manipulation of time as one of cinema's specific capacities. The fate of the series likewise led away from television and back toward cinema: by the time the series was completed, its commissioner, Marcel Jullian, had been replaced at Antenne 2 by a less sympathetic party, who refused to show the series on the grounds that it contained "technical problems."[96] The series was shown instead at the Rotterdam Film Festival in 1979 (despite having been finished in early 1978), in a special screening by *Cahiers du cinéma,* and at the Centre Pompidou.[97] Only two years after its completion, in April 1980, would it be broadcast, and then not as intended, as a twelve-episode series, but in three large blocks in a time slot reserved for great filmmakers ("Ciné-club").[98] Television, as Godard had predicted in *Six fois deux,* proved to be an untenable space for his experiments, simply because of their inability to surmount its closely guarded frontiers, and he strongly objected to the relocation of the program, claiming that "the time of broadcast was deliberately chosen to wreck my work."[99] As he commented in 1975,

> making cinema or television, technically, is sending twenty five postcards per second to millions of people . . . but no one has the means to do it, except for those who are at once everyone and no one, for example, the ORTF [French national television], or [media conglomerates] Thompson or Publicis.[100]

The increasing difficulty of finding a space in which to imagine a different television seemed to foreclose the possibility of any further utopian experiments. As though it could no longer be mobilized by television, a form whose promise appeared to be quickly fading away as deregulation and privatization loomed on the horizon, utopian thinking would seek different venues and raw materials as the 1980s began.

5

Utopia after Television

MEDIA MUTATIONS AND TRANSPLANTATIONS

By the early 1980s, European television had begun to undergo a dramatic transformation: far more than ever before, the principles (however loose and elastic) that had informed public service broadcasting and state control over broadcasting more broadly were being challenged and, in many cases, undermined through legislative and judicial action. Godard and Miéville's 1985 essay film *Soft and Hard* (produced by the United Kingdom's Channel 4, itself the result of a compromise between public and private broadcasting, a public network partially funded by the private ITV through advertising revenues) announces the importance of this change by reminding us of its historical context at its outset: "It was the era of the triumph of private television." Godard and Miéville's use of the word "triumph" implies that a battle had taken place and that the old public service model had lost. My contention in this chapter will be that as a result of this battle's outcome and the drastic changes that began in the 1970s and had been fully realized by the end of the 1980s—primarily legal deregulation of broadcasting, the erosion of the state monopoly, and the ascendancy of the private model—television's capacity to serve as a fertile site for utopian thinking, and as a set of raw materials that could be transformed and projected forward to imagine its utopian double, were largely undermined. This does not mean that the utopian impulse suddenly vanished from the European media landscape but rather that it tended to be directed elsewhere, rejecting television as a closed or ceded terrain and seeking other forms of media and other geographical locations on which to project itself. By attending to the elements of utopian thought and practice that persist in Godard's and Watkins's post-1970s work, we

179

can observe the sorts of geographical and media sites to which it migrates. The utopian impulse finds new geographical sites in Mozambique (for Godard) and in a denationalized transnational space and a strictly demarcated local one (for Watkins). It finds new media sites, meanwhile, in VHS and nonmediated face-to-face interactions (for Watkins) and, perhaps surprisingly, in cinema (for Godard). By analyzing these relocations, we can also detect changes in utopian thought more broadly: in some cases, it seems to become deeply invested in its own impossibility and preoccupied with the unrealized futures of the past (especially for Godard), whereas in others it adopts modes of thinking that conceive of the utopian gesture in oppositional rather than dialectical terms (especially for Watkins). Both of these tendencies, if read symptomatically, constitute responses to the undermining of postwar liberalism (for which "public service broadcasting," I would argue, can function as a metonym) and the difficulty of imagining any possible alternatives to the regimes that displaced it. This is hardly to say, however, that these new regimes (and here the word applies both in the conventional and the Rancièrian senses) do not offer new opportunities themselves: we can read more recent migrations of utopian thought to post–public service forms of media, such as the private television and Internet projects of Alexander Kluge, to which I will turn at this chapter's conclusion, as attempts to imagine utopian forms of media that no longer depend on the raw materials provided by the public service paradigm, thereby suggesting new models for the present and the future.

THE TRIUMPH OF PRIVATE TELEVISION

The move toward private television that so drastically altered Europe's media landscape appeared first in Italy (leaving aside the United Kingdom, which had been under a duopoly since the 1950s), when local commercial cable service was declared legal in 1975: dozens of noncable private television companies began to broadcast shortly after, and in 1976, the Italian Constitutional Court found the RAI monopoly unconstitutional when applied to local broadcasting.[1] Italy opened the floodgates to an almost entirely unregulated private television industry; while there were some limitations (private broadcasters could not network their individual

stations or show national news programs), an official regulatory body
was not established until 1985.[2] The result of this decision, however,
was not ultimately the proliferation of small, independent local stations
that would complement a national broadcaster but the acquisition and
consolidation of many local stations by a single owner, namely, future
prime minister Silvio Berlusconi.[3] By the early 1980s, Berlusconi had attained control of the majority of private television stations, nor was he to
leave the cinema untouched: by 1986, 60 percent of all film production
benefited from his financing.[4]

   In France, the privatization process came later (allowing Berlusconi
to get a piece of the pie) and met with more resistance but had a similarly
profound impact. In 1981, François Mitterrand ran for president on a
platform that advocated the "decentralization" and "pluralization" of radio
and television broadcasting, and a 1982 law declared audiovisual communication "free," putting an end to the state monopoly.[5] The year 1984
saw the establishment of Europe's first pay channel, Canal Plus (which
would go on to provide most of the funding for Godard's *Histoire(s) du
cinéma*), initially co-owned by state companies and private interests but
now a subsidiary of Vivendi.[6] In 1986, two new national commercial
networks (Le Cinq, largely controlled by Berlusconi, and M6) were
established, while in 1987, the state channel TF1 was privatized.[7] Part of
Mitterrand's strategy was to focus on public service rather than monopoly,
affirming that one could have the latter without the former;[8] Canal Plus's
concession to operate defined it as a public service broadcaster, yet it was
subject to very few guidelines.[9] Whether one believes that public service
can ultimately survive within the private sphere or not, the fact remains
that France's media landscape had almost completely changed in only a
few short years.

   The United Kingdom retained a greater stability than Italy or France
throughout the 1980s, although it established the previously mentioned
Channel 4 in 1980, then Sky Satellite (and later cable) television in
1982. Aggressive pushes were made to implement broadcasting reform,
culminating in a 1988 white paper that laid out plans for a move to a free-
market model. These plans aimed not to dismantle the BBC but rather
to transform the private but government-regulated ITV, selling off its

franchises to the highest bidder. A less dramatic version of the proposed changes was implemented in 1990, establishing a new regulatory body (the Independent Television Commission) that could grant broadcasting licenses for ten-year periods and a fifth national channel (the private Channel 5). Further satellite and pay channels were also established by the end of the decade.[10]

The implications of the advent of private television were monumental. As a producer for ZDF, one of Germany's public channels, remarked in 1994, "We had lots of money, a large audience, and with no competition, an excellent reputation. We could show what we wanted when we wanted, and success was almost guaranteed.... And then, we woke up and understood that we had lost our paradise."[11] To begin with, there were simply far more images available in Europe than ever before, a situation that completely undermined the monopoly logic of public service television. The pressure of competition often led public service broadcasters to more closely resemble their commercial counterparts, in terms of both their economic functioning and their programming.[12] The educational and cultural imperatives of public service largely fell by the wayside, sacrificed to competition: the sorts of programming that had been staples of the BBC (arts, documentaries, children's programs) were replaced by more serial drama and light entertainment on the main BBC channels and later found homes on the BBC's digital channels, indicating their marginalization and transformation into "niche" programming.[13] Italy's RAI responded to the challenge by increasing its entertainment programming from 18 to 57 percent, while "cultural, educational, children's, and other programming" fell from 73 to 32 percent.[14] Commercial channels were in most cases free to broadcast whatever they wished, and the changes in France's TF1's programming before and after its privatization make the differences between the two formats clear: in its very first year as a commercial channel, it ceased all documentary and educational programs, replacing them with entertainment shows that were often either directly modeled on American ones or simply imported from the United States.[15] The shift toward massive amounts of imported programming was typical across the continent, corresponding with a decline in European production.[16]

It was not, however, simply the character of the programming that was at stake but the whole concept of television itself, what it had meant and could mean in practice and in the cultural imagination. Television became, for one thing, less distinctly European and far more American, owing to the imitation and importation of American content. Nor, as French legislators argued in 1986, was it to be considered a public service.[17] It was no longer assumed that television, as Blumler puts it, should be approached "from a standpoint of social ethics, associating it with a cluster of values to be pursued purposively," and its public service mission was replaced by the "capture of the audience-as-market as the prime normative and pragmatic goal."[18] This turn away from the public service model corresponded, Umberto Eco argues, with a turn away from the outside world itself, as television increasingly came to function as a self-enclosed system: "Whereas Paleo-TV talked about the external world, or pretended to, Neo-TV talks about itself and about the contact that it establishes with its own public."[19] The new television insisted not on its usefulness but on its presence for and with the viewer, "emphasizing the needs of the individual and consumption rather than the communal or social principles which had underpinned PSB."[20]

This last characteristic suggests the extent to which this change reflects not only a larger ideological shift but also a dismantling of long-established hierarchies of power (which, in the case of countries like Italy and France, were perfectly willing and able to use broadcasting to pursue political agendas). As Franco "Bifo" Berardi, Marco Jacquemet, and Gianfranco Vitali note, the rise of Berlusconi (with the aid of Socialist prime minister Bettino Craxi) signaled both the ascendancy of a new class that "secularized" Italy, undercutting the established "churches" of Catholicism and Communism, and "the economic transition from an organic industrial system to a polymorphous infoproduction system."[21] These political and economic transitions were accompanied, as Eco suggests, by a turn to new modes of televisual communication. Previously one could still count on broadcasters to categorize different types of audiovisual information differently and thereby prescribe a particular kind of reading for each kind of text, even if programs like those of Watkins and Godard revealed the futility and danger of doing so. Private television finally eradicated the remnants of this precarious regime, Mauro Wolf argues, marking "the end of television's pedagogic model with its distinct scheduling divisions, rigidly balanced between the clearly separate communicative functions of entertainment, education and information."[22] Instead we find the "different communicative functions . . . firmly and continually linked to one another."[23]

As I argued in chapter 1, television had threatened to carry out this kind of collapsing of different forms of communication or practice and their corresponding modes of reception very early on, but older ways of conceiving of cultural categories (the radical separation of information from entertainment, or even from the image itself, the division between "reality" and fiction) provided a kind of check or containment. The practitioners of utopian television had detected the disruptions that this collapsing enacted on the *partage du sensible* and used them to imagine another future *partage* and the kind of media that it would allow. With the advent of private television, however, the disruptions that public service television had resisted were fully embraced and turned to the ends of commerce and power. In short, the utopian possible future suggested by television's most subversive attributes when they remained in some way hidden or "underground" became a dystopian real one upon their "above-ground" adoption by private television, which greatly reduced the possibility of using them to imagine something else. The barriers that previously kept the different types of discourse and apprehension mobilized by television in their place have arguably ceased to govern our cultural logic at all. As Berardi and his colleagues put it, noting the failure of forces on the center-left to anticipate this development due to their continuing adhesion to older ways of thinking, "television is not a medium for the creation of consensus or for a kind of rational persuasion. . . . Television is a means of pervasion, rather than persuasion. It operates on the cognitive modalities for reception, interpretation and decision, rather than on the ideological content of the message."[24] It was precisely this capacity that Watkins and Godard embraced (while Rossellini still clung, at least on the surface, to a model in which separation and containment could be achieved), yet the triumph of private television turned it to entirely different ends.

With the "triumph of private television," television—on the level of both actual practice and what could be imagined by taking that practice as its starting point—and utopian thinking move further apart. The most obvious solution to this problem would be simply to posit an anticommercial utopian television (a description we might assign to Watkins's *The Journey,* to which I will return shortly), one that rejects all aspects of television as it exists in order to fight against the new privatized media; in this case, something like an all-out declaration of war replaces the dialectical transformations of the past. This turn toward pure negation rather than dialectical transformation, in turn, creates new dangers: any attempt to replace television risks simply being an inverted reflection of what is rather than finding the seeds of what could be within it, unless one is willing to find new utopian possibilities within the very same conditions that destroyed the old ones.

These problems also raise wider historical and geopolitical implications, which extend far beyond media and necessitate a dramatic reconfiguration of the utopian impulse and its venues. At its broadest level, the decline of public service broadcasting and of television as a utopian site suggests the foreclosure of a particular historical narrative: if television itself was a powerful symbol of modernity, even futurity, its mutation suggests the end of that modernity and, perhaps, the closing off of the future that it occasionally revealed to us. In more concrete political terms, the triumph of private TV illustrates a broader abandonment of the public (as space or venue and as a collective viewership rather than a fragmented series of niches or markets); the destruction of an imaginary that could be seen, however dubiously, as the voice of a nation (hence collective); and the shift from a national media framework (which allows for television to speak as the voice of the state, understood as a set of civil institutions separate from private enterprise) to an international one (with the same owners, such as Berlusconi, controlling television in multiple countries). Television disintegrates as though in response to the Thatcherite dismissal of "society" itself. The privatization of the European airwaves, furthermore, corresponds roughly with the fall of Soviet Communism—that other lost utopia whose very existence served, at least in the West, as a sign of possible difference, a physically and imaginarily separate space.

It is hardly any surprise that utopian thought wanes in such circumstances, giving way instead to a condition, as Jameson characterizes it, marked by "a weakening of historicity or of the sense of the future; a conviction that fundamental change is no longer possible, however desirable."[25] Meanwhile, "omnipresent consumerism, having become an end in itself, is transforming the daily life of the advanced countries in such a way as to suggest that the Utopianism of multiple desires and consumption is already here and needs no further development."[26] Owing to the first factor, utopian thinking seeks an absolute "elsewhere" or an "outside" that can only negate rather than imaginatively transform what exists; owing to the second, meanwhile, it simultaneously becomes more likely to mistake the "already here" for the utopian, even within the context of the most seemingly oppositional projects. We find both of these movements in the late work of Peter Watkins, which provides an exemplary illustration of the new problems (and problematic solutions) that a utopian approach to media encounters after its rejection of television.

PETER WATKINS AND THE MONOFORM

Beginning in the 1980s, Watkins broke dramatically with the model he had used from his BBC works until the late 1970s. Broadly speaking, the shifts that Watkins carried out demonstrated an increasing distrust of and contempt for television as an institution, technology, and language. The alternative types of media that he formulated, however, tended to focus far more on new modes of production than his past works had, while showing little concern for the finished product. While his emphasis on transforming the production process in many ways recalls the collective film projects of the post-1968 moment, and seems to resonate more broadly with a "political modernist" approach, I will contend here that Watkins's post-1970s work is motivated by a very different set of assumptions and strategies than those of the works it resembles. In fact, films like *The Journey* (1987) and *La Commune (Paris, 1871)* (2000), while similar to earlier radical works in their emphasis on collective production, appeal to processes of denaturalization and defamiliarization, polemical approach, and tendency to treat the filmmaking process as an event-in-itself or "happening," are deeply informed by the changes brought about by the rise of private television and the political processes of which this rise was a symptom. They seek to respond to these changes and aspire (in many ways, far more openly than Watkins's earlier works) to the status of utopian projects, yet at the same time, they fall into deadlocks or contradictions that arise due to their substitution of a dialectical approach with a more purely oppositional one.

The shift in Watkins's attitude toward television and media more broadly emerged as a result of his deeper engagement with media analysis through research and courses taught at Columbia University in the mid-1970s, during which he and his students investigated the formal language of television news.[27] This research ultimately led to Watkins's formulation of the concept of the "Monoform," an idea most fully elaborated in his book *Media Crisis,* first published in 2003 in French. The Monoform, Watkins explains,

> is the one single language form now used to edit and structure cinema films, TV programmes.... The result is a language form wherein spatial fragmentation, repetitive time rhythms, constantly moving camera, rapid staccato editing, dense bombardment of sound, and lack of silence or reflective space, play a dominant and aggressive role.[28]

As a result of this uniformity, all content supposedly comes to carry the same charge, neutralized by form to such a point that all things seem to be of equal importance and value. An issue of great historical importance, such as slavery, which in itself would seem to carry the capacity to be shocking or destabilizing, is in *Roots* thus neutralized by being structured according to the same models as *Kojak* or *Love Story.*[29] These observations echo Jean Baudrillard's argument, already referenced in chapter 1 in relation to the idea that television imposes a uniform model on everything it broadcasts, about the way different classes of events enter into a kind of homogenizing totality as they "take part in the same process of political signification ... a closed system of models of signification from which no event escapes."[30] For Baudrillard, any political act, simply in being presented by the media, is in fact depoliticized by its subjection to a common register of enunciation and symbolic meaning: "transgression and subversion never get 'on the air' without being subtly negated as they are: transformed into models, neutralized into signs, they are eviscerated of their meaning."³¹ Similarly, Watkins believes that no politically radical (or even slightly critical) message or content can be expressed via the Monoform without losing its subversive power.

It is quite easy to see how this mode of thinking would forbid the dialectical transformation of elements of television that Watkins carried out in his earlier works, because any usage of Monoform elements is seen as locking the text into a "closed system," a form that dominates and distorts, completely crushing any forms of meaning that cannot be adapted to it. This problem is further exacerbated by Watkins's belief (not unlike that of certain film theorists of the post-1968 moment) that this form can only generate one possible relationship with and response from the spectator. Just as Watkins had earlier spoken of his films as a kind of irresistible, even violent attack on the viewer's subjectivity, he now sees the Monoform as a similarly irresistible force that reshapes our mental capacities: it "has led to seriously reduced attention spans; to a lack of tolerance for sustained process or for any form of communication that takes longer than ten seconds; to a growing loss of history (especially among young people); to an increased need for constant change."³² This process of "fragmentation" and perceptual reorientation, in turn, creates an individualist subjectivity no longer willing to participate in any collective behavior.³³ The implications of these ideas for Watkins's previous method are devastating, not only because they more or less rule out any adoption and subversion of the Monoform but also because their focus on the extent to which it tyrannizes and manipulates the spectator suggests the undesirability of *any* rhetorical use of audiovisual texts. This problem, which would seem to forbid any attempt to elicit the sorts of reactions that made *The War Game* so powerful, is the primary source of the contradictions that will be generated in *The Journey* and *La Commune*: if one is ethically prohibited from making an audiovisual work that elicits a strong reaction on the part of the spectator, can there be any point in making one at all? We might read Watkins's shift to an emphasis on collective production over the text-as-object and experience as a way to dodge this question, or at least to shift it to another front.

Watkins's emphasis on developing new production practices illuminates the differences between the Monoform theory and earlier theories
that cover much of the same territory. The concept of the Monoform,
Michael Wayne argues, recalls both Noël Burch's Institutional Mode of
Representation and Colin MacCabe's Classic Realist Text.[34] While on
the surface level, the similarities are clear—all of these theories posit a
dominant mode of production, ideological in its very form, that needs
to be contested through an oppositional formal language—Watkins's
production-centered counterstrategy differs greatly from the ones found
in earlier political modernist forms of practice. The problem of the Monoform's manipulative character, for example, appears to be a reiteration of
the form–spectator problem that arose from the overly deterministic positions of so-called *Screen* theory, which tended to favor theoretical models
that assumed that a single invariable spectator position was dictated by the
hegemonic mode of filmmaking. Such arguments often led to the positing
of counter-cinemas characterized first and foremost by the alteration of
film form, such as the Dziga Vertov Group's *Vent d'est.* Because Watkins
does not seek to create a new form that would also create a new sort of
spectatorial engagement, a strategy that would be overly manipulative
and hierarchical according to the Monoform theory, he abandons the
political modernist practice of political intervention through work on
form. In the Monoform theory, as in much political modernist discourse,
there is still a "bad object," but that object is to be corrected through
work on the level of production rather than by attending to the object's
form and its rhetorical properties; the problem, as we will see, is that
there cannot for Watkins be any good objects but only good processes.
Form can only gain a positive valence if it reflects the good or "correct"
production process, thus leading to a situation in which that "correctness"
is fetishized as an end in itself. This fetishism, as I will explain more fully
later, is underpinned by a form of ethical thinking in which both ends
and means are evaluated above all in terms of where they can be placed
in a bad–good binary opposition rather than in respect to their actual
particularities, functions, and effects.

To be "correct," and thus to evade the dangers of the Monoform, it is
necessary for Watkins that an audiovisual text be produced differently;

what is produced matters far less. While the implications of this problem will become clearer when we turn to an analysis of *The Journey* and *La Commune,* its very logic not only undermines any rhetorical use of audiovisual media but tends in its absolutism to value difference and opposition above all else. Thinking in such terms, it becomes very difficult to imagine another form of media that does not simply create a kind of negative reversal of the one that exists, one that, like the Dziga Vertov Group's *Pravda* and *British Sounds,* can only attest to the wrongness of what is rather than allowing us to glimpse what could be. In such a dualistic system, one can only posit a static negation rather than a dialectical transformation, although in Watkins's case, the main negation is to be that of the mode of production (seen as dictating form) rather than that of form itself.[35]

The two major works of Watkins's post-1970s career, *The Journey* and *La Commune (Paris, 1871),* though undermined by the dualistic and ethical thinking that underlies them and their prioritization of participatory production over finished product, can nonetheless be identified as utopian in character, although in a far different manner from his earlier works. Both of these projects attempt to enact an actualizable utopian program: the teaching and implementation of new media structures and modes of production and, through this, the constitution of new forms of community and relationships. In short, Watkins believes himself not to be creating a representation that enacts a utopian transformation of existing elements but rather to be carrying out a utopian process *directly.* Both works overtly seek to transform the world but do so specifically through the creation of ad hoc microcommunities, which might be described as small-scale models of the kind of ideal self-governing communities that would characterize a utopian society. In this sense, they are both concrete projects and representations, insofar as they are in some way obliged to "figure" their utopias. These figures are not, however, treated as art; they are not detached from any particular desired response or end, as *Punishment Park* was, nor do they embrace the utopian method as a means of speculation. Rather, they represent something more like instructions or commands, as though offering a manual for how to construct a utopian community. Watkins thus moves from the category of what Russell Jacoby calls "iconoclastic utopians," who "longed, waited, or worked for utopia but did not visualize it," to that of "blueprint utopians."[36] He does not use the audiovisual as a tool to imagine what could be, creating a text that hails us from a world yet to come, but rather insists on creating a replacement for the existing media (and, in *La Commune,* perhaps even a replacement of society as a whole) in the here and now. This leads to a categorical confusion, in which the very process Watkins is carrying out risks being identified with the utopian political goal to be achieved and thus treated as an end in itself. As we will see, it is perhaps in this respect that his works are particularly symptomatic of our present "posthistorical" world: rather than using the actual to imagine and construct the future, they largely fail to look beyond the present, unmediated moment.

WATKINS'S UTOPIAS

The Journey, shot between 1984 and 1986 and shown at the Berlin Film Festival in 1987, was primarily financed by the National Film Board of Canada and broadcast on a handful of local television stations in Canada and the United States. The fourteen-hour-long film treats the subjects of militarization (especially nuclear proliferation), government spending on the arms race, and global poverty and was produced with and features individuals from around the world (Scotland, the United States, Canada, Polynesia, France, the USSR, Mozambique, Japan).[37] The ambitious and unprecedented scope of the film suggests an effort to break out of the model Watkins had followed in Europe (first in the United Kingdom, then in Scandinavia throughout the 1970s): while it received financing from a public institution (the National Film Board), it was not a production of a state television network. It rejects, in its extreme length, the parameters of the usual film or television program, nor does it employ the clearly televisual language that marked Watkins's earlier films. Furthermore, it refuses to conceive of its public or its participants as national in character, replacing the collective national public as addressee with the individual nuclear family and a nationally delimited cast and crew with an international one.

The Journey's international participants are questioned by Watkins, usually as families and usually in their own homes, about their knowledge of the global arms race, the effects of nuclear weapons, their preparedness for nuclear attack, and international politics. They are also asked to reflect on their relationship to the mass media and other channels of information (educational institutions, government, the family itself). Watkins provides the families and other individuals with information about these subjects, including photographs and visual aids (charts, diagrams, etc.) that seek to communicate the scale of the arms race and spending on it. Additional individuals who are depicted and given the opportunity to speak include antinuclear activists and community groups, survivors of World War II (including a number of survivors of the nuclear bombings of Hiroshima and Nagasaki), and residents of areas of French Polynesia used for nuclear testing. Other segments of the film depict the families involved taking part in simulations of either nuclear attack or evacuation prior to nuclear attack, staged by Watkins. A final thread analyzes media coverage of the 1985 Shamrock Summit held in Ottawa between Canadian prime minister Brian Mulroney and U.S. president Ronald Reagan, revealing how news reports about the event promote certain perceptions of it and marginalize others, particularly by refusing to depict or listen to any of the many protestors present at the summit. This tightly controlled, exclusionary form of media serves as a foil to Watkins's form, as he dedicates hours to those who are not normally given the chance to speak publicly. As in his earlier films, Watkins serves as narrator for *The Journey* (although he is only seen on-screen near the very end of the film), adopting a voice that is at once knowledgeable and fallible, both to reflect his own biases and to disavow any position of authority held in relation to the viewer. All of these components are presented in tandem: rather than being arranged episodically, the film alternates throughout between all of its participants and all of the levels of discourse that it engages in, an approach Watkins first developed in *Edvard Munch* (1973) and *The Seventies People* (1974).

The Journey marks Watkins's first attempt at a truly collaborative and collectively authored production as well as his first attempt to treat the participants in the film, rather than the spectators, as pedagogical subjects, an approach informed by his teaching experience. Scholar and filmmaker Ken Nolley, who collaborated with Watkins on *The Journey,* explains that the film was intended to challenge "the idea of traditional

authorship and ownership in the cinema in a powerful way, attempting
to give greater voice and control to the many people who participated in
the process of its production, making them active, participating subjects
rather than passive, manipulated objects."[38] In its early stages, however,
the film seems to reproduce a very conventional pedagogical process in
which the pupils are treated as the unknowing objects of the master.
While Watkins begins his work with each family by showing them charts
and photographs, he seems to recognize that such information itself is
useless, insofar as it fails to break through defenses (both ideological
and perceptual) that prevent real engagement, and it is here that an apparently unquestioning return to the aggression of his earlier approach
becomes necessary. His interaction with the families takes on the tone
of a confrontation rather than a simple discussion, as the participants are
asked if they were previously aware of the information with which they
are presented, if they had discussed it at school or in their families, and
how it makes them feel. If they have not discussed it in their families,
Watkins asks them why not and forces them to reconcile their supposed
concern with the fact that they do not share it at home or in the work-
place. His role, then, metamorphoses from schoolmaster (as conveyer of
information) to something like a radicalized psychoanalyst (or, if one is
less sympathetic, a bully), forcing confrontation with both exterior and
interior conflicts that have been repressed and eliciting an autocritique.
Paradoxically, this forced confrontation simply relocates the attack on
domestic space carried out via television in *The War Game* onto a direct
person-to-person level; Watkins has not abandoned, as his rhetoric might
suggest, a hierarchical and antagonistic relationship with his subjects but
has simply shifted it to a more immediate (and, I would argue, less effective) level. Rather than smuggling his message into the domestic space
through television, Watkins must literally enter it to interact with his
audience, who in turn have taken on the (dubious) guise of "participants."
This shift from mediated communication to face-to-face communication,
which in its failure to do away with a hierarchical relationship between
filmmaker and his audience/participant shows itself to be more concerned
with "correct" production procedure than with its actual dynamics and
effects, is symptomatic of a broader shift toward an insistence that what

is valuable and radical must take place in the here and now, and in the form of an unmediated subjective experience. Whereas *Culloden* and *The War Game* both sought to create an intense perceptual experience for the spectator while jamming or subverting habitual modes of apprehension, here the only form of experience granted any value is one that entails doing something oneself, in person, in the here and now. One must do something "active" and "participatory" rather than being moved to new forms of experience by aesthetic objects. Having forced confrontations with his participants in the discussions described earlier, Watkins thus asks the families to move to the level of practice: unlike in the earlier films, in which the viewing of a staged scene was cast as capable of generating knowledge, here it is the *participation* in such a scene that is meant to generate knowledge. The film self-validates this approach, as participants in Watkins's nuclear attack simulations comment on the enlightening, empowering force of these experiences after their completion, attesting to their capacity for altering subjectivity and producing new kinds of knowledge. The spectator, meanwhile, can only watch, because knowledge is now treated as something that must be attained through practice. The only possible value of the enactments to the spectator, as Scott MacDonald notes, is as models, or as I suggested earlier, as a set of instructions: "the dramatizations are less interesting as film spectacle than as models of processes that could be developed by community groups, schools, and local media to assist people in informing themselves about the practical implications of current political and social policies."[39] The abandonment of the spectator necessitated by the Monoform critique, which would see any form of audiovisual rhetoric as inherently tyrannical, not only devalues (or even forbids) a focus on the finished product but also implicitly denigrates the act of spectatorship itself.

The Journey does, however, suggest how utopian hopes might be transferred to another form of media seen as outside the established system: home VCRs and video cameras are here positioned as the "off-the-grid" and personalized alternative to the anonymous public address and invariable position of the addressee characteristic of the Monoform. A dialectical approach to television is substituted by a hope placed in a new form of technology, which now takes on the status of enclave or co-optable space formerly assigned to television. Here, however, the dynamic of the earlier works, which critiqued the very tools they worked with, is replaced by one in which the medium assigned utopian potential is cast, at least on the surface, as purely positive and as a neutral means of communication and community formation. *The Journey* proposes a final step toward engagement to its participants: they are meant to serve as the core of a network of video-based communication that will span the globe, allowing such conversations and confrontations as Watkins has staged to continue and to offer the possibility of international activism.[40] Such a network never materialized, but the creation of one would be attempted once again with *La Commune*. Both films call on their participants to essentially duplicate what they have already carried out, once again demonstrating a far more deterministic attitude toward their subjects than the rather open-ended earlier films, which were content to elicit an emotional reaction without proposing solutions. Speculation and orientation toward a far-off goal are discouraged in favor of immediate results. Audiovisual work thus functions not as a unique mode of thinking that can be used to spur political practice but rather as a double of political practice, albeit a compensatory and unsuccessful one.

Watkins's proposal of a VHS-based international network is also problematic insofar as it contradicts and is ultimately undermined by his insistence on nonmediation and face-to-face interaction. The very form of media that here seems to fill the void left by television is positioned not as a way to go beyond existing circumstances, as a new tool offering new possibilities, but rather as a kind of substitute or second-best solution, which is implicitly lamented more than it is championed. This is because the film predominantly models situations that require the physical co-presence of the director and the participants. While *The Journey* appeals to home video as a material to be used, it is clear that for Watkins, the most important work connected to the series takes place face-to-face, when he speaks to families or directs them in staged emergency scenarios. VHS stands as the "prosthesis" for this process, not in the sense of being, as Marshall McLuhan would put it, an "extension of man" but rather in the sense of being a poor substitute.[41] While a prosthetic use of VHS might suggest a familiar utopian scenario, in which media is cast as extension of the self and as a tool for two-way communication, rather than as a "form" in itself, this utopian thrust is countered through the insistence that media can *only* ever be a substitute for something else. Coupled with *The Journey*'s implication that any mediated position or process is undesirable, this renders the film's placement of VHS far from a utopian technology; its raw materials are not used to imagine its transformation but rather refer us to an altogether different medium (or, better, the lack of one) that is taken as prior and preferable to it. The movement is not forward but backward.

The terms of *The Journey* project, even if we imagine it as an attempt to create independent and nonhierarchical media structures rather than a text or object, imply that any media consumption (including that of the film itself) is essentially passive and of little value when compared to "active" practice. Though I have already touched on some of the effects that this assumption has in terms of creating internal contradictions within the project, it can also be read as a manifestation of an overall theoretical orientation with a long history in leftist art and thinking about art and culture: just as Watkins's later work echoes many of the tenets of political modernist film theories, it is also rooted in paradigms of art that seek to turn the consumer into a producer. When read within their "belated" historical context, however, we can begin to see how Watkins's use of these paradigms transforms them into (or perhaps even reveals them to be, as though allowing us a kind of retrospective clarity) antiutopian vehicles of ideological maintenance. While I would not contend that any iteration of a strategy to turn spectators or consumers into producers necessarily falls victim to these problems—obviously the huge range and differing historical situations of such works forbid any such generalizations—I think that such strategies have become particularly problematic in the past twenty-five years or so and that the way they operate in Watkins's work illuminates these problems and their relationship with utopian thinking and practices in the present.

Not viewing but rather taking part in the process of production, "becoming producer," is valorized as the end state of Watkins's utopian project. He thus creates a dynamic in which action is valued over spectatorship, practice over contemplation or aesthetic experience; the former terms are associated with the acquisition of knowledge and positive political action, the latter with their opposites. These premises structure a familiar set of oppositions constructed in discourses about art that persist from Plato to Debord. These oppositions can be reduced, Rancière argues, to "one basic formula":

> Viewing is the opposite of knowing: the spectator is held before an appearance in a state of ignorance about the process of production of this appearance and about the reality it conceals. Second, it is the opposite of acting: the spectator remains immobile in her seat, passive. To be a spectator is to be separated from both the capacity to know and the power to act.[42]

Watkins's move from the imagining of another television to the planning of grassroots media education and activism frames itself as shifting the viewer from a position of spectatorship, passivity, and ignorance to one of activity, production, and knowledge, but conceives of that activity in a way that denigrates any spectatorial activity and makes production a fetishized end-in-itself, the ethically correct position among the oppositions Rancière describes. It is unclear, however, to what extent such oppositions need to be identified specifically with art; we might instead read their application to the spectatorial situation as a metaphor, in which terms that are viewed as ethical and/or political in character are only metaphorically present in the structure of an artwork or performance; the passivity of the spectator, in other words, is not the same as the passivity of the disengaged or oppressed citizen. As Claire Bishop notes of participatory art (a category in which we might place *The Journey*) and its relationship to politics, "artistic models of democracy have only a tenuous relationship to actual forms of democracy."[43] The same idea holds even if one sees Watkins's project as one that has nothing to do with art at all: in this case it would be the activity of "production" itself, detached from any artistic specificity, that serves as the site of a metaphorical projection of the political, as though participatory and collaborative forms of production were somehow inherently politically progressive or valuable. When viewed in relation to Watkins's far more "aesthetic" earlier works, however, it is also tempting to see the switch of emphasis from spectator to participant as an effort to transition from one form of practice to another, from art to politics, as though by changing the characteristics of the work–spectator relationship one could qualitatively change the field in which the work existed and functioned. To stop being a spectator means to act, hence to "do" politics.

Although, of course, there is nothing inherently wrong about wanting to overcome art (or whatever institutional and perceptual boundaries the *partage du sensible* has erected around it at any given moment), in this case we find not an erasure of boundaries between fields and practices but simply a switching between them, given that an ethical binary in which one side is completely rejected and opposed forbids any dialectical development. The idea that art and politics are two different things (the first being passive and bad, the second active and good) is thus strongly affirmed. The move from one category to the other, furthermore, risks being reduced to a kind of ethical performance, one that is more preoccupied with its own repositioning than with its effects, and thus remains in the realm of the figural, mistakenly identified with the political. While *The Journey* may not necessarily consider itself to be a work of art, I believe, as suggested earlier, that both it and *La Commune* are in many senses aligned with the broad category of "participatory" or "relational" art; this placement gains support from the extent to which Bishop's observations about participatory art seem to apply to both films. Bishop locates precisely the problem I have been describing in respect to Watkins's films in recent works of participatory art, arguing that, on one hand, they cast "concrete goals" as "more substantial, 'real' and important than artistic experiences," while, on the other, they fail to compare their own "social achievements" to those of "actual (and innovative) social projects taking place outside the realm of art."[44] If one takes *The Journey* to be a work of art, it fails because of its inability to mobilize the aesthetic powers of Watkins's earlier work (now forbidden by the Monoform theory) and because of another contradiction that Bishop has identified as characteristic of participatory art, namely, "the division between first-hand participants and secondary audience," with the latter being implicitly dismissed by the project's premises.[45] If one takes it to be a properly political utopian project, meanwhile, it fails because it did not give rise to the communications networks it hoped to form; its entire agenda thus begins to appear to be an ethical metaphor through which the director redistributes "positions" in a fetishistic manner, as though they were ends in themselves.

The symptomatic meaning of the way that Watkins deploys the ethical binary as a question of position (sometimes quite literally), and its implications for utopian thinking at a moment when television had largely lost its utopian status, becomes clearer in his 2000 television film *La Commune (Paris, 1871),* financed by and broadcast on (albeit in the middle of the night, to Watkins's fury) the public Franco-German television channel ARTE. The nearly six-hour-long film was shot (on video) in 1999 over the course of three weeks in Montreuil, an industrial suburb of Paris, and dramatizes the founding and fall of the Paris Commune, charting its seventy-two-day tenure. Unlike Watkins's earlier films, in which every effort was made to give the viewer an impression of reality equal to the television news broadcast, the setting is only partly realistic: while certain efforts at re-creating a period feel are evident (costumes, furniture), the set is never disguised as anything more, and its self-contained and delimited nature is made quite apparent (Figure 18). At the core of the film are its actors, mostly nonprofessionals. Those playing the Communards are modern-day activists and militants, recruited through social justice groups, while the bourgeois and Versaillais were recruited through an ad in *Le Figaro* calling for participants "who thought the defeat of the Commune a good thing."[46] The actors, who move freely in and out of character, were responsible for writing their own dialogue within the framework of situations laid out by Watkins, and much of the film is dedicated to their discussions (both in and out of character) about the Paris Commune, present-day political issues, and direct comparisons of how different issues were treated in the past versus the present (for example, the treatment of North Africans and wage equality for women).[47] The process of making the film is also dealt with in discussions throughout, and the conditions of this process are

FIGURE 18. The set of *La Commune* (2000) stops short of creating a full illusion, leaving the ceilings of the building that houses it visible.

elaborated at its outset. As though to emphasize its status as a record of this mock Commune and the activities of its inhabitants, *La Commune* is shot primarily in very long single takes.

The dimension of media critique usually present in Watkins's films, meanwhile, is integrated into the representation of the Commune itself: the action that we see is chronicled by two opposing news networks, Versailles and Commune TV, each of which represents a particular public–media dynamic. Versailles TV is polished in form and offers analyses via experts seated comfortably in a studio. Commune TV, meanwhile, seeks to allow the Communards themselves to comment on events, setting up a circuit of communication rather than a hierarchical information delivery system (Figure 19). Commune TV, however, also has its shortcomings, such as a lack of analysis, a tendency to favor short "sound bites," and a lack of political independence in respect to the Commune. Although Commune TV is cast as the preferable alternative, Watkins makes it clear that neither model is ideal, as a key scene in the film depicting the Communards accusing one of the Commune TV reporters (played by Gérard Watkins, the director's son) of detached passivity suggests that

FIGURE 19. The reporters of Commune TV represent a progressive but still flawed news media in *La Commune* (2000).

any form of mediation risks alienation from practice and participation, a message that mirrors the valorization of participatory and collective production that animates the film.

Here, as in *The Journey,* it is participation, the move from the position of consumer to that of producer, that represents the highest ideal. In line with this ideal, Watkins again places far more emphasis on the experience of the participants in the film than on the spectator who will be watching at home. Participants in the film were required to carry out historical research, both on the particular role that they were playing and on the Commune more broadly.[48] This research allowed them to contribute to the formulation of the film's script (although the term can only be used loosely, given the clearly improvisational nature of much of the dialogue), a practice that might be read as the participants' accession to the position of media producers, their collaboration in an act of artistic creation, or even a categorical shift from artistic to political practice.[49] It is, however, not their relationship to film-as-work (as authors and producers) that constitutes the primary and most profound experience of *La Commune*'s participants but rather their immediate experience of the film-as-process, as players in a temporally and spatially localized "happening." It is this level of immediate experience, both as individual performance and as the creation of a collective, that in *La Commune* allows the film's participants to develop new forms of subjectivity and subjective relationships with history. They speak from their own positions and imagine how they would have acted at the time of the Commune, but more importantly, they reflect on how acting as a Communard in the film itself might affect their present situation, either in terms of creating a sense of having inherited certain political struggles or in terms of offering them a place in a historical narrative that connects present and past. They are not, in short, producers of a film so much as they are experiencing something that is an end in its own right.

Much as *The Journey*'s emphasis on face-to-face interactions contradicted its promotion of VHS networks, the first-person experience of those involved in *La Commune* (which may indeed have been quite enlightening) becomes far more problematic when it is conceived of as the basis of a recorded audiovisual work rather than as a one-time happening that is a work in itself. While there is not necessarily any problem in seeing it as the latter, the fact remains that it is not *only* this—the title *La Commune* refers to a film and not to the events that it records. The tension between the potential value of the experience for its participants and the way that its use as raw material for a film complicates and even contradicts that experience—what Bishop would call the tension between primary and secondary audiences—can be illustrated through the film's use of what seem to be typically "Brechtian" techniques. The value placed on performance in *La Commune* demonstrates a preference for localized forms of interaction but combines them with an insistence on acting-as-pedagogy that we might trace back to Brecht's *Lehrstücke,* or learning plays. In the *Lehrstücke,* as in Watkins's film, learning is carried out through acting, which is undertaken primarily for the benefit of the actors themselves, not for an audience. As Jameson explains, "the text and its performance slowly blur and disappear into enlarged discussions, into fights about interpretation, and the proposing of all kinds of alternative gestures and stage business," a description that fits *La Commune* quite well.[50] Such a performance, however, as Jameson notes, would require us "to begin to invent a new conception for the kind of art and aesthetics that the *Lehrstück* seems to rehearse. It will have to avoid the reification of the usual language of art works and objects."[51] It is precisely such a conception that *La Commune* fails to develop, instead creating a fixed or reified work or object—the film itself—out of a process, and thereby giving rise to the contradictions that the insistence on being both work and process at once creates. Other seemingly "Brechtian" procedures present in *La Commune* are distanced from their usual function through an emphasis on participant over spectator. The breaks or ruptures that occur in *La Commune,* for example, no longer serve the Brechtian function of distancing or separation of elements: when an actor shifts out of character, it is not to disorient the spectator but rather to provide that actor with a particular experience. Similarly, the film's "halfway" settings—evocative enough to suggest a sense of place but hardly illusionistic—do not serve the purpose of reminding us of the staged nature of what we are seeing in anti-illusionistic fashion but instead were necessary to the experience of the film's participants, insofar as they created a space whose chief purpose was to be self-contained and demarcated enough to allow for it to be imaginatively transformed into another place and time.

Michael Wayne has suggested that what we are seeing in *La Commune* is perhaps more accurately described not as a Brechtian exercise but as a modern-day incarnation of "Third Cinema" and argues that this is what differentiates Watkins's practice from the ones usually associated with theories about dominant ideological forms (such as those of Burch or MacCabe) similar to his own.[52] I would argue, however, that this analogy is best mobilized to illustrate the *differences* between Watkins's practice and that of Third Cinema. By setting *The Journey* and *La Commune* alongside Octavio Getino and Fernando E. Solanas's *The Hour of the Furnaces* (1970) and their manifesto, "Towards a Third Cinema," we can see how Watkins's films adhere to a binary opposition between art and political practice that leads them to function as compensation rather than emancipation.[53] Like Watkins, Solanas and Getino consider postscreening discussions essential and appeal to the spectator to become part of a greater network, thereby joining a political struggle. Furthermore, this appeal is situated as a call to depart from the position of spectatorship.

The voice-over declares in the second section of *The Hour of the Furnaces,* "This is not a space for spectators, but only for the authors and main actors in the process that this film tries to document and explain. This film is a pretext for dialogue, for the search for different wills to meet." Watkins makes similar appeals for discussion in *The Journey,* punctuating each section of the film with a question mark and continually asking the spectator, "Did you know that?" while his insistence that the film be used rather than consumed suggests sympathy with Solanas and Getino's position. The latter, however, differ from Watkins in several crucial respects. Despite their concern with a revolutionary appropriation of media and offering an alternative, they do not, like Watkins, ultimately conflate *political* "spectatorship" or passivity with the spectatorship of the cinema audience. The "authorship" and "acting" that they refer to are not artistic or textual but political; a metaphor is recognized as such. Whereas Watkins calls on the spectator to accede to a superior position by becoming producer and participant of a work, Solanas and Getino, like the early Watkins, acknowledge cinematic spectatorship as a state that is not opposed to but rather *precedes* political engagement. The audiences of *The Hour of the Furnaces* are called on to "become actors" not by making a film but rather by joining in revolutionary struggle. Finally, *The Hour of the Furnaces* directs its viewer toward the future, toward what has not yet occurred, whereas Watkins offers a recording of a process that has already concluded and whose future extension can only be a feeble repetition.

It is ultimately the form of *La Commune,* rather than what it documents, that most clearly reveals the centripetal and self-contradictory character of the project, as well as its broader alignment with conceptions about utopia and experience that are far more characteristic of late neoliberal capitalism than of political modernism or Third Cinema. The pervasive use of extremely long takes, the preference for "coverage" and capturing as much as possible over composition and structure, all suggest that the point of the film's form is not to function in any rhetorical fashion whatsoever but simply to stand as evidence that the experiences it depicts have taken place. As Watkins puts it, "our 'form' is visible in the long sequences and extended length of the film which emerged during the editing. . . . The form enables the process to take place, but without the process the form in itself is meaningless."[54] Form is reduced to a function of process. It is the immediate experience, the momentary creation of a micro-utopia, that is fetishized over any subsequent formal work, suggesting a very different way of conceptualizing and realizing "another world" than the one we found in Watkins's hyperrhetorical earlier works. One might object that this approach is no different from the common political modernist procedure of demystifying production and showing the work-in-process. Indeed, Watkins's films may at times seem to be mimicking such strategies, but their reason for employing them is profoundly different than in earlier cases, insofar as such procedures are here motivated not by a desire to provoke the spectator's apprehension of process behind form, or the true material nature of any seemingly unified and complete work as text-in-process, but rather by a desire to respect and "give voice to" the participant. Self-reflexive procedures which could, in *The Journey* and *La Commune,* seem like a demystification of the finished, seamless product that hides its own production are in fact the opposite: they do not chip away at the polished surface of a seemingly effortless work to reveal the coded and wrought nature of all texts. They do not reveal the text as a polyphonic assemblage of signifying materials beyond the mastery of the author and uncontainable by fixed form but rather show us process to emphasize the ontological integrity of that process itself and the film's inviolate recording of it. They exchange the illusion of artifice that characterizes a "work" for the traces of a process that is revealed to us in its unbroken wholeness, attesting to the filmmaker's having carried out a democratic, participatory, and pedagogical filmmaking project, a true micro-utopia. The form of the film thus becomes nothing more than evidence of a particular mode of production and the guarantor of correct process, political organization, and positive ethical placement— all of which remain realized only within the parameters of the work itself rather than in a true political project through which the artwork would be transcended and move outward, as in Third Cinema. Utopia here seems completely *contained* in a single space and time, enacted and documented rather than projected forward.

There are, however, elements of the film that work against this sense of containment. These appear in its first few minutes, as the two reporters who will be covering the Commune for Commune TV welcome the viewer and explain that we are now seeing the space in which the filming of the project was completed the day before. The Commune is, in other words, depicted in its absence, as though it had appeared briefly only to fade back into memory. The way the sequence proceeds adds an additional layer of complexity as well: as a handheld camera navigates the now-empty set, the first reporter describes the people, objects, and events that recently populated it. At first, the description refers to the Commune itself, as though what we were seeing was in fact the actual eleventh arrondissement of Paris in 1871: "On the left is what remains of the town hall, where the revolutionary subcommittee enjoyed absolute power, until yesterday." As the second reporter takes up the voice-over, however, it is clear that he is referring not to the events of the 1871 Commune but rather to those of the reenactment: "Beyond this table is the local courtyard with its flies and cesspool, and the café where we filmed discussions with the actors about revolution and contemporary society." Here Watkins recalls the powerful use of contradictions found in the BBC films. Whereas there, however, the strongest sense of contradiction arose between our knowledge of the "falsity" of the image and our sense of its reality, here we find an interplay of absence and presence, on one hand (what is described is *not* visible), and between the film's two temporal layers (as representation of 1871 vs. as a document of an event occurring in 1999), on the other. The first contradiction evokes utopia as absence and might be seen as situating it as either a lost object (hence nostalgic) or something that may reappear again. The second contradiction prevents this reappearance from being seen as a mere ahistorical doubling, insofar as it emphasizes the difference between the 1871 Commune and the 1999 reenactment. While this second contradiction is sustained throughout the film, the first is not: never again is the 1999 event situated as lost or absent; rather, it is rendered to us in its full presence.

The logic that divides spectatorship from participation forbids that such distance remain between us and utopia, because this would render the film a form of mediation; instead, presence and immediacy must be reasserted. This was to take place through a group formed after the film's completion, Rebond pour la Commune, which held screenings and discussions about it. Rebond's task appears to have been an extrafilmic effort to remedy the supposed shortcomings of the film-object, acting upon it externally to reconvert it back into process and to overcome the persistent spectator–producer division. As the group explains on its website, its central aims are to extend the film-object beyond itself and to transform its spectators into participants, if only through an engagement in discussion:

> The main objective of this first experiment [a screening followed by a discussion with those who participated in the film] was to explore new forms of relation with the cinematic work by trying to move towards the exterior what was developing in the image.
>
> With the profusion of questions contained in *La Commune,* the projection of the film can be the site of a new collective conception for any organization, educational establishment, etc. The members of Rebond (actors in the film, militants, artists, historians), offer to share their experiences and reflections so that the film may be the occasion for a real meeting between words and moving images.[55]

In light of these statements, the film's pedagogical goal would seem to be realized not by the object itself, nor by the discussion that it elicits, nor by, as in the case of *The Hour of the Furnaces,* a move to direct political action. Instead, the end point is simply the encounter between participant (now member of Rebond) and spectator and the formation of another ad hoc collective: the primary goal here is avowedly a positional one, "to move towards the exterior what was developing in the image." Here, again, media is cast as a kind of prosthesis, as though the participants' experiences were "carried" by it and had to be reconverted back into unmediated experience (only their "sharing" allows the film screening to become "a real meeting between words and moving images"). At best, the former spectator takes his place among the exhibitors and commentators of Rebond, bringing others into a group whose primary aim is its own prolongation and expansion, a self-contained Commune that seeks to rescue spectators from their fallen position and bring them into its fold rather than spurring them outward toward political action.

The idealization of unmediated communication that we find both in and beyond the film itself goes far beyond being a mere critique of the media; rather, it suggests deep metaphysical underpinnings. As Isabelle Marinone argues, "*La Commune* curiously finished by excluding the question of media in favor of direct, simple, exchange, without mediation between the participants and the experience.... In this sense, the structure and the very process of the film constitute a return towards the pure word, without translation, without intermediary."[56] This invocation of the "pure word" suggests the nostalgia for purity and nonseparation that animates Watkins's project, a sign of both its ethical structure and its conflation of the mediation carried out by media with a political and even metaphysical mediation or separation; Watkins, as Rancière notes of thinkers of spectatorial "emancipation" more broadly, conceptualizes this emancipation "as re-appropriation of a relationship to self lost in a process of separation."[57] If complete immediacy and "pure word" are held up as the highest values, utopia can never be anything other than fully present, experienced without mediation. Utopia ceases to be something that is located elsewhere and whose imagining meets with perpetual resistance in the real, a resistance that must be acknowledged and understood rather than disavowed if it is to be overcome.

La Commune, then, while clearly a work that operates within a utopian framework, seems to symptomize a situation in which both utopian thinking and practice encounter numerous contradictions and risk serving a compensatory function that rests on the mistaking of subjective experience and re-placement for political action. If we look at this situation as a manifestation of an ethical way of thinking about art, individual experience occupies what, for Plato or Rousseau, would be the position of the "true" community, opposed to the "false" work. For Rousseau, Rancière writes, "what must replace the mimetic mediation is the immediate ethical performance of a collective that knows no separation between performing actors and passive spectators. What Rousseau counter-poses to the play of the hypocrite is the Greek civic festival where the city is present to itself, where it sings and dances its own unity."[58] As I have suggested previously, on one hand, this sort of binary creates a situation in which a practice can only be art or politics rather than transcending the boundaries between the two. In this particular instance, however, the position of the living community becomes one that is not integrated with or identical to society as a whole (as in the ideal of civic festivals) but rather radically separate and demarcated from it. I would suggest that in the present moment, a perceived opposition between community and art tends, on one hand, to draw the two closer together (as in the practices of so-called relational art), but in a way that the proposed solution, in which art becomes community, can only take place in a situation that is quite literally cordoned off from living community as it presently exists. Utopia thus abandons a temporal vector and turns to hyperspatialization, much as Jameson's characterization of postmodernism might lead us to expect: it is no longer temporally projected forward, as a notion that can only be imagined through the sublation of that which exists, but rather exists alongside us, thoroughly spatialized, thus recapitulating the enclaves of prosperity produced by capital to protect its custodians from those outside the walls.[59] The pseudo-utopian space, furthermore, is to be experienced in the here and now, not as a sign of what is to come but as a self-contained and self-enclosed substitute for what is, a kind of alternative present. *La Commune* constructs a model in which being in the right position means being separate from everything else and also insists that utopia be accessible to us *now,* going so far as to undo any sense of its possible absence or passing by "resurrecting" it outside of the filmed document. These tendencies, also visible in much of the work that falls under the rubric of participatory or relational art, illustrate how modes of thinking that valorize immediacy, presence, simultaneity, and separate or "pure" spaces can easily co-opt (and undermine) utopian thinking. *La Commune*'s reliance on such modes of thinking not only renders it ineffective in its own terms but allows it to stand as a symptomatic example of how these sorts of values, despite being intended to oppose what exists at present, end up being used to reaffirm it.

The notion of utopia as an ephemeral, demarcated, and spatialized experience rather than a form of temporalized and imaginary projection extends far beyond Watkins and frequently appears in the discourse surrounding participatory or relational art. As I have already suggested, Watkins's works strongly resemble other recent participatory projects, particularly insofar as they generate the characteristic set of contradictions identified by Bishop. Her analysis likewise notes the extent to which such projects fulfill the kind of compensatory function we see at work in Watkins, operating according to the conviction that "if social agencies have failed, then art is obliged to step in."[60] Bishop argues that the kinds of micro-utopias relational art offers, however, mirror more than challenge the forms of experience that have undone the political sphere, insofar as they are "predicated on the exclusion of those who hinder or prevent [their] realization,"[61] and seem to "dovetail with an 'experience economy,' the marketing strategy that seeks to replace goods and services with scripted and staged personal experiences."[62] In other words, they reflect that larger shift that finds subjectivities and relationships rather than material goods becoming the privileged products of the capitalist economy and offer the finest versions of such products. The particular relationships produced by relational art, Bishop argues, are hardly positive by definition and are subject to the same kind of fetishization and treatment as ends-in-themselves that I have argued so deeply compromise Watkins's post-1970s work: "all relations that permit 'dialogue' are automatically assumed to be democratic and therefore good," while "the quality of the relationships in 'relational aesthetics' are never examined or called into question."[63] The supposed value of the work, then, lies not in its capacity to activate or propel the user/participant outward, nor to propagate the formations of positive relationships outside the gallery, but simply to engage him in an unmediated, despectacularized form of sociality of indeterminate quality. The artwork or art "experience" is called on to enact that which should, but cannot, be achieved elsewhere, be it unmediated social relationships or political action: the false utopia of consumerism thus comes to substantially overlap with works that ostensibly challenge it, insofar as both function to fill the holes left by the disintegration of the political without any reflection on how they got there in the first place.

When utopia becomes present and experienced, it risks collapsing the entire temporal–historical logic that grants utopian thought its value as both a spur to imagining a better world and a tool for diagnosing the limits of what can be imagined in the present. In such situations, Bloch argues, we find an "embellishment" that mistakes what is present for what is to come, a "premature harmonization": "what exists is completed here, though in a largely idealistic-abstract way and never in a dialectically explosive and real way . . . an anticipation in space so to speak, not or only inauthentically in future and time."[64] It is particularly telling that it is, in Watkins's case, a re-creation of the Paris Commune that takes on this character, and here we might recall Bishop's claim that the current vogue for participatory art "accompanies the consequences of the collapse of really existing communism, the apparent absence of a viable left alternative, the emergence of the contemporary 'post-political' consensus, and the total marketisation of art and education."[65] Watkins's efforts to re-create the Commune, to bring past and present together through its historical "resurrection" in the bodies of modern militants, suggest both a commitment to the ideals that it embodied and a desire to protect these ideals. This protection, however, petrifies and reifies, containing Communism in a Montreuil warehouse and aligning it with the pleasures of the "experience economy." Who needs Communism (or utopia, for that matter), when one can get the same kick from its performance? Communism becomes *La Commune*.

Of course, it would be ridiculous to blame Watkins for any of this. Rather, his project represents—and here still retains value—an illustration of the limits of our imaginations, our inability to project a future or to repress our desires for immediate gratification and visible results in consumption and politics alike. As Jameson puts it, "this is the sense in which the vocation of Utopia lies in failure; in which its epistemological value lies in the walls it allows us to feel around our minds, the invisible limits it gives us to detect by sheerest induction, the miring of our imaginations in the mode of production itself."[66] Watkins's Commune is thus symptomatic of the post-Communist world more broadly, and the shape that it takes attests to the difficulty of finding any forms to which utopian thinking might attach itself that are not thoroughly obeisant to the cultural logic of late capitalism. Nonetheless, this Commune is problematic precisely because it does not see these walls and thus risks affirming or compensating for the present rather than carrying out a critique of it. If it cannot recognize its own limitations, its own captivity to the present, Watkins's failed Commune is nothing other than the re-iteration or repetition of the political failure that surrounds it—it does not remind us what is impossible or possible but luxuriates in its own present, not as an alternative but as a microcosmic reproduction of the totality in which it is situated.

GODARD AND THE UNFULFILLED PROMISES OF CINEMA

Like Watkins, Godard sought out new utopian sites after the execution of his major television works. As noted earlier, the first of these was geographical in character and offered the possibility of reviving postwar European hopes for television or the belated fulfillment of promises not kept in another place. In 1977, Godard and Miéville's Sonimage company entered into contact with representatives from Mozambique, which had gained its independence from Portugal only two years prior, about developing its national television system. While the precise intentions of the project remain—as with many things Godard—a bit nebulous, Godard writes in *Cahiers du cinéma* no. 300 (an issue that he guest-edited, or rather created, as a lengthy collage of texts and images), "Sonimage proposed that Mozambique should take advantage of the country's audio-visual situation to study television before it existed, before it flooded the entire social and geographical body of Mozambique (even in only twenty years)."[67]

For Godard and Miéville, the project thus represented an opportunity to do precisely what they had imagined in *Six fois deux,* but in a context in which an actual full-fledged implementation could be pursued: to create another television. Mozambique, gaining its independence later than many other African nations, functioned as a space in which alternatives could still be imagined. As Daniel Fairfax writes, "what attracted Godard to the concept was his notion of Mozambique as a country which, when it came to images, was 'virgin territory'—film and television were unknown, and photography was extremely rare, so most of the population had simply never seen a mechanically-reproduced image."[68] This scenario itself, however—that of the European "master" coming to teach the Africans a lesson—could hardly fail to suggest a kind of pater-nalism and hierarchy, a problem that Godard was well aware of. Beside a picture of him in Mozambique printed in *Cahiers* no. 300, we find the caption, "An image that should not be seen anymore. The white 'bwana.' The specialist."[69] Nor were others working for the government, such as the Mozambique-born Brazilian filmmaker Ruy Guerra, who headed the National Film Institute, altogether comfortable with Godard's working methods: "Guerra," Manthia Diawara writes, "felt that Godard was spending too much money on producing and theorizing, not actually making his films."[70] There were too many questions and not enough answers, too much theorizing and not enough action. Sonimage's contract with Mozambique was dissolved by the end of 1978.

Godard would later plan a television project based on his experiences in Mozambique, a multipart series titled *Birth (of the Image) of a Nation* that would include both staged sequences (with an actor and actress playing the Sonimage filmmakers) and documents from the trip.[71] This project never came to fruition, but perhaps of greater interest is the "failure" in Mozambique itself. Diawara suggests that despite the expectations of some in Mozambique, Godard and Miéville may never have intended to actually make any films or television programs there: "Maybe Godard was not even interested in producing the images as much as he was in trying to define these images, trying to lay the groundwork, preparing the kind of television they should construct given the world situation."[72] Diawara's suggestion raises the question of how the actual possibility of implementing another television, a realizable program, might relate to the imagining of one. Unlike Watkins, who responded to a declining faith in television by rejecting mediation entirely and attempting to directly enact utopian programs, Godard refused to place faith in the possibility of any such program. Speaking to Colin MacCabe after the termination of the Mozambique project, he explains, "It's too far away and the chance is over because it is a country.... TV is too big."[73] The project is too big, too all-enveloping, to imagine its successful execution, and moreover, "it is a country," a problem that Diawara associates with the difficulty of working under any sort of political control, but which might also be read as a problem of imagining a totality, an actualized national system, rather than the local and tentative imagining of *Six fois deux.*[74]

Instead of attempting to build a new television, Godard simply returned to cinema; this raises the question of whether he believed at this point in his career that the medium still held utopian potential and would be capable of delivering on its past unfulfilled promises—the very ones we saw being picked up by television in chapter 1. Godard's return to commercial cinema directly followed his experiences in Mozambique, with his "comeback" film, *Sauve qui peut (la vie),* being released in 1980. The most immediately evident utopian aspects of Godard's early 1980s films can be found in their concern with the same sort of ad hoc, small-scale communities that we find in Watkins. Just after his comments on Mozambique cited in the previous paragraph, Godard continues, contrasting the enormous scale of television with the smaller one of cinema: "A movie is interesting because it's smaller, everyone is living in a small place. A movie is a small place—it's a hundred people during six months."[75] Godard's 1982 film *Passion* depicts just such a place, chronicling the difficulties of a film director and his relationship with those around him. As in *La Commune,* we find the representation of something like a utopian community, but here it is ironic, tongue in cheek, and fated to fall short of expectations. What prevents these utopias from achieving any coherency is the fact that they so strongly resist the (on-screen) director's desire to master them, and it is precisely this resistance that keeps them from solidifying into more recognizable and orderly hierarchies, just as the television of *Six fois deux* refused to do. In this representation of utopian failure, we might say that Godard reaffirms the importance of keeping utopia at arm's length.

Perhaps more relevant to our concerns here are Godard's subsequent works, and his *Histoire(s) du cinéma* in particular, insofar as they undertake a more prolonged meditation on the connection between utopia and cinema. We might begin to consider the implications of this work by placing it, through the connecting motif of the Paris Commune, alongside that of Rossellini and Watkins. Near the end of his life, Rossellini hoped to make a film about the Paris Commune.[76] Ultimately, the subject was rejected as too complicated and replaced by a film on the (young) Marx and Engels, to be titled *Working for Humanity.* That film, which would have followed 1976's *The Messiah,* was never produced owing to Rossellini's death in 1977, although a screenplay was completed. Rossellini's film on Communism would surely have situated its subject as a turning point in a historical narrative, full of use-value for the present. Like all of his films, they would have insisted that true fidelity to the past, to history, entailed ensuring that it not be drowned out by the present. Watkins's Commune, in contrast, is a single frozen block of time that petrifies the past (both of the Paris Commune and of its own making) in an effort to make it present. While images of Watkins's film appear in Godard's 2006 work *Vrai faux passeport*, in a sequence that I will return to shortly, the Commune also appears in *Histoire(s)* 1A (1988), in the form of images from Grigori Kozintsev and Leonid Trauberg's 1929 *The New Babylon*. Kozintsev and Trauberg's film pits the forces of the Commune against those of commercialism and capitalism (the latter represented through an adaptation of elements from Zola's *Au Bonheur des dames*), as the shopgirl Louise joins the Communards and is subsequently executed. Godard's Commune references, single still images from the film, do not attempt to give the Commune representation as the staging and indirect trace of a "documented" history (as Rossellini's would have), nor does he attempt to create its modern-day counterpart, as Watkins does. Rather, the Commune appears as a fragment of a filmic fiction (not incidentally of the early Soviet period), in which it has already been transformed into something very different. The image of Louise that we see in *Histoire(s)* 1A is grainy and high in contrast (Figure 20), a copy of a copy (much like the black-and-white photocopies of film stills that appear in *A True History of Cinema and Television*). Written on it, we find the word "rêver." The passage where this image appears in *Histoire(s)* revolves around the phrases *usine de rêve* (dream factory, a reference to Hollywood) and *il faut rêver* (one must dream), along with the juxtaposition of Hollywood "Babylon" (represented by erotic pinup images in the moments that surround this image) with images from early Soviet cinema, including one of the dead Lenin from one of Vertov's *Kino-Pravda* newsreels, illustrating an opposition between the commercialism of the former and the revolutionary character of the latter. This Commune—and indeed, everything Godard shows us in the *Histoire(s)*—is very far away from us and highly mediated, but the suggestion remains that it still calls on

FIGURE 20. Louise, the protagonist of *The New Babylon* (1929), as depicted in Godard's *Histoire(s)* 1A (1988).

us to "dream" of its realization, in order to counteract the consumerist, hedonistic dreams provided by Hollywood.

What might this passage have to say about utopia, television, and cinema? The simplest answer would be that cinema itself is, or was, for Godard, the most truly utopian art form, but that its potential was squandered, and it can only be viewed as a lost opportunity; it is a tragedy of the past, much like the Commune. Like the Commune, it represents a failure, a promise that was not or could not be kept but that may nonetheless be passed on to the future as heritage. Christopher Pavsek begins his book *The Utopia of Film* by invoking an essay of the same name by Alexander Kluge and suggests that, for Kluge, the history of cinema can be viewed as "the history of unrealized possibilities, thwarted ambitions, and disappointed hopes; the 'promises that are contained in the history of film' [a quote from Kluge] have not been met and are too little known, but they persist, especially for those sensitive to their call, awaiting their realization."[77] Although what this history means for Kluge cannot be precisely equated with what it means for Godard, I would suggest that these lines provide an excellent starting point for a consideration of Godard's *Histoire(s)*. As presented by *Histoire(s)*, cinema appears as a series of deaths and failures: among them, Michael Witt notes, we find an initial "death" at the hands of sound cinema, then the failure of cinema to properly warn of or document the Holocaust.[78] As Daniel Morgan writes, "the failure at issue is that people were unable to recognize what they were seeing [in films] as allusions to events that were beginning to take place, and Godard holds that cinema was itself responsible for this public blindness, that it failed to make itself appropriately understood."[79]

This "death" or failure, what we might call an incapacity or abdication of the responsibility to truly see, Godard believes, is followed and doubled by the advent of television, which further contributes to cinema's death. Television is no longer positioned as even a potential site of an overcoming or move beyond cinema but rather as betraying both its own promises and those of the cinema before it. Godard's objections to television are many, and he treats it as a metonym for a broader cultural shift. First, it supplants cinema with a series of stereotyped images that replace vision with language, turning the image itself into a kind of text. "On television," he laments in 1985, "it is no longer a matter of showing things, but of speaking."[80] Television, he notes elsewhere, "reads" the image, scanning it line by line rather than capturing it all at once as traditional (chemical) film processes do.[81] Godard's other objections to television concern the small size of the image and its replacement of a collective, egalitarian viewing situation that facilitated a community's ability to see itself with a single spectator who is a passive subject of a predetermined message.[82] Nor is television, like cinema, an art; rather, it is "commerce, transmission."[83] It uses images to obscure rather than to reveal the real, as we see in a passage from *Vrai faux passeport*, made for Godard's 2006 *Voyage(s) en utopie* exhibition at the Centre Pompidou, to which I will return: here an excerpt from Watkins's *La Commune*, marked by superimposed text as "true," counters the "false" images of television reporting about French military exercises that precede it. In keeping with Godard's convictions about the ability of cinema, even fictional cinema, to reveal the real, it is the staged journalism in Watkins's film, rather than the "real" journalism of French television, that offers us what the film calls a "passport to the real."

Godard also deals with the relationship between cinema and television through his use of the term *projection,* although this concept itself (like most in Godard) should be read metaphorically: we need not assume that it literally describes what cinema can do and television cannot but can instead read it as a desire, an ideal that need not be bound up with any particular medium. Like so many of Godard's key terms, *projection* is a highly polyvalent one. Sometimes *projection* refers to the practice of film projection itself and is valorized because of its connection to the act of collective spectatorship (allowed by the size of the image and the viewing environment). At other moments it takes on the character of a psychoanalytic process (one recognizes oneself in a "projection"), and it is also used (both positively and negatively) to describe the power dynamic characterizing the relationship between the viewer and the screen. Television is rejected because the only thing it "projects" is its own viewer, but it is also described as "transmitting" rather than projecting, forcing the viewer into a fixed position, much like Watkins's Monoform. Godard's usage of the concept is hardly stable and changes over time; the most extensive account of the term, considering nearly all of its possible valences, appears in Morgan's *Late Godard,* but I would like to inflect it here in a specifically Blochian sense, connecting it with the idea of an "anticipatory extension" of the past or present into the future.[84] This connotation will be key in considering the connection between cinema, television, and utopian thinking in Godard's late works, and indeed, he himself seems to suggest it in *Les enfants jouent à la Russie* (1993), which features the line, "The origin of projection: where the idea of projecting something was born before the invention of cinema, the invention of utopia."

The Godard of the 1980s rules out the possibility of television being utopian because, quite literally, it does not project. Television's role in the *Histoire(s)* is thus primarily that of an antagonist. Yet it would be overly simplistic to reduce it to this role, to something that can only be rejected or fought against. For one thing, as Morgan argues, it is television that leads Godard to begin seeing projection as a defining characteristic of cinema: "television changes how Godard thinks about *cinema*; he starts to posit the site of viewing or reception as the central criterion for differentiating film from other media. It's in this context that he defines cinema in terms of projection."[85] A new media ecology in which television dominates thus serves to revalorize an element of cinema that might have formerly gone unnoticed. Godard himself, furthermore, relied on television for financing throughout the 1980s and 1990s, even in that "age of the triumph of private broadcasting" that he mentions in *Soft and Hard*. *Histoire(s)* itself would not likely have been possible without the funding of Canal Plus—France's first private television channel—and the support of Georges Duby, a professor of history and proponent of television as a means of education, and later chair of the new (public) channel for culture and education, la SEPT (now ARTE).[86]

This does not mean that *Histoire(s) du cinéma* is only or specifically a television program, at least not in the sense that the series of the 1970s were, but it does indeed have much to say about television and its relation to cinema, often by employing the concept of projection. In his interview with Serge Daney in *Histoire(s)* 2A (1997), Godard declares that his project to create a history of cinema is impossible precisely because it has to be done on television, and "television reduces. It projects, projects you, but we lose consciousness, because it projects the spectator, whereas the spectator of cinema is attracted." Godard's comment here picks up on similar ones made in *Soft and Hard,* in which he argues that in cinema, "the I was projected and magnified; it could get lost, but the idea could be found again, there was a sort of metaphor." Television, meanwhile, "projects us, and so we no longer know where the subject is." We do not recognize (or even construct) ourselves at all but become something like the product of the process itself. This television, unlike the one imagined by Godard and Miéville in *Six fois deux,* is essentially meant to keep us in our place, to present us with a fixed (and imposed) identity rather than forcing us to lose ourselves in projection only to find ourselves again. When there is no longer projection, or only the tyrannical projection of the spectator by the apparatus, something essential is lost. Projecting an image of *Contempt* on a wall at the end of *Soft and Hard* after first showing it on a television screen, Godard asks, "This project of getting bigger, of becoming subjects, where has it gone?" Television may not literally have caused this project to fail (indeed, Godard offers plenty of other reasons for its failure), but it serves as the emblem for a situation in which all images are known in advance and, as a result, the subject becomes little more than a "projection" of these standardized images. No communication, no displacement takes place. Because it does not project, we might also say that television has no future. Television becomes Godard's metaphor for lack of communication and lack of future, yet the texts that mobilize this metaphor depend on the "triumph of private television" and the new economy of images—perhaps even another new *partage du sensible,* which exponentially multiplies what can be seen and when, and quite literally provides the sources for *Histoire(s),* many of which were taped off of television.

If television represents the absence of a future, hence the impossibility of utopian thought, can cinema do any better? To put it in Godardian terms, can it still project? After his forays into television, Godard's attitude toward cinema clearly became more retrospective, as though it were mainly useful for contemplating the past rather than envisioning the future. Rather than projecting television forward, as did *Six fois deux, Histoire(s) du cinéma* looks backward at cinema. This shift demonstrates what Alain Bergala has described as a change in Godard's relationship with history. In the 1960s, Bergala writes, Godard walked "with the same hurried step as his era," speaking of and to the present, whereas now "he speaks of the tyranny of the present, of that present that advances by erasing the past."[87] History is no longer something that happens but something that has happened, "a more distant history."[88] Certainly more than the death of cinema is at stake here; it is as though history itself had stopped in its tracks, thus making the future vanish. As Morgan notes, Godard's work from the late 1980s onward raises the frightening possibility that many things have arrived at their end: "he explicitly positions his work as an engagement with the idea of the end of the century and a related set of anxieties about the end of various endeavors: state socialism, revolutionary politics, perhaps even modernity and the Enlightenment."[89] For Bergala, this question of endings is inextricably linked with death: Godard no longer speaks to an immediate public, "to convince, to simultaneously teach and terrorize," but "imaginarily addresses himself to the dead."[90] As Bergala and others have noted, Godard in this sense seems very much to resemble Walter Benjamin's angel of history (a figure referenced in *Histoire(s)*), looking back at the catastrophe of history. Can one still see utopia anywhere, or has it been blocked from sight by a television that erases the past while fabricating the present?

HISTOIRE(S) DE L'UTOPIE

One way to answer this question would be to look for the utopian impulse in Godard's turn toward the past itself rather than seeing it, as Bergala does, as an "address to the dead." Although Benjamin (who is cited in several of Godard's works) is often used to discuss the *Histoire(s),* it seems to me that Bloch is perhaps equally, if not more, useful; a turn toward the past that is also utopian makes perfect sense in Blochian terms, because "unbecome future becomes visible in the past."[91] Monica Dall'Asta, although still drawing on Benjamin, suggests how this idea might apply to the *Histoire(s).* She argues that we could see Godard's use of images from the past in *Histoire(s)* in Benjaminian terms, creating "an infinitely explorable image, an implosion of time, the abbreviation or recapitulation of the entire course of history in a single evanescent picture."[92] This operation is explicitly linked to Benjamin in Godard and Miéville's *The Old Place* (2000), which cites a passage from the *Arcades Project*: "It is not that what is past casts its light on what is present, or what is present casts its light on what is past; rather the image is the place wherein that which has been, comes together in a flash in the now, to form a constellation."[93] But what then? To connect past and present might simply mean to remember, to memorialize, or to momentarily revive rather than to necessarily imagine a future. Dall'Asta's suggestion that Godard somehow *changes* history in his interventions suggests a potentially utopian orientation and brings his operation more in line with that of Bloch. All that did not happen in history, all of the possible futures of cinema are, she argues, "falsified" by the passage of time—they become impossible, paths not taken. Godard, however, intervenes and "appropriates time's power of falsification so as to falsify its own falsifications."[94] The possible futures are in some sense reactualized; this constitutes not "a restoration or reconstruction of the truth, but aspires rather to a creation, an invention, of the truth."[95] Cinema's failures thus become, as in Pavsek's description of Kluge's "utopia of film," a collection of promises—of a cultural practice that would genuinely show ourselves and our world to us and that would live up to its responsibility to the real—not to be lamented as past and lost but to be projected into the future. This promise is also a political one, as signaled by the word "rêver" over the image of the communard Louise: the hope contained in cinema is inextricable from the hope for an emancipated society, one that would confront the real face-to-face, using the powers of the image to see rather than to obscure.

Histoire(s), then, might be read as utopian insofar as it entails the recovery of the seeds of the future from the past. But are these seeds still fertile? Can they still in any way take root, or be used to think the future? There remains a need to project forward, even if one cannot imagine quite how to do so or what one might find there, and this is perhaps one way to interpret the function of Godard's often repeated paraphrase of St. Paul that "the image will come at the time of the resurrection." *Histoire(s),* in short, is not the enactment of the resurrection, the utopian projection in which the image is finally fulfilled. As Godard himself argues, this is impossible, because television "reduces" and cannot project; Morgan agrees and argues that *Histoire(s)* engages in "recording, rather than producing, the experience of projection."[96] It does not actualize the kind of knowledge or historical consciousness that true projection would, yet "functions at once as an act of mourning and as a utopian memory for the future, a kind of time capsule."[97] One may thus, as Morgan does, argue that the image has a "deferred temporality," one that will only "come at the time of the resurrection," "placed into the future, its creation ratified and secured only by its subsequent acceptance."[98] But if no one is left to accept it, if the very conditions that would allow for its ratification vanish along with the death of cinema and the particular historical situation that it metonymizes for Godard, can it still retain any utopian value? If Godard cannot bring about this resurrection, who can? "Resurrection" remains simply a kind of placeholder—it does not explicitly refer to an art of the future, or a new society, or anything that one can grasp in linguistic or figural terms.

FIGURE 21. Children wave to a cruise ship in *Film socialisme* (2011), doubling the citizens of Odessa who wave to the battleship *Potemkin*.

We might, however, read this placeholder as keeping an open space for some future subject. Pavsek, who makes the broader argument that Godard's pessimism is in fact balanced by a hopefulness about his (and the cinema's) legacy, illustrates something resembling this scenario through his masterful reading of the final scene of 2010's *Film socialisme,* to which I will now turn.[99] The scene in question juxtaposes excerpts from Eisenstein's *Battleship Potemkin* showing the citizens of Odessa greeting the battleship with images of a young girl and boy waving to the cruise ship that is one of the film's main settings (Figure 21). Through this juxtaposition, Pavsek explains, the *Potemkin* is made to "coincide" with the cruise ship, which is in other senses a true dystopia; the promise of the past is recognized in the present, disguised as it might be.[100] The voice-over, meanwhile, which blends Paul Valéry's "Psaume sur une voix" and Denis de Rougement's *Penser avec les mains,* connects the French words "manifestation" (political demonstration, a reference to the *Potemkin* scene) and "mains" (hands): "The demonstration [*manifestation*] was full of joy, of happiness.... The soldiers began shooting from above because 'manifest'... and in 'manifest' there is 'hand' [*et dans manifeste, il y a main*]." For Godard, hands are often a sign of action and vitality and remain, as in painting, the means through which thought takes on material form (as in his manipulation of video images). In between the two parts of the phrase, between the words "happiness" and "soldiers," we hear what Pavsek describes as an interruption, as the lines "There's the work. It's your turn" are pronounced.[101] In some sense, this figuration of the future is one of the most clichéd ones possible, the handing off of responsibility to children. Yet here we are certainly far from empty cliché: the film as a whole deals with the notion of heritage (of lost gold, of European political and artistic culture, of images themselves), and the two children themselves are doubles of those in the film's previous section, who are depicted as more capable than their parents of reckoning with the political heritage of Europe; the *manifestation* is in their *mains*. The children's wave is part of a wider temporal collapse: they are, on one hand, doubling the joy of the citizens of Odessa waving to the battleship *Potemkin* but, on the other, waving good-bye to Europe (or a certain epoch of European history, a certain burden of historical failure), as embodied by the cruise ship. Godard is certainly aware of the potential for this trust in the young to be seen as a clichéd sentiment, as Valéry's poem, read by the voice-over, continues: "Not a worn-out sentiment. An ideal, a smile that dismisses the universe." The French verb in question in the last sentence is *congédier*, but as Pavsek notes, it is translated in the German version of the *Histoire(s) du cinéma* book (in which the same text is cited) with the German *aufheben*.[102] This is of course the verb used by Hegel, usually translated as "to sublate"—the smile is not a rejection or abandonment of what is but a supersession or incorporation into something else. A similar smile, I would add, can be seen on Louise's face at the end of *The New Babylon*, as she smiles and laughs while her husband digs her grave (Figure 22): she may die, but the Commune lives on, and the film closes with images of the words "Vive la Commune!"

If cinema, like the Commune or even the project of the Enlightenment, is mortal (and, as Godard would have it, somehow incarnated in himself), it will indeed die, but the promises that it carried within it, its legacy to the future, will find some other way to live. These promises, however, need not (and perhaps cannot) be experienced as they were in the past; it will not be the cinema that saves cinema. Godard's utopia is

FIGURE 22. "A smile that dismisses": Louise laughs at death in *The New Babylon* (1929).

ultimately not *in* cinema or television (or at any rate, no longer is); these served as ways to express the utopian impulse for a time but have now passed away. For Godard, it may even be the case that art itself has ceased to be utopian—if cinema was indeed the "last chapter" in its history, as he tells Serge Daney, this is perhaps because it could no longer fulfill a certain cultural function.[103] Yet this demise may itself clear the way for the imagining of something after art: something that dismisses but perhaps also overcomes and transcends. Failure and death allow for memory and subsequent resurrection, not in any theological sense, but in that they leave a place open for a future subject and their eventual fulfillment. As in *Six fois deux,* success must always be deferred to ensure that we do not mistake what lies before us as the utopia to come.

We find a similar way of thinking about cinema, failure, and utopia in Godard's 2006 exhibition at the Centre Pompidou, *Voyage(s) en utopie.* The much-discussed exhibition was widely received as a catastrophe, but it has also been well documented as a replacement for the "real" or planned exhibition, titled *Collage(s) de France*. As with so many of Godard's projected works, the *Collage(s)* exhibition was never realized and only exists as a trace or, we might say, a "scenario" for its future realization in the small-scale model that remained at the center of the *Voyage(s)* exhibition. Given the ridiculousness of many of Godard's demands, however, one wonders if the exhibition's refusal and demise was perhaps not entirely intentional. As André Habib argues, "the ultimate refusal of the institution—in these and other cases—seems to have been paradoxically what allowed an exhibition to exist, precisely because it could expose itself as a ruin, an unfinished project."[104] This same pattern, Habib argues, runs throughout Godard's career: a "performance of failure" is "deeply tied to a mode of 'utopia.'"[105] Jameson's reading of *Passion* makes a similar proposition, observing in that film's depiction of a thwarted collective (one that recalls Godard's description of filmmaking as a kind of utopian endeavor) "the stunning dynamic of a collective social machine without a center" and inquiring as to whether the "final project," just like the video "scenario" for the film that Godard executed afterward, "is not itself its own visible 'scenario': not a world, but the possibility of a world, or at least the probability of that possibility."[106] This idea of not realizing a world, but rather suggesting its possibility, is borne out by much of Godard's career and illuminates the utopian logic that lies behind his obsession with failure; the failures of cinema discussed in *Histoire(s)*, Habib argues, shed "a light on the 'power' he believes 'cinema' (that he somehow embodies) should have had. Hence, each one of these 'failures' opens an 'imagine if,' unveiling the utopian potential of cinema."[107]

Habib's argument suggests that it is precisely, in Godard's eyes, cinema's failure that keeps it alive, and we might also think here of those images of failure and death that occur at the end of so many early Soviet films, from Eisenstein's *Strike* to the fall of the Commune in *The New Babylon*. What both cinema and revolution did not do reminds us of what they could do or could have done. I see no reason why we might not say the same of television, particularly given the parallels between the comments on failure at the end of *Six fois deux* and those about cinema's death and failure. These unfulfilled futures of television, furthermore, are present in *Histoire(s)* itself: what is it to show *Histoire(s)* on television if not precisely to undo television's ways of seeing from within? The formal practice of *Histoire(s)* likewise draws out the possibilities of television, revalencing its conventional practices: it depends, of course, on video technology largely used for television but also makes use of images and texts in a way that recalls their frequent televisual superimposition. Its rapid movement through a vast number of images illustrates, as Witt argues, "Daney's advocacy of the use of the remote control to deprogram the television schedules and to create a more personal form of television through the playful art of 'zapping' (channel surfing)."[108] Furthermore, the very "unreadability" of the text—the impossibility of grasping the onslaught of sounds and images that move by at a high speed, making us feel that they are always too fast and our perception too slow—anticipates the scrolling text, multiple "frames," and overall excessiveness that have come to characterize television (particularly news channels) in this century. The difference, of course, is that such techniques as they are normally used do not in any sense want to help us "see"; rather, they make sure that perception is always filled, the eye always busy, continuously occupied with the same invariable forms of word and image and frozen in a perpetual present. In Godard, meanwhile, this busyness becomes the sublime of history and of thought itself, ungraspable but worth reaching for, continually producing the new in every interstice and insisting on the need to make the past present so that it may become future. But the moment of synthesis, that point at which the eye would grasp all, or at which meaning or the road to utopia would become clear, is perpetually deferred. It must be, so that in its death cinema may continue to call on us to realize it, if only in some other form, and to continue to remain faithful to the utopian impulse.

KLUGE'S GARDEN AND THE PASSING OF TELEVISION

Pavsek notes that for Kluge, too, "the cinema...lives on because the moment of its realization was missed."[109] Kluge furthermore, recalling Godard, situates television (and new media more broadly) as displacing both cinema and history. Yet Kluge has made far more of a commitment to television than Godard ever did: he began his television production at the very moment when public service television came under threat, in a remarkable act of resistance against the overall trajectory of the medium in Europe. Kluge first gained a foothold in private channel SAT1 in 1985 by forming a company (Neue Medien Ulm) and acquiring 1 percent of the channel, which allowed him to provide 1 percent of its programming.[110] Subsequently, legislative measures provided an even greater opening, as a 1987 law obligated commercial stations to provide programming slots for "independent cultural producers."[111] In 1987, Kluge then formed a television production company—DCTP (Development Company for Television Programs)—and ever since has produced weekly programs for a number of private channels.[112]

We find something similar to Godard's "time capsule" or "utopian memory for the future" in the way that Kluge's television programs bring together fragments of the past. Klaus Kreimeier compares his *Ten to Eleven,* broadcast on German private television since the late 1980s, to Benjamin's *Arcades Project* (to which Kluge has also dedicated one of his programs): "One is able to use the whole pictorial universe of film and television, as Benjamin utilized the Paris National Library: to pull together material for a work that would describe and conceptualize an entire century."[113] Unlike the fragments of conventional television, Kluge's fragments retain their historical character; they form, Christian Schulte writes, "open constellations whose individual elements have not congealed into ahistorical information."[114] Television holds these fragments but, in doing so, allows a kind of relocation to take place, a migration between media; as Tara Forrest writes, "the aim of the programmes is to provide what Kluge describes as 'cultural windows' for the 'old media' within the comparatively 'new' medium of television."[115] Television becomes, in a sense, a home or shelter for "old media," at a moment when they appear to be under threat; as Kluge himself puts it, "since I can't make them disappear, then instead we must use these New Media to protect the film medium."[116]

While I will to return to this idea of "protection" in a moment, it bears noting that Kluge's programs, like the *Histoire(s),* also draw on the forms of television in their assembly of a "time capsule," transforming the "old media" to which they give shelter. As Peter C. Lutze notes, Kluge had already incorporated elements of television, particularly advertising, into his film work, and his use of its techniques—"repetition, variation, rapid pacing, and musical selections that unite diverse images"—only became more pronounced when working on television itself.[117] Perhaps the most consistent characteristic of his programs is their extensive use of text, both superimposed over and separate from images, as in Godard. Words often scroll across the screen, almost too quickly to read, and the quick, slide show–like progression of images that accompany them adds to the sense of an informational overload, mimicking what Kluge and Negt had earlier referred to as television's tendency toward "compression."[118] But as Godard and Miéville did in *Six fois deux* and *France tour,* Kluge frequently offers a decisive slowing down of television's pace as well: the dominant format used in his programs is the interview (often with artists, intellectuals, or academics but also with actors playing characters), and these discussions often take up the entire duration of the program (ranging from ten up to forty-five minutes). The programs' intellectual discourse, meanwhile, is decidedly heterogeneous and fragmentary; the result is something like the superimposition of discourses we see in Godard, described by Schulte as the "lively manipulation of apparently irreconcilable schools of thought, whose frozen identities can perhaps, at some points, be thawed."[119] This fragmentary character, as noted earlier, is also reflected in the programs' formal structure, which keeps the elements of television discourse themselves from cohering (much like the separate "segments" in *France tour*). This lack of coherence on the formal level, Schulte contends, "makes it clear that the genres of television are constructed, and therefore are alterable, and its performances, aimed at effectiveness and a sense of completion, do not have any substance, but are based from the beginning on partitions, on exclusions (e.g., of spontaneity)."[120] Kluge, like Godard and Watkins, reveals the boundaries and efforts at containment of different types of discourses characteristic of television to be nothing more than arbitrary (and highly ideological) constructions whose overturning can be carried out through a repurposing of the very same forms that it employs.

Kluge's television programs have been criticized by German network executives as "ratings killers" and "stone-age television," in terms that recall the objections to the poor "technical quality" of Godard and

Miéville's television programs.[121] The fact that Kluge's programs should appear "prehistoric," however, seems perfectly fitting, given his decidedly anachronistic pursuit of a radically different kind of television at the very moment that the sorts of institutions that once facilitated it are withering away. Kluge sees cinema as obsolete, and for this very reason an ideal means to disrupt the "ever-expanding present," and he seems to push television in the same direction.[122] His television is perhaps more anachronistic than any of the other examples discussed here, a relic of the past that has been "excavated" (to invoke one of Kluge's preferred metaphors) and put to use in the present.[123]

I end with a discussion of Kluge, however, not as much to suggest the vantage point from which utopian thought and method might approach television today as to provide a glimpse into the new sorts of utopian raw materials that its successors offer. If what we might call a televisual distribution of the sensible is no longer operative, having given way to the even more radical availability and remapping of sounds, images, and text enabled by the Internet and on-demand streaming video platforms (now typically included with cable TV service), what might this new paradigm have made thinkable, and how might one use it to revitalize the utopian imagination? Kluge has gestured beyond television by gathering a large number (although still only a partial sample) of his television programs on DCTP's website,[124] in a project he refers to as the "Garden of Information" (Figure 23). Perhaps the most interesting aspect of the site is the way the texts are organized. Kluge, on the website, explains that they are grouped into "loops" *(Schleifen)* comprising twelve to thirty-six segments. These range from two-minute-long visual essays to the longer interview-based programs described earlier; the individual programs, which are themselves often composed of identifiable segments or "modules," thus become attachable to other heterogeneous modules, which can be watched "in order" (an order that is itself hardly necessary and imposed after the fact) or shuffled through at will. Different collections of loops, meanwhile, are gathered under a "context" *(Kontext)*. The overall organization suggests both a tentative whole but also that this whole can be broken down and rearranged at will by the user. The Garden of Information resembles at once an archive and, as the name suggests, something constantly in the

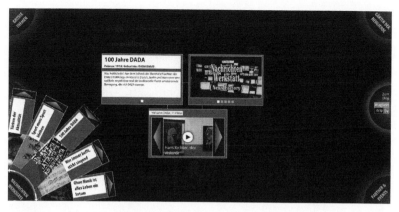

FIGURE 23. Alexander Kluge's online Garden of Information, here displaying one of several video clips contained in a "loop" dealing with Dadaism.

process of change and growth, organic not in its aspiration to wholeness but rather in its living character and its resistance to any fixed form.

How might we think about this project in utopian terms? I would like to conclude with a speculative sketch intended to suggest how the forms taken by new media might be approached by a utopian method, but in such a way that also links them (while mindful of their novelty) to past paradigms of media, art, and thought. In the most obvious sense, Kluge's garden takes on a utopian aspect simply because of its name, which suggests an Edenic space of both protection (to recall Kluge's comments about "protecting" old media) and accumulated knowledge. If, however, we conceive of it as an archive—a key term for scholars of numerous disciplines, whose importance and implications I can only begin to explore here—the situation becomes more complex. Despite its continuing relevance in contemporary artistic practices, the archive form has long been subject to critique and treated, particularly when connected to visual culture, as the site of a dialectic between memory and forgetting. Benjamin Buchloh offers a succinct and powerful analysis of this dialectic in his discussion of Gerhard Richter's *Atlas,* a collection of visual materials (primarily photographs) that the artist has been accumulating and arranging since the 1960s. For Buchloh, Richter's *Atlas* demonstrates the oscillation between different conceptions of the archive (and the photographic archive in particular) that were already visible in the 1920s. In 1924, Aby Warburg began work on his *Mnemosyne Atlas,* which Buchloh describes as "a model of the mnemonic in which Western European humanist thought would once more, perhaps for the last time, recognize its origins and trace its latent continuities into the present."[125] While the emphasis on memory here situates the project somewhat differently, we might align Warburg's project with Rossellini's: both construct something like a historical archive that seeks to preserve the memory of the European past with the hope for its usage in the present and future, although, as I will return to in more detail in a moment, neither of course had access to the new media that allow the archive to take on a new form. The supposed purpose of Warburg's *Atlas,* to follow Buchloh, comes into conflict with an effect generated by the form of the archive itself: while it collects fragments of "extreme temporal and spatial heterogeneity," it also renders them homogeneous in "their simultaneous presence in the space of the photographic, anticipating the subsequent abstraction from historical context and social function in the name of a universal aesthetic experience by André Malraux in his *Le Musée imaginaire.*"[126] For Buchloh, both of these tendencies become visible in Richter's *Atlas,* in which the mnemonic purposes served by family photographs come into conflict with the forgetting engendered by images in a commodity culture, demonstrating that "the registers of fetishistic desire and of sign exchange value had gradually displaced presence, corporeality and the mnemonic experience."[127]

We might see the kind of archives that are usually offered by online services like YouTube and Netflix, or home media like streaming cable boxes, as more fully realizing the antimnemonic, dehistoricizing tendencies of the archive, insofar as their contents are, particularly when we move beyond the more "democratic" space of YouTube, quite literally sounds and images as commodities, interchangeable objects whose function has been reduced to their exchange value. We could thus write a narrative of decline much like the one we traced in chapter 1 between cinema and television, in which a new technology enables a more efficient and complete ideological subjection of the visible world to commodity logic. There are also clear differences that arise when we move from "classical"

television to new media: whereas television offered audiovisual commodities in a "punctual," fleeting form—not available "on demand" but only for
a single moment, hence in some sense ephemeral and thus clearly historically situated—new media preserve them indefinitely. Whereas television
addressed an identifiable collective spectator, insofar as all viewers had to
watch at once and were conceived of as a specifically national audience,
new media speak to individuals and to no one in particular, and what
is seen is dictated by the viewer's choice. Both changes can plausibly be
described not as emancipatory, but as manifestations of broader developments in capitalist culture that place a premium on consumer agency and
choice in a way that obscures (and compensates for) declining political
agency and choice and that turn ephemeral "events" (as we might call the
old form of television broadcast) into durable commodities.

New media, then, could easily be read as another instance of the "bad"
archive, in which the promise of Warburg is replaced by the ambivalence
of Richter. But utopian material inheres in this very situation, even within
the displacement of the collective spectator by the individual, and the
ephemeral event (which we might see as more properly historical, insofar
as it is explicitly connected with a particular place and time) with the
timeless commodity. In this latter shift, for example, we might detect a
sublation or overcoming of precisely those terms that have long allowed
us to distinguish between cinema and television, namely, the opposition
between technologies of preservation and technologies of transmission;
new media do both at once, far more than television did, and their ability to make anything present at any time depends on the existence of
an archive. While the archive as collection of ahistorical commodities
makes this overcoming appear to be a response to consumer demand—
everything exists in the now, whenever the consumer wants it, because
what is transmitted always "waits" in storage—we might equally say
that the notion of transmission now always presupposes a past: there is
no transmission without storage, without an archive. Seen in this light,
the dialectic of memory and forgetting, of history and timelessness,
identified by Buchloh as a characteristic of the archive begins to appear
less settled in favor of the latter, negative terms. Texts delivered via new
media begin to seem as though they always hail us from the past, an idea

that is further strengthened by the short commercial life span of media commodities, whose need to appear present comes back to haunt them as they so quickly transform into remnants of the past. The sounds and images that we encounter can thus be recast not as durable, timeless goods but as fragments of history.

Once these sounds and images are awakened, they encourage us to respond to them differently than past audiovisual texts. Francesco Casetti argues that our position in respect to the new media display is quite different than the one we occupied before the cinema or television screen, conceived of as windows: "we cannot look out of a display screen, nor can we fill our eyes with it, nor can we lean out of it. Instead we ask something of it, as at an information window. We work on it, as at a table."[128] These are, of course, "active" responses, and we might well read them as nothing more than the telling alignment of the passivity–activity dichotomy contested by Rancière and the false sense of agency and choice offered by contemporary capitalism. In most cases, as when one watches a film from a streaming cable box or on Netflix, there is nothing particularly disruptive about these activities: we "ask" things before our displays because we depend on them and on their constant "refreshment," as one depends on a narcotic, and we "work" on them to ensure that what they offer can be precisely fitted to our desires (breaking them into chunks, replaying single scenes, etc.). Before an archive that still explicitly addresses us from the past, however, the meaning of these characteristics becomes rather different, as though they had been resituated, to recall Jameson, as "components of a different system." Kluge's garden represents something like this, a utopian revalencing of the often-criticized archive or, more precisely (since archives come in many forms and have indeed been subverted and "made utopian" in the realm of contemporary art, as Paolo Magagnoli has argued),[129] of the new media archive exemplified by sites like Netflix. In an archive like Kluge's garden, we are presented not with ahistorical and already-closed texts that address our desires and needs immediately but rather with fragments of history that require us to rearrange them, that remain contingent and incomplete, and that contain within themselves a Blochian "unbecome future" that calls out for the spectator to locate and realize it. Philipp Ekardt suggests something along these lines, albeit on a smaller scale and in a more delimited context, in arguing that Kluge's DVDs and website facilitate acts of "correlation" between different points in time, insofar as the user can combine fragments from different moments in the director's career, creating a Benjaminian "constellation."[130] The new media archive thus appears not as much as a total submission of sounds and images to the ahistorical world of the commodity as the site of their rehistoricization. The fact that Kluge calls this archive a "Garden of Information," of course, also reminds us of the Internet's status, much like that of television in the past, as a supposedly "informational" form of media. Here, however, there may also be a suggestion of how we might redefine the term itself, much as was necessary in the wake of television: here information refuses to be abstracted or dehistoricized and will not be reduced to a series of interchangeable commodities. Instead, information requires a response, and perhaps even a form of completion or realization. Kluge's archive insists on the need, again, to recall Casetti's terms, to first ask something of the past ("as at an information window") and then to go to work on it; it fights against the tendency of the commodified archive, which we might well associate with the Internet itself, to blot out the historicity of its own contents but also refuses to let them remain as they are, just as Godard refuses to abandon a past that is, as he often reminds us in allusion to Faulkner, not dead and "not even past." A crucial step in drawing out the utopian potential inherent in the new media archive, therefore, is to orient a form that is so often seen as a way of exploring the past, or the relationship between past and present, toward the future, as both Godard (albeit not quite yet in new media form) and Kluge have done. A utopian does not approach the archive as a Foucauldian genealogist but rather, to recall Jameson's definition of the utopian method, inverts this procedure. He does not seek to reconstruct the discursive formations of the past to write a history of the present, as Foucault did, but rather looks in the past for the seeds of the future.

The "bad new days" of new media provide, perhaps despite themselves, the means to direct us toward new forms of utopian thinking and suggest new ways of using sounds and images as utopian raw material. Even as they betray certain promises (for example, the one contained in collective address), they show how others might be kept alive in new form and how the very tools that would be used to bury the past can insist on the need for its realization in the future. This is where the atomized spectator's status as no-one-in-particular becomes particularly valuable: those who will play in Kluge's garden, like those future subjects who will receive Godard's "time capsule," can be imagined as still yet-to-come.[131] The place of the subject who waves back at the *Potemkin* is left open, and this subject can be located in front of the computer screen just as easily as she could be located before that of the cinema or the television. "There's the work," we might say, recalling the voice-over in *Film socialisme*: an unbecome future calls on us to excavate and attend to the promises of the past, in whatever form they might present themselves. The fragments of history preserved in Kluge's garden are nothing less than the seeds of time; the fruit they bear will not be ours to taste, but the garden still needs tending.

Acknowledgments

This book is the product of a lengthy process, and it has passed through a number of different forms on its way to completion. Here I would like to thank those who contributed to it in one way or another over the years. To begin with, my thanks to all of those who provided support, guidance, and feedback during my time as a graduate student at Yale University. First among them should be Dudley Andrew, who has always shown unflagging confidence in my work and has been instrumental in my formation as a scholar. Next come John MacKay and Francesco Casetti, who have followed my academic career from the beginning and have provided valuable feedback and insight at every step of the way. In addition to these three, my thanks to the others who took the time to read and respond to this project at the dissertation stage, including Katie Trumpener and Barry McCrea. Many others contributed to my graduate work, including J. D. Connor, Aaron Gerow, Millicent Marcus, Charles Musser, and Brigitte Peucker.

I also owe a debt of gratitude to others I encountered along the way, such as Garrett Stewart, whose Mellon Dissertation Seminar at the University of Iowa gave me the space and time to finish the first version of this project, not to mention a chance to spring Godard's *La Chinoise* on a captive audience of fellow dissertators. Perhaps the greatest debt is owed Fredric Jameson, not only for his visionary and inspiring work and his insightful comments on this project but also for his profound personal generosity. I also express my gratitude to Malcolm Turvey, whose interest in and support for my scholarship date back to our very first meeting, and to Thomas Elsaesser, in whose class I first encountered the work of Jacques Rancière. Adriano Aprà and Danny Fairfax were both immeasurably helpful in providing me with research materials. Much is owed

Sally Shafto for her careful reading of this book and her meticulous work on the index. Then there is Anne Kern at SUNY–Purchase College, who has always gone above and beyond the call of duty in her support for me and who is one of the finest colleagues that any academic could wish for; the same can be said of Su Friedrich at Princeton, who also happens to be a brilliant filmmaker. My deepest thanks to my colleagues at Sarah Lawrence College, whose warmth and generosity over the past months have made the completion of this book far easier than it might otherwise have been. I would be amiss if I did not also acknowledge my students at SUNY–Purchase, Princeton, and Sarah Lawrence: their enthusiasm proves to me on a daily basis that, contrary to rumor, cinema is far from dead.

I have not yet mentioned all of the friends who made this book possible, both by taking the time to read or listen to its earlier iterations and by simply being present in my life. They include (but are not limited to) David Assouline, Alice Lovejoy, Alexandra Magness, Jeremi Szaniawski, and George Weinberg. Ksenia Sidorenko merits a sentence all to herself, being both the first person to read this book in its entirety and my closest confidante during its writing; it would not have been possible without her. Equally indispensable and irreplaceable are my parents, Mark and Kathy Cramer, who never even batted an eye when I told them I was going to graduate school for film studies and who have always had complete trust and confidence in me. Nor can I omit my brother, Elliott Cramer, whose prodigious talents and enormous heart never fail to astound.

Finally, I thank my anonymous reviewers for their invaluable feedback as well as everyone at the University of Minnesota Press. My deepest gratitude to my editor, Danielle Kasprzak, for her confidence in the project and for shepherding it to completion, and to her assistant, Anne Carter, for making this process as smooth and easy as possible.

Notes

INTRODUCTION

1 Roberto Rossellini, *La Télévision comme utopie,* ed. Adriano Aprà, trans. Diane Bodart (Paris: Éditions Cahiers du Cinéma, 2001).

2 Ruth Levitas, *The Concept of Utopia* (New York: Philip Allan, 1990; repr. Oxford: Peter Lang, 2011), 4–6. Page numbers refer to the 2011 edition.

3 Ruth Levitas, *Utopia as Method: The Imaginary Reconstitution of Society* (New York: Palgrave Macmillan, 2013), esp. 153–220.

4 Fredric Jameson, *Valences of the Dialectic* (London: Verso, 2009), 423.

5 Ibid., 433.

6 Ibid., 434.

7 Ernst Bloch, *The Principle of Hope,* 3 vols., trans. Neville Plaice, Steven Plaice, and Paul Knight (Cambridge, Mass.: MIT Press, 1986).

8 Ibid., 1:9.

9 Ibid., 1:144.

10 Jérôme Bourdon, "L'idea di 'servizio pubblico' nella tv europea," in *Storie e culture della televisione italiana,* ed. Aldo Grasso (Milan: Mondadori, 2013), 137.

11 Jérôme Bourdon, *Du service public à la télé-réalité: Une histoire culturelle des televisions européennes* (Bry-sur-Marne, France: INA, 2011), 28.

12 Bloch, *Principle of Hope,* 1:154.

13 Jacques Rancière, *The Politics of Aesthetics,* trans. Gabriel Rockhill (London: Continuum, 2004), 13.

14 Ibid., 12.

15 Ibid., 13.

16 Ibid.

17 Davide Panagia, "'Partage du sensible': the distribution of the sensible," in *Jacques Rancière: Key Concepts,* ed. Jean-Philippe Deranty (Durham, U.K.: Acumen, 2010), 98.

18 Rancière, *Politics of Aesthetics,* 20.

19 Ibid., 13.
20 See Fredric Jameson, *Archeologies of the Future* (London: Verso, 2005), 14: "If in a first moment I have characterized the Utopian's relationship to her social situation as one of raw material, we may now ask what kind of building blocks the historical moment provides. Laws, labor, marriage, industrial and institutional organization, trade and exchange, even subjective raw materials such as characterological formulations, habits of practice, talents, gender attitudes: all become, at one point or another in the story of utopias, grist for the Utopian mill and substances out of which the Utopian construction can be fashioned."
21 G. W. F. Hegel, *Science of Logic,* trans. A. V. Miller (Atlantic Highlands, N.J.: Humanities Press, 1989), 107.
22 Jameson, *Valences,* 415. On the utopian program, also see Jameson, *Archeologies,* 2–4.
23 Jameson, *Valences,* 413.
24 Ibid., 434.
25 Fredric Jameson, *The Seeds of Time* (New York: Columbia University Press), 130.
26 Bourdon, *Du service public à la télé-réalité,* 225.
27 Bloch, *Principle of Hope,* 1:9.
28 Ibid.
29 See, e.g., Sheila C. Murphy, *How Television Invented New Media* (New Brunswick, N.J.: Rutgers University Press, 2011).
30 As Bourdon notes, attacks on public service broadcasting were often used to demonstrate the failings of the welfare state more broadly; see "L'idea di 'servizio pubblico' nella tv europea," 142–43.
31 For the relationship of Socialist governments to media privatization in France and Italy, see Eli Noam, *Television in Europe* (New York: Oxford University Press, 1991), esp. 99–109 and 153.

1. THE PROMISE OF TELEVISION

1 Jonathan Bignell and Andreas Fickers, "Introduction: Comparative European Perspectives on Television History," in *A European Television History,* ed. Jonathan Bignell and Andreas Fickers (Oxford: Blackwell, 2008), 29.
2 Ibid., 30.
3 Massimo Scaglioni, "Cavalcare la tigre. Tv italiana e culture storiche," in Grasso, *Storie e culture della televisione italiana,* 28.
4 Siegfried Zielinski, *Audiovisions: Cinema and Television as Entr'actes in*

History, trans. Gloria Custance (Amsterdam: Amsterdam University Press, 1999), 11–12.

5   Ibid., 12.

6   Gunther Anders, "The Phantom World of TV," in *Mass Culture: The Popular Arts in America,* ed. Bernard Rosenberg and David Manning White (Glencoe, Ill.: Free Press, 1957), 358.

7   Scaglioni, "Cavalcare la tigre," 37–39.

8   Ibid., 33.

9   Sylvie Pierre, *Jean d'Arcy, penseur et stratège de la television* (Bry-sur-Marne, France: INA Éditions, 2012), 82.

10   Watkins cannot be said to have been associated with the cinema in the same way, given that his first major works were made for (and, as I will argue, as) television, although his earlier short films were made within the context of the United Kingdom's robust amateur film culture.

11   Theodor W. Adorno, "Prologue to Television," in *Critical Models,* trans. Henry W. Pickford (New York: Columbia University Press, 2005), 50.

12   Theodor W. Adorno, "How to Look at Television," *Quarterly Review of Radio and Television* 8, no. 3 (1954): 216.

13   Christopher Pavsek, *The Utopia of Film: Cinema and Its Futures in Godard, Kluge, and Tahimik* (New York: Columbia University Press, 2013), 2. I will return to the question of cinema's status as utopian, and what Pavsek calls "the promises contained in the history of film," in chapter 5.

14   As Pavsek writes of *Potemkin,* "it is utopian in its universal appeal to the great collectives who comprise its audiences and in its ability to speak to them across the divides of language and the barriers of illiteracy. It is utopian not only in its commitment to the project of revolution and the constitution of a new society, but also in its status as the most modern of the arts." Pavsek, *Utopia of Film,* 6. By the 1950s, though, perhaps television had come to occupy the position of "the most modern of the arts."

15   Zielinski, *Audiovisions,* 147–48.

16   J. C. W. Reith, *Broadcast over Britain* (London: Hodder and Stoughton, 1924), 185.

17   Richard Collins, "'Ises' and 'Oughts': Public Service Broadcasting in Europe," in *The Television Studies Reader,* ed. Robert C. Allen and Annette Hill (London: Routledge, 2004), 39.

18   The 1927 charter is accessible online in the BBC Royal Charter Archive, located at http://www.bbc.co.uk/bbctrust/governance/regulatory_framework/charter_archive.html.

19 Jay G. Blumler, "Public Service Broadcasting before the Commercial Deluge," in *Television and the Public Interest: Vulnerable Values in West European Broadcasting*, ed. Jay G. Blumler (London: Sage, 1992), 7.

20 Ibid., 7–14.

21 Reith, *Broadcast over Britain*, 17.

22 Ibid., 34.

23 Ibid.

24 Asa Briggs, *The BBC: The First Fifty Years* (Oxford: Oxford University Press, 1985), 55; Matthew Arnold, *Culture and Anarchy* (Oxford: Oxford University Press, 2009).

25 Franco Monteleone, *Storia della radio e della televisione in Italia*, 3rd ed. (Venice: Marsilio, 2003), 289.

26 Scaglioni, "Cavalcare la tigre," 37–38.

27 Quoted in Bourdon, *Du service public à la télé-réalité*, 205.

28 Pierre, *Jean d'Arcy*, 83.

29 Ibid., 67. Pierre likens d'Arcy's attitude to that of Rossellini on several occasions.

30 Bourdon, *Du service public à la télé-réalité*, 33.

31 Fabrice d'Almeida and Christian Delporte, *Histoire des médias en France* (Paris: Flammarion, 2010), 190.

32 Thierry Vedel and Jérôme Bourdon, "French Public Service Broadcasting: From Monopoly to Marginalization," in *Public Service Broadcasting in a Multichannel Environment*, ed. Robert K. Avery (White Plains, N.Y.: Longman, 1993), 32.

33 Noam, *Television in Europe*, 3.

34 Ibid., 127. It bears noting that the private ITV was, like the BBC, expected to fulfill a public service mandate.

35 Jay G. Blumler, "The British Approach to Public Service Broadcasting: From Confidence to Uncertainty," in Avery, *Public Service Broadcasting*, 3.

36 Michael Tracey, *The Decline and Fall of Public Service Broadcasting* (Oxford: Oxford University Press, 1998), 24.

37 Reith, *Broadcast over Britain*, 181.

38 Bloch, *Principle of Hope*, 1:153–56.

39 Stuart Hall, "Encoding/Decoding," in *Culture, Media, Language: Working Papers in Cultural Studies, 1972–1979*, ed. Stuart Hall, Dorothy Hobson, Andrew Lowe, and Paul Willis, 117–27 (London: Routledge, 1980).

40 Raymond Williams, *Television* (New York: Schocken Books, 1975; repr., London: Routledge, 2003), 22. Page numbers refer to the 2003 edition.

41 William Urrichio, "Television's First Seventy-Five Years: The Interpretive

Flexibility of a Medium in Transition," in *The Oxford Handbook of Film and Media Studies,* ed. Robert Kolker (New York: Oxford University Press, 2008), 289.

42 Peter Bürger, *Theory of the Avant-Garde,* trans. Michael Shaw (Minneapolis: University of Minnesota Press, 1984).

43 Theodor W. Adorno, "Commitment," in *Aesthetics and Politics* (London: Verso, 1977), 179.

44 Ibid., 180.

45 Jean-Paul Sartre, *What Is Literature?,* trans. Bernard Frechtman (New York: Philosophical Library, 1949), 79.

46 Ibid., 159.

47 Ibid., 291.

48 Jacques Rancière, "The Paradoxes of Political Art," in *Dissensus: On Politics and Aesthetics,* trans. Steven Corcoran (London: Continuum, 2010), 135–36.

49 Ibid., 136. Rousseau's argument can be found in his 1758 "Lettre à M. D'Alembert sur les spectacles"; see Jean-Jacques Rousseau, *Politics and the Arts: Letter to M. D'Alembert on the Theatre,* ed. and trans. Allan Bloom (Ithaca, N.Y.: Cornell University Press, 1960).

50 Adorno, "Commitment," 183.

51 Ibid., 186.

52 Ibid.

53 Ibid., 185.

54 Jacques Rancière, *Aesthetics and Its Discontents,* trans. Steven Corcoran (Cambridge: Polity, 2009), 29.

55 Jacques Rancière, "The Aesthetic Revolution and Its Outcomes," in *Dissensus,* 118.

56 Adorno, "Commitment," 191.

57 Rancière, *Aesthetics and Its Discontents,* 40.

58 Ibid.

59 Fredric Jameson, *Brecht and Method* (London: Verso, 1998), 3.

60 John Grierson, "First Principles of Documentary," in *Grierson on Documentary,* ed. Forsyth Hardy (London: Faber and Faber, 1966), 36.

61 Ibid.

62 Ibid., 41.

63 John Grierson, "The Documentary Idea: 1942," in *Grierson on Documentary,* 112.

64 Brian Winston, *Claiming the Real: The Documentary Film Revisited* (London: BFI, 1995), 11.

65 Ibid., 46.

66 Ian Aitken, *Film and Reform: John Grierson and the Documentary Film Movement* (London: Routledge, 1990), 37–47.

67 Dziga Vertov, "The Essence of Kino-Eye," in *Kino-Eye: The Writings of Dziga Vertov,* ed. Annette Michelson, trans. Kevin O'Brien (Berkeley: University of California Press, 1984), 49–50.

68 Ibid., 49.

69 Dziga Vertov, "Kinoks: A Revolution," in *Kino-Eye,* 20.

70 Ibid., 11.

71 Ibid., 19.

72 Dziga Vertov, "On the Significance of Nonacted Cinema," in *Kino-Eye,* 37.

73 On Vertov's imagining of television as part of an "all-encompassing putting-into-view of the world," see Richard Dienst, *Still Life in Real Time: Theory after Television* (Durham, N.C.: Duke University Press, 1994), 4–5.

74 Zielinski, *Audiovisions,* 120.

75 Adorno, "Prologue to Television," 50.

76 On the "ideology of the visible," see Jean-Louis Comolli, "Technique and Ideology: Camera, Perspective, and Depth of Field," in *Movies and Methods,* ed. Bill Nichols (Berkeley: University of California Press, 1985), 2:40–57.

77 Anders, "Phantom World of TV," 359–61.

78 Bürger, *Theory of the Avant-Garde,* 54.

79 Ernst Bloch and Theodor W. Adorno, "Something's Missing: A Discussion between Ernst Bloch and Theodor W. Adorno on the Contradictions of Utopian Longing," in *The Utopian Function of Art and Literature,* by Ernst Bloch, trans. Jack Zipes and Frank Mecklenburg (Cambridge, Mass.: MIT Press, 1988), 2.

80 Ibid., 2–3.

81 Zielinski, *Audiovisions,* 52.

82 David Joselit, *Feedback: Television against Democracy* (Cambridge, Mass.: MIT Press, 2007), 6–7.

83 Ibid., 14.

84 Williams, *Television,* 27.

85 Asa Briggs, *The History of Broadcasting in the United Kingdom,* vol. 1, *The Birth of Broadcasting* (New York: Oxford University Press, 1995), 45.

86 Reith, *Broadcast over Britain,* esp. 93–143 and 165–77.

87 Williams, *Television*, 14.
88 Bourdon, *Du service public à la télé-réalité*, 13.
89 Ibid., 33.
90 Geoffrey Cox, *Pioneering Television News* (London: John Libbey, 1995), 13.
91 Bourdon, *Du service public à la télé-réalité*, 123.
92 Monteleone, *Storia della radio e della televisione in Italia*, 341.
93 Bourdon, *Du service public à la télé-réalité*, 39.
94 Ibid., 40.
95 Walter Veltroni, *I programmi che hanno cambiato l'Italia: Quarant'anni di televisione* (Milan: Feltrinelli, 1992), 49.
96 Aldo Grasso, *Storia della televisione italiana*, 3rd ed. (Milan: Garzanti, 2004), 134.
97 Mary Ann Doane, "Information, Crisis, Catastrophe," in *Logics of Television*, ed. Patricia Mellencamp (Bloomington: Indiana University Press, 1990), 225.
98 Ibid., 223.
99 Ibid., 224.
100 André Bazin, "A Contribution to an *Erotologie* of Television," in *André Bazin's New Media*, ed. Dudley Andrew (Berkeley: University of California Press, 2014), 110.
101 Bourdon, *Du service public à la télé-réalité*, 123.
102 Williams, *Television*, 71.
103 Ibid., 88–91.
104 Jean Baudrillard, *For a Critique of the Political Economy of the Sign*, trans. Charles Levin (St. Louis, Mo.: Telos, 1981), 175.

2. TELEVISION AS ENLIGHTENMENT

1 André Bazin, "Cinema and Television," in *My Method*, ed. Adriano Aprà (New York: Marsilio, 1995), 94. Originally published as "Cinéma et télévision. Un entretien d'André Bazin avec Jean Renoir et Roberto Rossellini," *France Observateur*, July 4, 1958. I have given references to the translated version of *My Method*, the most substantial collection of Rossellini's interviews and writings in English, when possible; the English version, however, omits about half of the material found in the Italian original.
2 Fereydoun Hoveyda and Eric Rohmer, "An Interview with *Cahiers du cinéma*," in Aprà, *My Method*, 152. Originally published in *Cahiers du cinéma*, no. 145 (July 1963).

3 Sergio Trasatti, *Rossellini e la televisione* (Rome: La Rassegna, 1978), 291.

4 The single best introduction to the form and content of Rossellini's pedagogical films is Adriano Aprà's "Rossellini's Historical Encyclopedia," in *Roberto Rossellini: Magician of the Real,* ed. David Forgacs, Sarah Lutton, and Geoffrey Nowell-Smith (London: BFI, 2000), 126–48. Also useful, particularly in its consideration of Rossellini's relationship to historical scholarship, is David Forgacs, "Rossellini's Pictorial Histories," *Film Quarterly* 6, no. 3 (2011): 25–36.

5 Tag Gallagher, *The Adventures of Roberto Rossellini* (New York: Da Capo Press, 1998), 559–60.

6 Raymond Bellour, "Voix d'images," *Trafic,* no. 50 (May 2004): 57.

7 The major studies in English are Gallagher's critical biography and Peter Brunette, *Roberto Rossellini* (Oxford: Oxford University Press, 1987). The most comprehensive work in Italian is Gianni Rondolino, *Roberto Rossellini* (Turin: UTET, 1989).

8 Patrick Werly, ed., *Roberto Rossellini: de la fiction à l'histoire* (Lormont, France: Bord de l'Eau, 2013).

9 Gallagher, *Adventures,* 559.

10 Ibid., 656. It bears noting that Gallagher's skepticism toward Rossellini's television project has much in common with Brian Winston's attacks on John Grierson, mentioned in the previous chapter. In both cases, art and information are seen as fundamentally incompatible, and their fusion is thus attacked as a duplicitous political gesture in which one serves as alibi or "cover" for the other.

11 Hoveyda and Rohmer, "An Interview," 152.

12 Roberto Rossellini, "Conversazione sulla cultura e sul cinema," in *R. R. Roberto Rossellini,* ed. Edoardo Bruno (Rome: Bulzoni, 1979), 29. Originally published in *Filmcritica,* no. 131 (March 1963).

13 Ibid.

14 Roberto Rossellini, *Utopia autopsia 10^{10}* (Rome: Armando, 1974).

15 Max Horkheimer and Theodor W. Adorno, "The Culture Industry: Enlightenment as Mass Deception," in *Dialectic of Enlightenment,* trans. Edmund Jephcott (Stanford, Calif.: Stanford University Press, 2002), 94–136.

16 Dwight MacDonald, "A Theory of Mass Culture," in Rosenberg and White, *Mass Culture,* 59–73. For Clement Greenberg's formulation, see his "Avant-Garde and Kitsch," in *Art and Culture: Critical Essays,* 3–21 (Boston: Beacon, 1961).

17 Roberto Rossellini, "Neorealismo e kitsch," in *Il mio metodo,* ed. Adriano Aprà (Venice: Marsilio, 1987), 125–26.

18 Roberto Rossellini, "I mezzi audiovisivi e l'uomo della civiltà scientifica e industriale," in *Il mio metodo,* 260.

19 "Roberto Rossellini vous avez la parole!," in *Il mio metodo,* 147–48. Originally published in *Filmklub-Cinéclub,* October 1958.

20 Ibid., 148.

21 As Jameson notes, utopian texts favor a completely overhauled totality, demonstrating "a revolutionary and systemic concept of change rather than a reformist one." See his *Archeologies,* 39. In Rossellini's case, of course, we do not see the representation of a modified totality but rather an effort to completely renovate a single sphere, that of mass communications, in its entirety.

22 James Beveridge, *John Grierson: Film Master* (New York: Macmillan, 1978), 250. Elsewhere, however, the efforts of the documentarians Grierson, Rotha, and Flaherty are rather cryptically dismissed in passing: "As for the most serious initiatives, even if they were not extremely effective, such as the now-defunct English and Canadian documentary movements, and the works of men like John Grierson, Paul Rotha, and Robert Flaherty, which are now but a past memory, we have, with much respect, much to object." See Rossellini, "Per un buon uso degli audiovisivi," *Bianco e nero,* no. 5 (2001): 78. This rejection may have as much to do with Rossellini's desire to break from past practices as it does with their particular methods.

23 Rossellini lived in Paris from 1954 until 1956, during which time he interacted extensively with the critics of *Cahiers du cinéma* and employed François Truffaut as his personal assistant. For the fullest accounts of Rossellini's stay in Paris, see Rondolino, *Roberto Rossellini,* 230–36, and Gallagher, *Adventures,* 455–60.

24 Roberto Rossellini, *Fragments d'une autobiographie* (Paris: Ramsay, 1987), 19.

25 Hoveyda and Rohmer, "An Interview," 145.

26 Ibid., 149.

27 Fereydoun Hoveyda and Jacques Rivette, "An Interview with *Cahiers du cinéma,*" in Aprà, *My Method,* 109. Originally published in *Cahiers du cinéma,* no. 94 (April 1959).

28 See Herbert Marcuse, "The Affirmative Character of Culture," in *Negations: Essays in Critical Theory,* trans. Jeremy J. Shapiro (Boston: Beacon Press, 1968), 88–133.

29 On this kinship, see Fredric Jameson, "Reification and Utopia in Mass Culture," in *Signatures of the Visible*, 9–34 (London: Routledge, 1990).

30 Adriano Aprà and Maurizio Ponzi, "An Interview with Roberto Rossellini," in Aprà, *My Method,* 65. Originally published in *Filmcritica,* no. 156–57 (April–May 1965).

31 Roberto Rossellini, *Un esprit libre ne doit rien apprendre en esclave,* trans. Paul Alexandre (Paris: Fayard, 1977), 65.

32 Hoveyda and Rivette, "An Interview," 110.

33 Roberto Rossellini, "Un cinema diverso per un mondo che cambia," in *Il mio metodo,* 305. Rossellini's statement seems deliberately phrased to emphasize the opposition of his pedagogical project to his postwar neorealist films.

34 Rossellini, *Utopia autopsia,* 198.

35 Roberto Rossellini, "Agostino e la crisi della civiltà greco-romana," in Trasatti, *Rossellini e la televisione,* 161. Originally published in *L'osservatore romano,* August 2, 1972.

36 Rossellini, *Un esprit libre,* 73.

37 Edoardo Bruno, "Seconda Intervista," in Bruno, *R. R. Roberto Rossellini,* 117. Originally published in *Filmcritica,* no. 190 (August 1968).

38 Ivano Cipriani, "Roberto Rossellini dice addio al 'Centro' e alla TV italiana," in Trasatti, *Rossellini e la televisione,* 144. Originally published in *Paese sera,* November 15, 1969.

39 Beveridge, *John Grierson,* 249.

40 Jérôme Bourdon, with Juan Carlos Ibáñez, Catherine Johnson, and Eggo Müller, "Searching for an Identity for Television: Programmes, Genres, Formats," in Bignell and Fickers, *A European Television History,* 119.

41 Rossellini, *Utopia autopsia,* 14.

42 Ibid., 73. Rossellini here freely adopts a passage of Marx that he frequently cites, in which the latter writes, "The concrete is concrete because it is the concentration of many determinations, hence unity of the diverse." See Karl Marx, *Grundrisse,* trans. Martin Nicolaus (Harmondsworth, U.K.: Penguin, 1973), 101.

43 Rossellini, *Un esprit libre,* 73.

44 Rossellini, *Utopia autopsia,* 189.

45 Ibid., 14.

46 Ibid., 26–27; Rossellini, *Un esprit libre,* 120. In his comments on "intellectual difference," Rossellini comes remarkably close to positions on pedagogy espoused by Jacques Rancière in *The Ignorant Schoolmaster,* trans.

Kristen Ross (Stanford, Calif.: Stanford University Press, 1991), a text
I will return to later.

47 Rossellini, *Utopia autopsia,* 180–81.

48 Rossellini, *Un esprit libre,* 142.

49 Ibid., 143.

50 Jean Collet and Claude-Jean Philippe, "An Interview with *Cahiers du cinéma,*" in Aprà, *My Method,* 175. Originally published as "Roberto Rossellini: *La prise de pouvoir par Louis XIV,*" in *Cahiers du cinéma,* no. 183 (October 1966).

51 Lietta Tornabuoni, "Ventotto domande a Rossellini," in Trasatti, *Rossellini e la televisione,* 158. Originally published in *Appunti del servizio stampa del R.A.I.,* August 1970.

52 Ibid., 134.

53 Roberto Rossellini, "Riflessioni e considerazioni per una educazione integrale," in Bruno, *R. R. Roberto Rossellini,* 81. Originally published in *Filmcritica,* no. 264–65 (May–June 1976). This statement is clearly based on St. Paul's in his first letter to the Corinthians 13:12: "For now we see through a glass, darkly, but then face to face: now I know in part; but then shall I know even as also I am known."

54 Quoted in Rossellini, *Utopia autopsia,* 195, and *Un esprit libre,* 101–2.

55 Rossellini, *Utopia autopsia,* 195.

56 The obvious example here is Bazin's claim that photography can "lay bare the realities": "Only the impassive lens, stripping its object of all those ways of seeing it, those piled-up preconceptions, that spiritual dust and grime with which my eyes have covered it, is able to present it in all its virginal purity to my attention and consequently to my love." See Bazin, "The Ontology of the Photographic Image," in *What Is Cinema?,* ed. and trans. Hugh Gray (Berkeley: University of California Press, 1967), 1:15.

57 Rossellini, *Fragments,* 13.

58 Mario Garriba, "Cinema anno zero," *Filmcritica,* no. 374 (May 1987): 235.

59 Jacques Rancière, *Les Écarts du cinema* (Paris: La fabrique, 2011), 99.

60 Alain Bergala and Jean Narboni, eds., *Roberto Rossellini* (Paris: Éditions Cahiers du Cinéma, 1990), 45.

61 Aprà, "Rossellini's Historical Encyclopedia," 135.

62 Raymond Bellour, *L'Entre-Images 2* (Paris: P.O.L., 1999), 111.

63 For a detailed technical account of Rossellini's use of the process, see Beppe Mangano, "Gli specchi di Rossellini," *Filmcritica,* no. 374 (May 1987): 242.

64 See, e.g., John Hughes, "Recent Rossellini," *Film Comment*, July/August 1974, 21, which argues that the mirror shots in *Augustine* "indicate the illusoriness of the fiction of history."

65 Àngel Quintana, "La méthode de travail de Rossellini et son chemin vers la pédagogie de l'image," in Werly, *Roberto Rossellini*, 36.

66 Peter Wollen, "'Ontology' and 'Materialism' in Film," in *Readings and Writings: Semiotic Counter-Strategies* (London: Verso, 1982), 196.

67 Ibid., 201.

68 Ibid.

69 Tornabuoni, "Ventotto domande a Rossellini," 157.

70 Wollen, "'Ontology' and 'Materialism' in Film," 203.

71 Aprà and Ponzi, "An Interview," 166.

72 Michèle Lagny, "De Socrate à Descartes: faire 'voir' la pensée?," in Werly, *Roberto Rossellini*, 57.

73 Raymond Bellour, "Le cinéma, au-delà," in Bergala and Narboni, *Roberto Rossellini*, 83. Jacques Aumont too places Rossellini alongside Vertov, while adding Grierson as another similar case; see *Théories des cinéastes* (Paris: Nathan, 2002), 101.

74 Roberto Rossellini, "Cinema: nuove prospettive di conoscenza," in Bruno, *R. R. Roberto Rossellini*, 46. Originally published in *Filmcritica*, no. 135–36 (June–August 1963).

75 Ibid.

76 Rossellini, *Fragments*, 14.

77 Bürger, *Theory of the Avant-Garde*, 49.

78 Rossellini, *Fragments*, 40.

79 Bruno, "Seconda Intervista," 117.

80 Bürger, *Theory of the Avant-Garde*, 54.

81 Rossellini, *Fragments*, 18.

82 Jacques Rancière, "The Aesthetic Revolution and Its Outcomes," in *Dissensus*, 128.

83 Ibid., 129.

84 Max Horkheimer and Theodor W. Adorno, "Odysseus or Myth and Enlightenment," in *Dialectic of Enlightenment*, 35–62.

85 Rossellini, *Fragments*, 30.

86 Rossellini, *Utopia autopsia*, 29.

87 Adorno and Horkheimer, *Dialectic of Enlightenment*, 9.

88 Aprà and Ponzi, "An Interview," 160.

89 Giuliana Bruno, "America," *Filmcritica*, no. 374–75 (May–June 1987): 127–28.

3. INFORM, EDUCATE, AND AESTHETICIZE

1 The frequent association of Watkins's early films with subsequent fiction films using documentary forms leads John Cook to position the filmmaker as the "father of modern docudrama." Cook, "'Don't Forget to Look into the Camera': Peter Watkins' Approach to Acting with Facts," *Studies in Documentary Film* 4, no. 3 (2010): 227–40.

2 See Watkins's own narratives of the suppression of his work in "An Open Letter from Peter Watkins," *Velvet Light Trap*, no. 13 (Winter 1975): 53–54; Watkins, "*Punishment Park* and Dissent in the West," *Film/Literature Quarterly* 4, no. 4 (1976): 293–302; Watkins, "Media Repression: A Personal Statement," *Cine-tracts* 3, no. 1 (1980): 1–7.

3 For an account of Watkins's early career, see Joseph Gomez, *Peter Watkins* (Boston: Twayne, 1977), which I draw upon here.

4 James Chapman, "The BBC and the Censorship of *The War Game* (1965)," *Journal of Contemporary History* 41, no. 1 (2006): 88.

5 "Peter Watkins: An Interview," *Film Society Review* 7, no. 7–9 (1972): 76–77.

6 Ibid., 79.

7 "Left, Right, and Wrong: An Interview with Peter Watkins," *Films and Filming* 16, no. 6 (1970): 29.

8 Lester Friedman, "The Necessity of Confrontation Cinema—Peter Watkins Interviewed," *Literature/Film Quarterly* 11, no. 4 (1983): 240.

9 Ibid.

10 The overwhelming realism of *The War Game* was both blamed for its banning by the BBC and widely reported to cause adverse emotional and even physiological effects. See James M. Welsh, "The Modern Apocalypse: *The War Game*," *Journal of Popular Film and Television* 11, no. 1 (1983): 25–41.

11 Milton Shulman, *The Ravenous Eye* (London: Cassell, 1973), 242.

12 Ibid., 243.

13 Ibid., 244.

14 Ibid., 242.

15 Raymond Durgnat, "The Great British Phantasmagoria," *Film Comment*, May/June 1977, 50.

16 John Corner, *The Art of Record* (Manchester, U.K.: Manchester University Press, 1996), 15–16.

17 Grierson, "First Principles of Documentary," 36.

18 Corner, *Art of Record*, 16.

19 S. M. J. Arrowsmith, "Peter Watkins," in *British Television Drama,* ed. George W. Brandt (Cambridge: Cambridge University Press, 1981), 225.

20 Corner, *Art of Record,* 16.

21 Antoine de Baecque, *L'histoire-caméra* (Paris: Gallimard, 2008), 224–25.

22 Roland Barthes, "The Reality Effect," in *The Rustle of Language,* trans. Richard Howard (Berkeley: University of California Press, 1986), 141–48.

23 Bill Nichols, *Representing Reality: Issues and Concepts in Documentary* (Bloomington: Indiana University Press, 1992), 142.

24 Peter Watkins, *Media Crisis,* new ed. (Paris: Editions Homnisphères, 2007), 13.

25 Roman Jakobson, "On Realism in Art," in *Language and Literature,* 19–27 (Cambridge, Mass.: Belknap Press of Harvard University Press, 1987).

26 Nichols, *Representing Reality,* 20.

27 On the scope of the research carried out by Watkins for most of his films, see de Baecque, *L'histoire-caméra,* 244–46. For *The War Game* specifically, see Gomez, *Peter Watkins,* 46–47.

28 Here I assume a clash in tense between image and word based on an interpretation of the filmic image as present (both in terms of tense and in terms of our experience of it as nonabsence), as argued by Christian Metz in "On the Impression of Reality in the Cinema," in *Film Language,* 3–15 (Chicago: University of Chicago Press, 1974).

29 Vivian Sobchack, *Carnal Thoughts: Embodiment and Moving Image Culture* (Berkeley: University of California Press, 2004), 70–71.

30 Ibid., 63

31 Ibid., 67.

32 Michael Hirschorn, "He Saw It Coming," *Atlantic Monthly,* November 2008, 51–52.

33 Grierson, "First Principles of Documentary," 36.

34 Bazin, "A Contribution to an *Erotologie* of Television," 113.

35 Welsh, "Modern Apocalypse," 28.

36 Jacques Grant, "Peter Watkins," *Cinéma 73,* December 1973, 110.

37 Quoted in Gomez, *Peter Watkins,* 119; see also S. M. Eisenstein, *Film Form,* trans. and ed. Jay Leyda (New York: Harcourt Brace, 1949), 84.

38 S. M. Eisenstein, "The Montage of Attractions," in *Selected Works,* vol. 1, *Writings 1922–1934,* trans. and ed. Richard Taylor (London/

Bloomington: BFI Publishing and Indiana University Press, 1988), 34. Eisenstein later writes that theater and film share this "basic material."

39 Ibid., 34, 39.

40 Ibid., 39; Sobchack, *Carnal Thoughts,* 55.

41 "Peter Watkins: An Interview," 81–82.

42 James M. Welsh and Steven Philip Kramer, "*Film and History* Interview: Peter Watkins," *Film and History* 7, no. 1–2 (1977): 40.

43 Kenneth Tynan, "A Warning Masterpiece," *Observer* (London), February 13, 1966.

44 "Peter Watkins: An Interview," 75.

45 Gomez, *Peter Watkins,* 108.

46 Calvin Green, "Punishment Park," *Cineaste,* Spring 1972, 32.

47 "Peter Watkins: An Interview," 74.

48 Ibid., 75.

49 Welsh and Kramer, "*Film and History* Interview: Peter Watkins," 8.

50 George Melly, "Dissenter's Nightmare," *Observer* (London), February 13, 1972.

51 Williams, *Television,* 71.

52 Carol Clover, *Men, Women, and Chain Saws: Gender in the Modern Horror Film* (Princeton, N.J.: Princeton University Press, 1992); Linda Williams, "Film Bodies: Gender, Genre and Excess," *Film Quarterly* 44, no. 4 (1991): 5.

53 Watkins, *Media Crisis,* 136.

4. RADICAL COMMUNICATIONS

1 Antoine de Baecque, *Godard: biographie* (Paris: Grasset, 2010), 408–11.

2 Although he is not referring to the specific theoretical problems I will address here, Raymond Bellour makes a similar point, noting that, for Godard, a move for television was necessary to preserve cinema, to renew in some sense the "mystery of its presence and its distance," but also because it had imposed "a permanent modification of the conditions of production and reception of images and sounds." See Bellour, *L'Entre-Images 2,* 117.

3 Serge Daney, "Le thérrorisé (pédagogie godardienne)," in *La Rampe* (Paris: Gallimard/Cahiers du Cinéma, 1982), 86. Originally published in *Cahiers du cinéma,* no. 262–63 (January 1976).

4 Peter Wollen, "Godard and Counter-Cinema: *Vent d'est,*" in *Narrative, Apparatus, Ideology,* ed. Philip Rosen, 120–29 (New York: Columbia University Press).

5 De Baecque, *Godard,* 425.

6 For details on this project, see ibid., 441–42, as well as Julie Perron's film *Mai en decembre: Godard en Abitibi* (2000).

7 On the political limitations after the immediate post-May period, see Steve Cannon, "Godard, the Groupe Dziga Vertov and the Myth of 'Counter-Cinema,'" *Nottingham French Studies* 32, no. 1 (1993): 77.

8 On Godard's involvement with various *gauchiste* newspapers, see Michael Witt, "Godard dans la presse d'extrême gauche," in *Jean-Luc Godard: Documents,* ed. Nicole Brenez, David Faroult, Michael Temple, James Williams, and Michael Witt, 165–73 (Paris: Éditions du Centre Pompidou, 2006).

9 De Baecque, *Godard,* 488; Richard Brody, *Everything Is Cinema: The Working Life of Jean-Luc Godard* (New York: Metropolitan Books, 2008), 350.

10 Marcel Martin, "Le Groupe 'Dziga Vertov,'" in *Godard par Godard,* ed. Alain Bergala (Paris: Éditions de l'Étoile/Cahiers du Cinéma, 1998), 1:343. Originally published in *Cinéma 70,* no. 151 (December 1970).

11 David Faroult, "Never More Godard," in Brenez et al., *Jean-Luc Godard: Documents,* 121.

12 Brody, *Everything Is Cinema,* 337.

13 Jean-Luc Godard, *Introduction to a True History of Cinema and Television,* trans. Timothy Barnard (Montreal: Caboose, 2014), 343.

14 De Baecque, *Godard,* 445.

15 Stéphane Bouquet and Thierry Lounas, "Défense du cinéma: Entretien avec Jean-Henri Roger," *Cahiers du cinéma,* "Cinéma 68" (unnumbered special issue), 38.

16 Jean-Luc Godard, "India," in Bergala, *Godard par Godard,* 1:199. Originally published in *Cahiers du cinéma,* no. 96 (June 1959).

17 Jean-Luc Godard, "Premiers 'sons anglais,'" in Bergala, *Godard par Godard,* 1:337–38. Originally published in *Cinéthique,* no. 5 (September–October 1969).

18 De Baecque, *Godard,* 463.

19 Michael Goodwin and Greil Marcus, *Double Feature* (New York: Outerbridge and Lazard, 1972), 30.

20 Colin MacCabe, *Godard: Images, Sounds, Politics* (Bloomington: Indiana University Press, 1980), 42–43.

21 For this opposition, see Godard's comments in Goodwin and Marcus, *Double Feature,* 30, and "Le Groupe 'Dziga Vertov,'" in Bergala, *Godard*

par Godard, 1:343. For Roger's comments, see Bouquet and Lounas, "Défense du cinéma," 38.

22 Yvonne Baby, "Pour mieux écouter les autres," in Bergala, *Godard par Godard,* 1:365. Originally published in *Le Monde,* April 27, 1972.

23 De Baecque, *Godard,* 446.

24 Ibid., 447–48.

25 Ibid., 465–66.

26 Ibid., 473–78.

27 Colin MacCabe, *Godard: Portrait of the Artist at Seventy* (New York: Farrar, Strauss, and Giroux, 2003), 216.

28 A fetched image, Godard and Gorin explain, is one that already exists and that the filmmaker merely films, whereas a built one is constructed by the filmmaker. See Goodwin and Marcus, *Double Feature,* 21.

29 Guy Debord, *The Society of the Spectacle,* trans. Donald Nicholson-Smith (New York: Zone Books, 1994).

30 "Pravda" (from handout distributed during February 1970 screening), in Bergala, *Godard par Godard,* 1:340.

31 Groupe Lou Sin, "Le groupe 'Dziga Vertov' (1)," *Cahiers du cinéma,* no. 238–39 (May–June 1972): 37.

32 Adorno, "Prologue to Television," 50.

33 On the relationship between word, image, and information in Godard's pre–Dziga Vertov Group films, see Michael Cramer, "Idées vagues/images claires: Image, Pedagogy, and Politics in the Films of Jean-Luc Godard, 1966–1969," *October,* no. 157 (Summer 2016): 90–106.

34 Rancière, *Aesthetics and Its Discontents,* 28.

35 De Baecque, *Godard,* 450–51.

36 Louis Althusser, "Ideology and Ideological State Apparatuses," in *Lenin and Philosophy and Other Essays,* trans. Ben Brewster (New York: Monthly Review Press, 1971), 109.

37 Gerard Leblanc, "Lutte idéologique et *Luttes en Italie,*" *VH101,* no. 9 (Fall 1972): 88.

38 Marc Cerisuelo, "Jean-Luc, Community, and Communication," in *A Companion to Jean-Luc Godard,* ed. Tom Conley and T. Jefferson Kline (Chichester, U.K.: Wiley-Blackwell, 2014), 309.

39 Michael Witt, *Jean-Luc Godard: Cinema Historian* (Bloomington: Indiana University Press, 2014), 2.

40 Alain Badiou, "La fin d'un commencement: notes sur *Tout va bien,* de Jean-Luc Godard et Jean-Pierre Gorin," in *Cinéma,* ed. Antoine de Baecque (Paris: Nova, 2010), 394–95.

41 Bertolt Brecht, "Against Georg Lukács," in *Aesthetics and Politics*, 69.
42 Godard, *Introduction to a True History of Cinema and Television*, 88.
43 Michael Witt, "On and under Communication," in Conley and Kline, *A Companion to Jean-Luc Godard*, 323.
44 Ibid., 324.
45 Interview with *Téléciné*, no. 202 (September–October 1975): 11.
46 Jean-Luc Godard, "Penser la maison en termes d'usine," in Bergala, *Godard par Godard*, 1:380. Originally published in *Libération*, September 15, 1975.
47 On *Communications*, see Brody, *Everything Is Cinema*, 235.
48 Yvonne Baby, "Faire les films possible là où on est," in Bergala, *Godard par Godard*, 1:382. Originally published in *Le Monde*, September 25, 1975.
49 Bruce Clarke, "Information," in *Critical Terms for Media Studies*, ed. W. J. T. Mitchell and Mark B. N. Hansen (Chicago: University of Chicago Press, 2010), 136.
50 Ibid., 138.
51 MacCabe, *Godard: Images, Sounds, Politics*, 153.
52 Baby, "Faire les films possibles là où on est," 1:385.
53 Joselit, *Feedback*, 5–6.
54 Baby, "Faire les films possibles là où on est," 1:385.
55 MacCabe, *Godard: Portrait of the Artist at Seventy*, 243.
56 De Baecque, *Godard*, 537.
57 Philippe Dubois, "Video Thinks What Cinema Creates," in *Jean-Luc Godard: Son et Image*, ed. Raymond Bellour and Mary Lea Bandy (New York: Museum of Modern Art, 1992), 173.
58 Jerry White, *Two Bicycles: The Work of Jean-Luc Godard and Anne-Marie Miéville* (Waterloo, Ont.: Wilfrid Laurier University Press, 2013), 83.
59 David Sterritt, *Seeing the Invisible: The Films of Jean-Luc Godard* (Cambridge: Cambridge University Press, 1999), 251.
60 Godard, *Introduction to a True History of Cinema and Television*, 370.
61 Michael Witt, "Altered Motion and Corporal Resistance in *France/Tour/Détour/Deux/Enfants*," in *For Ever Godard*, ed. Michael Temple, James S. Williams, and Michael Witt (London: Black Dog, 2007), 205.
62 MacCabe, *Godard: Images, Sounds, Politics*, 134.
63 Ibid., 132.
64 Quoted in White, *Two Bicycles*, 81–82.
65 MacCabe, *Godard: Portrait of the Artist at Seventy*, 254.
66 Godard, *Introduction to a True History of Cinema and Television*, 228.

67 Michael Cramer, "Television and the Auteur in the Late '50s," in *Opening Bazin*, ed. Dudley Andrew with Hervé Joubert-Laurencin (Oxford: Oxford University Press, 2011), 269–70.

68 MacCabe, *Godard: Images, Sounds, Politics,* 139.

69 Philippe Durand, "Jean-Luc Godard fait le point," *Cinéma pratique*, June 1973, 157.

70 Ibid., 156.

71 Witt, "On and under Communication," 330.

72 MacCabe, *Godard: Portrait of the Artist at Seventy*, 255.

73 Gilles Deleuze, "Three Questions about 'Six fois deux,'" in Bellour and Bandy, *Jean-Luc Godard: Son et Image*, 37.

74 Ibid.

75 Margaret Ganahl and R. S. Hamilton, "One Plus One: A Look at *Six Fois Deux*," in *Camera Obscura*, no. 8–10 (Fall 1982): 109.

76 Deleuze, "Three Questions about 'Six fois deux,'" 40.

77 Gilles Deleuze, *Cinema 2: The Time-Image*, trans. Hugh Tomlinson and Robert Galeta (Minneapolis: University of Minnesota Press, 1989), 179–80.

78 Witt, "On and under Communication," 330.

79 Deleuze, "Three Questions about 'Six fois deux,'" 35.

80 Ibid., 40.

81 Godard, *Introduction to a True History of Cinema and Television*, 229.

82 De Baecque, *Godard,* 541.

83 Ibid., 540.

84 The television publication *Télé 7 jours,* de Baecque notes, wrote that "if the cinéaste raves in dark cinemas, fine, but not when he introduces himself into the living rooms of our fellow citizens on Sunday evenings through television. We must yell 'halt!'" See de Baecque, *Godard,* 541.

85 MacCabe, *Godard: Images, Sounds, Politics,* 159.

86 De Baecque, *Godard,* 550.

87 Ibid.

88 Jean-Luc Godard, "*France tour détour deux enfants*: Déclaration à l'intention des héritiers," in Brenez et al., *Jean-Luc Godard: Documents,* 302.

89 Philippe Dubois, "Video Thinks What Cinema Creates," in Bellour and Bandy, *Jean-Luc Godard: Son et image,* 175–77.

90 The name of Godard's interviewer character in the film is Robert Linhard, a reference, as Michael Witt notes, to prominent Maoist leader and journalist Robert Linhart, with whom Godard had worked at *J'accuse.*

Witt, "Godard dans la presse d'extrême-gauche," in Bellour and Bandy, *Jean-Luc Godard: Documents,* 167–68.

91 Constance Penley, "Les Enfants de la Patrie," *Camera Obscura,* no. 8–10 (Fall 1982): 35.

92 Ibid.

93 Claire Strohm, "Moi je," in *Cahiers du cinéma, Spécial Godard,* November 1990, 72. In contrast, Strohm notes, "*Six fois deux* escapes from the terrorism of thought that directs *France/tour.* Here, Godard can do nothing against the speech of others, and furthermore he does not oppose his own to it."

94 Witt, "Altered Motion and Corporal Resistance in *France/tour/détour/deux/enfants,*" 205–7.

95 Jean-Luc Godard, "Propos Rompus," in Bergala, *Godard par Godard,* 1:462. Originally published in *Cahiers du cinéma,* no. 316 (October 1980).

96 De Baecque, *Godard,* 553–54.

97 Ibid., 554.

98 Ibid.

99 Witt, "On and under Communication," 332–33.

100 Baby, "Faire les films possibles là où on est," 1:385.

5. UTOPIA AFTER TELEVISION

1 Noam, *Television in Europe,* 152.

2 Ibid., 153–58.

3 Petros Iosifidis, Jeanette Steemers, and Mark Wheeler, *European Television Industries* (London: BFI, 2005), 35.

4 Noam, *Television in Europe,* 157.

5 D'Almeida and Delporte, *Histoire des médias en France,* 253–56.

6 Bourdon, *Du service public à la télé-réalité,* 61; Noam, *Television in Europe,* 103.

7 Noam, *Television in Europe,* 106.

8 D'Almeida and Delporte, *Histoire des médias en France,* 254.

9 Ibid., 259.

10 Noam, *Television in Europe,* 142–46.

11 Bourdon, *Du service public à la télé-réalité,* 36.

12 Iosifidis et al., *European Television Industries,* 11.

13 Ibid., 13.

14 John F. Kramer, "Italian Entrepreneurial Initiatives: Public Service Broadcasting in Transition," in Avery, *Public Service Broadcasting in a*

Multichannel Environment, 124. The comparison is between 1974 and 1983.

15 Iosifidis et al., *European Television Industries,* 38.

16 Ibid., 55.

17 Vedel and Bourdon, "French Public Service Broadcasting," 38.

18 Jay G. Blumler, "Introduction: Current Confrontations in West European Television," in Blumler, *Television and the Public Interest,* 2.

19 Umberto Eco, "A Guide to the Neo-Television of the 1980s," trans. Robert Lumley, in *Culture and Conflict in Postwar Italy,* ed. Zygmunt G. Barański and Robert Lumley (New York: St. Martin's Press, 1990), 246.

20 Iosifidis et al., *European Television Industries,* 11.

21 Franco "Bifo" Berardi, Marco Jacquemet, and Gianfranco Vitali, *Ethereal Shadows: Communications and Power in Contemporary Italy,* trans. Jessica Otey (New York: Autonomedia, 2009), 29.

22 Mauro Wolf, "The Evolution of Television Language in Italy since Deregulation," in Barański and Lumley, *Culture and Conflict in Postwar Italy,* 287.

23 Ibid.

24 Berardi et al., *Ethereal Shadows,* 39.

25 Jameson, *Valences,* 413.

26 Ibid.

27 Peter Watkins, "Notes on the Media Crisis" (Barcelona: Museu d'art Contemporani de Barcelona, 2010), http://www.macba.es/uploads/20100526/QP_23_Watkins.pdf. For Watkins's discussion of his teaching, see Scott MacDonald, "An Interview with Peter Watkins," *Journal of the University Film and Video Association* 34, no. 3 (1982): 48–50.

28 Watkins, *Media Crisis,* 18.

29 MacDonald, "An Interview with Peter Watkins," 49.

30 Baudrillard, *For a Critique of the Political Economy of the Sign,* 175.

31 Ibid., 132.

32 Watkins, *Media Crisis,* 23.

33 Ibid., 3.

34 Michael Wayne, "The Tragedy of History: Peter Watkins's *La Commune,*" *Third Text* 16, no. 1 (2002): 63.

35 This is identified as a key problem in political modernist practice by D. N. Rodowick: "in a binary the terms in conflict are always constructed as identical to themselves as well as in opposition to each other. In this manner binary thinking excludes any alternative not accounted for by

the dualism itself." See Rodowick, *The Crisis of Political Modernism* (Berkeley: University of California Press, 1995), xxvi–xxvii.

36 Russell Jacoby, *Picture Imperfect: Utopian Thought for an Anti-utopian Age* (New York: Columbia University Press, 2005), 32–33.

37 For an account of how Watkins engaged the film's participants in both fund-raising and putting together production teams, see Scott Mac-Donald, "Process Is Product; Product Is Process: Peter Watkins' *The Journey*," in *Peter Watkins' "The Journey": A Film in the Global Interest*, ed. Ken Nolley (Salem, Ore.: Willamette University, 1991), 24–25.

38 Ken Nolley, "Making *The Journey* with Peter Watkins," *CineAction!*, no. 12 (April 1988): 5.

39 Scott MacDonald, *Avant-Garde Film* (Cambridge: Cambridge University Press, 1993), 179.

40 Nolley, "Making *The Journey* with Peter Watkins," 9.

41 Marshall McLuhan, *Understanding Media: The Extensions of Man* (New York: McGraw-Hill, 1964).

42 Jacques Rancière, *The Emancipated Spectator*, trans. Gregory Elliott (London: Verso, 2011), 2.

43 Claire Bishop, *Artificial Hells: Participatory Art and the Politics of Spectatorship* (London: Verso, 2012), 5.

44 Ibid., 19.

45 Ibid.

46 Frédéric Bas, "Chacun devait écrire ses dialogues," *Cahiers du cinéma*, no. 546 (May 2000): 11.

47 Ibid.

48 Isabelle Marinone, "Une opposition aux mass media audiovisuels," in *L'insurrection médiatique: Médias, histoire et documentaire dans le cinéma de Peter Watkins*, ed. Sébastien Denis and Jean-Pierre Bertin-Maghit (Pessac, France: Presses Universitaires de Bordeaux, 2010), 52.

49 Bas, "Chacun devait écrire ses dialogues," 11.

50 Jameson, *Brecht and Method*, 64.

51 Ibid.

52 Wayne, "Tragedy of History," 64.

53 Fernando Solanas and Octavio Gettino, "Towards a Third Cinema," in *Movies and Methods*, ed. Bill Nichols (Berkeley: University of California Press, 1976), 1:44–64.

54 Watkins, *Media Crisis*, 191.

55 Text from the website of Rebond pour la Commune, formerly at http://rebond.org/, now defunct.

56 Marinone, "Une opposition aux mass media audiovisuels," 54.

57 Rancière, *Emancipated Spectator,* 15.

58 Ibid., 62.

59 Fredric Jameson, *Postmodernism, or the Cultural Logic of Late Capitalism* (Durham, N.C.: Duke University Press, 1990), 16.

60 Bishop, *Artificial Hells,* 275.

61 Claire Bishop, "Antagonism and Relational Aesthetics," *October,* no. 110 (Autumn 2004): 68.

62 Ibid., 52.

63 Ibid., 65.

64 Bloch, *Principle of Hope,* 1:149.

65 Bishop, *Artificial Hells,* 276–77.

66 Jameson, *Seeds of Time,* 75.

67 *Cahiers du cinéma,* no. 300 (May 1979): 73. Translation from White, *Two Bicycles,* 50.

68 Daniel Fairfax, "Birth (of the Image) of a Nation: Jean-Luc Godard in Mozambique," *Acta Univ. Sapientiae, Film and Media Studies* 3 (2010): 58.

69 *Cahiers du cinéma,* no. 300 (May 1979): 95.

70 Manthia Diawara, "Sonimage in Mozambique," in *I Said I Love. That Is the Promise: The Tvideo Politics of Jean-Luc Godard,* ed. Gareth James and Florian Zeyfang (Berlin: B-Books, 2003), 105.

71 Godard lays out a synopsis for the program in "Birth (of the Image) of a Nation" in *Cahiers,* no. 300 (May 1979): 77.

72 Diawara, "Sonimage in Mozambique," 111.

73 MacCabe, *Godard: Images, Sounds, Politics,* 156.

74 Diawara, "Sonimage in Mozambique," 93–99.

75 MacCabe, *Godard: Images, Sounds, Politics,* 156–57.

76 The only mention of such a project I have encountered comes from Silvia D'Amico Bendico, who mentions Rossellini's desire to make a film about the Commune in Comolli's 2006 film *La Dernière utopie.*

77 Pavsek, *Utopia of Film,* 1.

78 Michael Witt, "The Death(s) of Cinema According to Godard," *Screen* 40, no. 3 (1999): 333–35.

79 Daniel Morgan, *Late Godard and the Possibilities of Cinema* (Berkeley: University of California Press, 2013), 179.

80 Antoine Dulaure and Claire Parnet, "Dans Marie il y a aimer," in Bergala, *Godard par Godard,* 1:603–4. Originally published in *L'autre journal,* January 1985.

81   Alain Bergala, Serge Daney, and Serge Toubiana, "Le chemin vers la parole," in Bergala, *Godard par Godard*, 1:512. Originally published in *Cahiers du cinéma*, no. 336 (May 1982).

82   Morgan, *Late Godard*, 209–10.

83   Jean-Luc Godard and Serge Daney, "Dialogue entre Jean-Luc Godard et Serge Daney," *Cahiers du cinéma*, no. 513 (May 1997): 49.

84   Morgan, *Late Godard*, 208–212.

85   Ibid., 207.

86   Witt, *Jean-Luc Godard: Cinema Historian*, 43.

87   Alain Bergala, *Nul mieux que Godard* (Paris: Éditions Cahiers du Cinéma, 1999), 225.

88   Ibid., 227.

89   Morgan, *Late Godard*, 204.

90   Bergala, *Nul mieux que Godard*, 226–27.

91   Bloch, *Principle of Hope*, 1:9.

92   Monica Dall'Asta, "The (Im)possible History," in Temple et al., *For Ever Godard*, 356.

93   For Godard's use of this passage, see Witt, *Jean-Luc Godard: Cinema Historian*, 183.

94   Dall'Asta, "(Im)possible History," 362.

95   Ibid.

96   Morgan, *Late Godard*, 236.

97   Ibid.

98   Ibid., 235.

99   Pavsek, *Utopia of Film*, 71–77.

100   Ibid., 73.

101   Ibid., 74.

102   Ibid., 77.

103   Godard and Daney, "Dialogue entre Jean-Luc Godard et Serge Daney," 49.

104   André Habib, "Godard's Utopia(s) or the Performance of Failure," in *The Legacies of Jean-Luc Godard*, ed. Douglas Morrey, Christina Stojanova, and Nicole Côté (Waterloo, Ont.: Wilfrid Laurier University Press, 2014), 224.

105   Ibid., 225.

106   Jameson, *The Geopolitical Aesthetic* (Bloomington: Indiana University Press, 1995), 166.

107   Habib, "Godard's Utopia(s)," 228.

108 Witt, *Jean-Luc Godard: Cinema Historian,* 177.
109 Pavsek, *Utopia of Film,* 150.
110 Peter C. Lutze, "Alexander Kluge's 'Cultural Window' in Private Television," *New German Critique,* no. 80 (Spring–Summer 2000): 175–76.
111 Tara Forrest, "Raw Materials for the Imagination: Kluge's Work for Television," in *Alexander Kluge: Raw Materials for the Imagination,* ed. Tara Forrest (Amsterdam: Amsterdam University Press, 2012), 306.
112 Ibid.
113 Quoted in Lutze, "Alexander Kluge's 'Cultural Window,'" 188.
114 Christian Schulte, "Television and Obstinacy," in Forrest, *Alexander Kluge: Raw Materials for the Imagination,* 319.
115 Forrest, "Raw Materials for the Imagination," 305.
116 Quoted in Lutze, "Alexander Kluge's 'Cultural Window,'" 174.
117 Ibid., 178.
118 Oskar Negt and Alexander Kluge, *Public Sphere and Experience: Towards an Analysis of the Bourgeois and Proletarian Public Sphere,* trans. Peter Labanyi, Jamie Owen Daniel, and Assenka Oksiloff (Minneapolis: University of Minnesota Press, 1993), 117.
119 Schulte, "Television and Obstinacy," 322–23.
120 Ibid., 321.
121 Forrest, "Raw Materials for the Imagination," 306.
122 Pavsek, *Utopia of Film,* 171.
123 On "excavation" and Kluge's (and Oskar Negt's) conception of history, historical experience, and its usefulness in the present, see Fredric Jameson, "On Negt and Kluge," *October,* no. 46 (Autumn 1988): 154–55, 162–63.
124 http://www.dctp.tv/.
125 Benjamin H. D. Buchloh, "Gerhard Richter's *Atlas*: The Anomic Archive," *October,* no. 88 (Spring 1999): 122.
126 Ibid., 124.
127 Ibid, 141.
128 Ibid., 169.
129 Magagnoli's argument refers to works by Zoe Leonard, Rachel Harrison, and Jean-Luc Moulène. See Paolo Magagnoli, *Documents of Utopia* (New York: Wallflower Press, 2015), 87–117.
130 Philipp Ekardt, "Alexander Kluge's Digital Constellations," *October,* no. 138 (Fall 2011): 116.

131 As Ekardt notes, this characteristic of Kluge's work is also connected to the status of the digital as a storage medium: because all of the information contained on his DVDs and on his website "will never be exhaustively retrieved in any single act of viewing or reading," "indefinite futurity enters the body of the work itself, which never fully constitutes itself for a single viewer or reader." See Ekardt, "Alexander Kluge's Digital Constellations," 117.

Index

Michael Cramer is assistant professor of film history at Sarah Lawrence College.